THE Swampland OF SHAME

How Mentors and Transformative Events
Helped Me Navigate My Way Out of the Swamp

PETER F. PROUT

The Swampland of Shame
Copyright © 2022 by Peter F. Prout

Cover photo courtesy of Jeremy Bishop

Tellwell Talent
www.tellwell.ca

ISBN
978-0-2288-8020-2 (Hardcover)
978-0-2288-8019-6 (Paperback)
978-0-2288-8021-9 (eBook)

TABLE OF CONTENTS

FOREWORD v

PRELUDE.. ix

Part One
People, Events & Destiny.................................... 1

Part Two
A Second Chance... 101

Part Three
Canada: And Graduate Studies......................... 165

Part Four
Coming Home... 193

Part Five
"Half Time"..223

Part Six
Exiting the Swampland Of Shame 253

Part Seven
How God Intervened 283

APPENDIX..303

NOTES 311

ACKNOWLEDGEMENTS 333

FOREWORD

This is a powerful book about one man's life journey, focusing on the scary issue of shame.

Peter's father treated him badly, which caused him intense shame. Those feelings of failure and shame have run deep throughout Pete's life. Other actions, however, that caused Pete shame were his own choices. But in talking about them with honesty and insight, this book will give others the courage to own their personal shame and, most importantly, grow from it.

I have watched Peter over many years deal with his own shame, sometimes with initial avoidance, but with the courage required to 'lift up stones and see the shame beneath', thus seeing shame for what it really is, and making changes that release him from the potential captivity to shame.

I have known Peter, as a very close friend, for over half of his life. Our friendship initially developed around the common interests of sport and our deep love for our respective families, as well as our faith. It grew into a close friendship and continues to grow. Unlike many men he and I learned to share our deepest feelings and hurts as mates. We have gotten better at that over time.

Pete's insight, wisdom and generosity of spirit have helped me enormously in my own personal growth, including over the past few years when I have faced some major personal challenges of my own. He is very important in my life's journey, and I would have struggled without him, particularly recently.

From our early days of friendship, I was aware of how life events had 'knocked Peter around.' Firstly, the unrelenting emotional abuse he received from his father, leading him to have a deep sense of failure and shame that infiltrated his thinking about many life challenges he faced. Secondly, I was aware of how his near-death experience during his posting with the Australian Army in Southeast Asia, profoundly impacted him physically, emotionally and spiritually. But he has not sat around being bitter about these factors, rather he has grown from them. I so admire that.

These are the four key ingredients that I see in Peter that enable him to climb out of what he calls the 'swamp of shame'.

Firstly, he is willing to examine the causes of shame - issues that were out of his control, such as his father's behaviour, his military experiences, and his own bad decisions and actions. What I admire about that is, whereas most people avoid honest examination of their past, saying "what is the point of examining the past when you can't change it", Pete 'owns his actions' and seeks resolutions accordingly.

Secondly, Pete has not just blamed others, or life circumstances for everything that has happened to him. He is willing to own his responsibilities, and not spend his life blaming others. Again, this ownership is impressively courageous and, in my view, unique.

Thirdly, he doesn't remain at the point of insight into his behaviour rather, he seeks to change and take steps that enable him to learn and grow from his shame. In his book, Pete describes mentors that have helped him along his journey, but in the end the decision to change is his choice, and I admire his willingness to change and grow, including in these later stages of his life.

Finally, I have a deep admiration for his desire to turn his own mistakes into something that helps others avoid them, or to grow from them. I noticed in my early years as his friend that Pete turned his negative experiences with his own father, into actions such as trying to be a really good dad himself, and, as a teacher, to be a strong, affirming father-figure to his students.

Now, as he reflects on his life, Pete has identified ways in which his own experiences and choices could, if understood and embraced by other people, particularly men, enable them to grow to be better people.

This book will encourage readers that, no matter how shameful their actions, they can choose to change and grow and not wallow in their own 'swamp of shame.'

Bruce Robinson, Author, Husband, Father and Grandfather

MD W. Aust., MBBS (UWA), DTM&H Liv., FRACP, FRCP, FAAHMS

Professor, UWA Medical School, Internal Medicine

PRELUDE

"An unexamined life is not worth living"

Socrates (470-399 BC)

Kieran Perkins is one of my Aussie heroes. When he burst onto the world swimming stage in the 1990s, I was regularly swimming 1500 metres, twice weekly, for my main exercise. Kieran came second in the 1500 metres at the Commonwealth Games in Auckland in 1990, second in the same event at the World Championships in Perth in 1991 and won gold in Barcelona in 1992. Second and third places at Barcelona went to the two men who had defeated Kieran in Auckland and Perth. In 1994, at the Commonwealth Games in Vancouver, Kieran proceeded to smash the world record for both the 1500 and 800 metres.

Kieran was my champion.

However, between the Commonwealth Games in 1994 and the 1996 Olympics in Atlanta, Kieran was 'written off' by all kinds of people. Personal issues plus emerging young swimmers gaining public attention, meant that Kieran was considered a 'has been,' no longer a champion. He was publicly shamed by sports journalists and some members of the Australian public, and, upon reflection, I was aggrieved as I perceived Kieran enduring his personal battle with shame.

Indeed, Kieran struggled to get fit for the Australian Swim Team for the 1996 Olympic Games. History reveals that Kieran managed to scrape into the 1500 metres final and was relegated to the 'death lane eight' for the event. Kieran was not considered a contender for the winner's list.

As the Olympic Final for the 1500 metres developed, it was evident that someone neglected to inform Kieran that he should not win from lane eight! His rhythm was strong and perfect, his shoulders shone in the pool with the purple glow swimmers get as they expend every possible store of energy for the event. The huge heart of the champion lifted him to one final victory that was so glorious. What an amazing moment. I wept unashamedly as he climbed out of the pool to walk over to hug his partner. Kieran [1] was a champion again.

In examining my own life, I experienced being a champion in my family, my work, my church and my social connections. However, due to a range of circumstances, including bad decisions on my part, I also experienced shame. Shame is a tough reality. It is a place to flounder, give up and lose hope, or it can be a place to search within and determine to be a champion again.

I have stared down shame, ready to be a more reflective champion again. I have been blessed with insights, experience and a willingness to confront shame and embrace vulnerability. Accordingly, I want to encourage others who may have been champions, and for whatever reasons, believe they no longer are. You are, and you can be again.

I don't swim now. I walk. I completed the Camino de Santiago (Way of St Francis) in 2015, and the Portuguese Camino de Santiago in 2016. During both these times of exertion and sometimes deep and not so easy reflections, I willingly confronted my shame and gained courage again. None of this was easy. In fact, I have struggled constantly throughout writing my story with the inner voice of shame asking:

> *"Are you sure you can do this; who do you think you are; why would anyone be interested in your story?"*

A motivating factor for sharing my story emanated from my 70th birthday and a realisation that I was just beginning another chapter of growth and confidence in my own sojourn. I was energised and more passionate about what I still had to offer in my professional and personal life.

Upon reflection, I also appreciated the many people who had been mentors and sources of great encouragement and inspiration to me. I wanted to honour them in my intentional recollections about my life and experiences.

The greatest positive impact on my life, however, is my unshakeable belief and trust in God. I trust that sharing these experiences and insights in depth will be edifying and encouraging for anyone reading this book, for such is my hope. In the wise words of Hugh Mackay: [2]

> *"Australians will never acquire a national identity until all Australians acquire identities of their own."*

Three Themes

- I will share impacts of shame throughout my life including setbacks, failure, loss, fury, and remorse, all fixed in dark times as first born in my family, including my relationship with my father, my mother, two younger brothers and a sister.

• I identify numerous events and significant people that influenced me to seek personal and spiritual growth, thus experiencing love, inspiration, hope, grace and wonder, all of which led me to healing and the authentic life I now embrace.

• Above all else, I acknowledge that achievements and learning in my life are due to peers and elders/mentors who throughout my life experiences have given me significant feedback and guidance.

My Focus Audience

I hope my story will be an encouragement and help to other men in their life journeys. Make no mistake, we are all impacted by shame in our lives; I trust I will clarify this assertion adequately in my story. Further, real men seeking to be leaders in their families, workplace and community constantly go through a process of self-examination in the endeavour to become 'better men,' and to sharpen every level of their intelligence. I sincerely applaud every step you take towards knowing yourself more deeply, and to celebrating the man you become.

PART ONE
People, Events & Destiny

Chapter 1

Love in the Beginning

I have two younger brothers, Harry (Henry) and Ross (Rosco), and one youngest sister, Di. I was first born and as long as I can remember my mum called me Pedro, which I loved. Throughout my life I never recalled mum being pregnant, but she kept bringing babies home. It seemed my mother could do anything.

I remember always being proud of my brothers, and of my little sister in particular. My greatest shock in relation to my brothers and sister was one day after school in April 1952, when I came running home from school and called out at the back door:

"G'day mum," only to be greeted by Jill Took at the stove saying:

"Your mum isn't here."

Jill was a neighbour, probably in her teens, who must have been summoned when mum went into labour, and hospital. Living in a close-knit farming community offered these kinds of support. I was seven years old, but I can still remember the shock at hearing Jill's words. If mum wasn't home, where was she? What has happened in the world? Where else could mum possibly be?

Of course, she was in hospital with my newborn sister. I could not believe it when mum came home with this treasured bundle of a beautiful sister. Amazing. I think mum coming home with our baby sister would be close to my number one memory from that time. I was seven years old and I was immediately drawn to want to protect her, albeit with mixed success. With three brothers to 'look after her,' I think Di came to appreciate there were some dangerous outcomes of having three brothers as her 'guardians.' Fortunately, when we wanted to do 'brother stuff,' mum would find things for Di to do. For example, Di was awesome with her little hands at pushing fruit into bottles for preserving.

Meanwhile, we would be building structures on an island in the river, catching gilgies in the river, trapping rabbits, looking for an old gold mine we knew existed somewhere in the bush behind the farm, sitting in the mulberry trees stuffing our bellies with mulberries or fig trees in season, and other activities that were simply sublime. I am always grateful for my 'farming background,' and for my special siblings who are more important to me now than they ever were.

Birthplace

I was born in Katanning [1] on February 2, 1945, in Coleraine Private Hospital which is now a private home in the town. Katanning is a sizeable regional town in Western Australia (WA), noted for many significant people and events. It was the first town in WA to have a secondary industry (the roller flour mill established by the Piesse brothers, Frederick and Charles). Percy Gratwick, a posthumous Victoria Cross (VC) winner in World War Two was a resident of the town. Similarly, Essendon Australian Rules footballer Mark Williams, and Lydia Williams, former goalkeeper for Australia's National Soccer Team, the Matildas, were also born in Katanning. Katanning was formally gazetted as a town in 1898 and was the first in WA to have streetlights.

Before my birth my mother had been a Head Nurse at the Katanning Hospital and my father worked on behalf of The Department of Native Affairs as it was known then, as a storeman at the Carrolup Native Settlement, about 15 kilometres out of town. In the late 1990s Carrolup was criticised in the Press as a place of oppression of Aboriginal children. However, people who knew my parents well assured me that my mother made sure the living conditions for the children were clean and tidy, and there was access to excellent health care. I cannot verify if my parents were living on the settlement or in town, but I can confirm that my mother loved and respected our Aboriginal people. She passed this attitude on to me, my siblings, and to each of my daughters.

Carrolup [2] was initially established under the direction of the Protector of Aborigines, a government department established in WA in 1915. The settlement under that management was closed in 1922, with residents transferred to Moore River Settlement. This was a bleak period of early European settlement in WA, as it was believed we were acting in the best interests of Aboriginal people by bringing children born of young Aboriginal girls and white fathers to Moore River to be schooled in the ways of white Australians.

I am personally aggrieved at what we did to our Aboriginal people in the process of white settlement in Australia, more so since the practice of taking children from their parents didn't stop until the 1970s. There is a graphic true story of Moore River Settlement told in the movie *Rabbit Proof Fence*, which I recommend to those seeking to learn more about this period of history.

Carrolup was reopened in 1939 as a farm training school for Aboriginal boys and my dad was working as a storeman at the school when I was born. I am not sure how dad came to be working there, although his mother, my Nana, owned the Dardanup General Store so dad would have known how to manage a similar service at Carrolup. By 1944, there were 129 children in government care at Carrolup but in 1949 the Carrolup school was closed and the government withdrew children in 1951. Carrolup was renamed Marribank [3] and handed over to the Baptist Churches of WA from 1952 to 1988.

There are numerous paintings by children from Carrolup held in the WA Japingha Gallery. [4] Amazingly, an American art dealer had taken many of the paintings to Boston where they were stored in an attic. They were eventually repatriated back to WA by the WA Art Gallery. By the 1970s, Marribank was running as a cooperative development centre offering family support programmes in cottages on the old mission site. However, Marribank was finally closed as an operational centre for Aboriginal people in January 1989.

Soon after I was born, my parents accepted a posting to work among Aboriginal people in the Kimberley region of WA. We travelled by State Ship from Fremantle, the port city of Perth, to Port Hedland, a coastal town approximately 1600 kilometres north of Perth. Upon reflection, later stories I heard from independent sources about my mother's care and love for Aboriginal youth at Carrolup were consistent with her attitude and behaviour towards the same people in the Kimberley Region.

The Kimberley and Tilley

According to research by my brother Ross, dad was initially employed as acting head of the Department of Local Affairs in

Port Hedland. Ross also learned we were only in Port Hedland for a short time before we moved to Broome, another coastal town 600 kilometres further north of Port Hedland, where dad was relieving head of the Local Department of Native Affairs and mum found work as a nurse at the Broome Native Hospital. Dad had a number of responsibilities in his work in Broome, including acting as defence council for Aboriginal people.

From Broome my parents moved again, this time to Halls Creek, [5] an inland town approximately 680 kilometres east of Broome where mum nursed at the Halls Creek Hospital operated by the Australian Inland Mission. Meanwhile, dad was still acting on behalf of the Department of Native Affairs as a storekeeper for the Aboriginal people at Moola Bulla Station, near Halls Creek.

I always noticed the love in my mother's voice as she informed me that while she was working, she would leave me in the care of a young aboriginal girl named Tilley. At the end of her nursing shift, mum would go down to the creek – Halls Creek – where I would be happily playing with the Aboriginal kids. Mum would remark that when she came to the creek to get me after work, I would often be holding forth much as a two-year old does, in front of adults who were enjoying my antics.

In later years, I confess I am astounded that Tilley and her mob accepted me so totally. I often wonder how they could have loved and cared for me when their own children were being snatched away. Young girls, including Tilley, were often raped by stockmen and other white males, and were then deemed unfit to mother their children (I also understand that not all stolen children were taken as a result of rape). I feel so blessed that they could love a little white kid in the midst of the pain they suffered. My mother also reported that Tilley was devastated when she had to say goodbye when we returned from Broome to Fremantle by ship in 1947.

Tilley insisted on walking ten kilometres pushing me in a pram just to spend that final time with me before we left. I often try to imagine what must have gone through Tilley's mind and heart as she had to hand me over to my mother for the last time. Her own baby had been taken and now another.

Indeed, my mum shared with me how hard it was for her to take me from Tilley, and to say good-bye to her. How blessed I was to be loved by this young aboriginal girl, yet it does pain me to think of the grief she had to bear on my behalf. When I try and make sense of this, I defer to my God whom I know hears the cry of broken hearts, and I entrust Tilley's heart and soul to his care.

My parents also spent time at Noonkanbah Station, where dad was the storeman for the station and mum was the nurse. It was here that mum saw Aboriginal people treated harshly by white stockmen and the Station Manager. When mum raised this with the manager, he simply informed her to mind her own business, and that since she was only at the station for a short time, she had no authority.

As a child, I learned so much from mum in relation to concepts of justice and fairness for the Aboriginal workers and their women and children. I noted how it touched mum's heart as she shared many of her 'Kimberley experiences' with me and my brothers and sister. Later in her life mum also shared these experiences with her grandchildren. I honoured mum for this, and was later grateful to see how my own daughters responded actively with love and respect towards all Aboriginal Australians.

Years later, in 2014 when travelling through the Kimberley with my brothers, we tried to find out what happened to Tilley.

First, we visited the old town of Halls Creek where we identified the foundations of the hospital. Looking down a slope and seeing the creek, my heart quickened, and I was filled with awe, grief and joy that I was with my brothers in the place where our mother had worked and loved her people. As we walked down to the creek and I stepped into the dry creek bed, I was overwhelmed with so many feelings. At that moment, I wished I was a poet to adequately describe my emotions.

After our visit to Halls Creek, we followed a tip from contacts in Broome, including the great Aboriginal leader and Member of Parliament, Patrick Dodson whom I met on a previous visit to Broome, who mentioned an elder in Fitzroy Crossing, a town close to Halls Creek, who might remember Tilley. We found the man who acknowledged Tilley had lived in Fitzroy Crossing, but that she had died in recent years.

If only I had undertaken this search in earlier years. It was one of those 'dread in the depth of your gut' feelings as I processed this news, like somehow your physical body has temporarily lost connection with your soul and spirit, and you feel all alone in the world. I still wish I could have hugged Tilley and told her how much I loved her. I imagined her as a little woman I could have smothered in my arms and share what I had done with my life, including never forgetting her. Hopefully, in heaven I will find Tilley by a billabong and we can chat for as long as it takes.

Following time with my parents in the Kimberley, I was soon to be joined by siblings and other significant changes that helped shape my life.

Chapter 2

Early Days of Shame and Wounding

After we left the Kimberley in late 1947, my parents settled on a dairy farm in the Ferguson Valley in the southwest region of Western Australia. Growing up on the family farm, I experienced mixed blessings and harsh realities. With my brothers and our sister, we had 110 hectares of back yard to play in, including the Ferguson River and two creeks. I have some rich memories of playing with my siblings during this time, although fear of my dad dominated my overall childhood.

Upon investigating possible reasons for the latter phenomenon, I was informed in my adult years that early in my childhood, my father demonstrated signs of jealousy towards me. Indeed, my father began calling his wife, 'mum,' and even though she asked that he desist, he continued. Throughout my life that is the only way I recall him addressing my mother. On one particular occasion when I was in my early 30s, I invited both my parents to attend my commissioning for work. My dad declined and when I inquired of my mother, she accepted. Immediately, my dad responded:

> *"That is what you have wanted to do all your life Peter, take your mother from me."*

At the time, I was staggered by my father's assertion and I don't recall how I responded, albeit I am sure I would have 'let the moment pass.' However, as I recalled a close family friend's observation concerning my early childhood, my dad's comment made some sense to me.

Hard Times on the Farm

As first born and from some of my earliest memories, I came under the supervision of my father who was quick, ferocious and frequent to physically and emotionally punish my errors, perceived, or actual. His constant and repetitious berating of my competence and intelligence included:

> *"You're a useless bastard, and you will never ever be any good for anything."*

Following this assessment of my future prospects, I would usually be confronted with further verbal abuse such as:

> *"Why did you do that"*, or
> *"How many times do I need to tell you"*, or
> *"There are two ways to do things, my way and the wrong way"*

Guessing dad's way at the time was a challenge in itself, and examples of my confusion stemming from this latter point, including punishments I experienced, included the following:

- Before we moved to selling whole milk, we separated milk and only sold the cream. The skim milk was used to feed calves being weaned, and for pigs. To feed the pigs, the skim milk was pumped through pipes to a large drum in the pig pens from where it would later be distributed by bucket to individual troughs. Normally, a hose at the end of the pipe from the dairy went into this large drum. But on one occasion, when I was around ten years old, dad instructed me to put the hose into a pig trough. I was too scared to question his instruction, or to seek clarification as abuse would always follow that, so, against my better judgement, I placed the hose in the closest trough, then hurried back to the dairy. Of course, the trough quickly filled, and the milk then spilled on to the ground and was wasted in one of the pig pens.

Just before milking finished, dad left the dairy to feed the pigs out of the drum. He came storming back to the dairy, grabbed me by one arm, and beat me with an old fan belt (from a vehicle). which was his favourite instrument, accusing me as he did of being a 'useless bastard' for putting the hose in a trough. Before leaving the dairy, he said I was to miss dinner that night because the pigs also had to go hungry. I was too afraid to go home so I sat in the dark in the milking shed to shore up courage before I did so. Deep down I knew all this was unfair. I also recall thinking it was my fault and that I probably could not be relied upon to do the right thing.

- Every weekend, I was normally so overwhelmed with verbal and physical abuse that I was unable to think, or to respond with any clarity. At the time, I had no way of identifying the emotions I was experiencing. I just recall being a jabbering mess. Dad would then go on to confirm me that I was not thinking because I was useless. Talk about a loop of horror. I would just quiver in fear in these times and weep in despair of ever being able to please my dad or to earn his affection.

- A further example of unjust punishment occurred during milking. One of my brothers left a gate open to a hay shed and some cows got into the hay after they were milked. It was impossible for me to have opened the gate since I was in the milking shed the whole time. Nevertheless, when dad discovered cows in the shed pulling bales of hay apart, he stormed back to the shed where I was finishing cleaning, grabbed me again by the arm and started belting me for leaving the gate open. It didn't matter that through my tears, I said I didn't do it. In dad's mind, I was the useless one who always did these things.

When challenged by dad about my perceived stupidity, I would normally respond with:

"I didn't think."

Of course, I couldn't think straight in those moments. I was too scared, even terrified at times. During my working career as a teacher and later with pre-service teachers at university, I would stress the importance of giving students time to respond to a question or instruction. This is simply because we know the child and teenage brain is dominated by emotional responses to anything that might trigger the amygdala to release powerful hormones. In the words of Daniel Goleman: [1]

To slow down thinking, and to prepare for flight.

Just when you need to be able to think, the amygdala is saying; 'no way, just hide for now!' In moments of fear and failure, there was no way I could explain or defend my behaviour. I find it difficult now to appropriately explain my actions and responses, but I hope the example is useful for you as you consider similar circumstances of your own. The learning point from these kinds of experiences is to understand that, our brain is doing exactly as it is designed to do – protect us from harm.

Based upon my reflections and learning from these early experiences with my dad, I firmly believe we should eliminate the word, 'why' from our vocabulary. I suggest this in relation to seeking understanding from our children in particular. If, in an emotionally charged moment of discipline with our children, we ask, 'why,' they will have no logical response simply because their brain is shutting down and seeking to 'fight,' or 'flee.' Rather, we can ask questions such as:

(1) *"What happened?"*
(2) *"Who else was there?"*
(3) *"When did this happen?"*
(4) *"What can you tell me about this?"*
(5) *"Where did this occur?"*
(6) *"Where were you when it happened?"*

These questions allow our children (and students when we are teaching) to take an objective stance, rather than a challenge to defend their behaviour that was quite possibly a result of haste, response in fear, or a learned personality response or action. In any case, we seek to discern the circumstances surrounding an event rather than immediately apportion fault or blame. Accordingly, I taught my student teachers how to ask questions and then allow their students time to discuss with a partner before attempting what is more likely to be, an intelligent and considered response. Dad didn't have time for that on the farm, nor did he have access to this knowledge and understanding of how our brain functions.

A further example may help here. There may have been times when you were asked a question to which you always knew the answer. However, in the moment of being 'asked without notice,' you might have stammered, or given a confused response, after which you felt really stupid. We have all experienced these moments and we will prosecute the cause and response later in this chapter.

Cringing From Shame

We had a lovely gentle cow on the farm named Whopper, since she had been a huge calf. Despite her size, Whopper had a quiet nature and she loved to be patted, at any time. Every night after milking it was my job to release the cows to an overnight paddock, normally close to the dairy so they could easily be brought into the shed in the morning. One evening, the cows were in the 'home paddock,' so named because the house and the dairy were in this paddock; farmers are always so logical in naming animals and paddocks/fields.

I was walking back to the house from the dairy when I stopped to pat Whopper. After another berating about the right and wrong way to clear cow shit from the milking area, I was tired, despondent and confused. I sat down by Whopper and she began nuzzling me and gently pushing me into a foetal position, making soft mooing sounds as she did. She continued this for as long as I responded by lying quietly. It was such an amazing experience, although I am a tad embarrassed including it in my story. I was fifteen and I just felt loved in that moment, even understood. In retrospect, I understand this was the beginning of my propensity to mindfulness, described by Pete Walker [2] as:

> *"...benign curiosity about all of your inner experiences."*

In other words, I was already seeking to understand my life experiences and to gain a degree of comfort in place of the emotional insecurity I experienced in my dad's presence. I also understand I was experiencing what Brene Brown [3] refers to as:

> *"Shame; one of the most primitive human emotions that we experience; something we find most difficult to talk about; and, that it will control our lives when we don't talk about it. Further, it is a belief that we are flawed and therefore unworthy of love and belonging."*

Among the markers of shame, I experienced were, believing I was (1) useless and no good, (2) incapable of doing the 'right thing', (3) untrustworthy, (4) stupid, (5) incompetent, and (6) unworthy. Following further reflections over recent years, I understand that what I once understood as 'false guilt' is actually shame. As a result of my dad's constant berating, I felt badly about myself and therefore condemned myself as 'guilty' when in fact I was tormented by shame. In this respect, Edward Welch [4] claims:

> *"...shame remains an essential feature of punishment around the world."*

He adds that parents and teachers have often used shame as a way of demeaning or reprimanding their children and students. Welch notes:

> *"...we see extreme measures of shame adopted by rogue soldiers and military regimes as a way of publicly humiliating and shaming others, including women and children as a way of exercising power."*

I mentioned above that I 'felt' shame. In his in-depth, and confronting analysis of shame, Jon Ronson [5] claims, with respect to 'feeling' shame, that the term:

"...feeling of shame ...is the wrong word."

He illuminates this view, quoting James Gilligan, as follows:

> *"It may be somewhat paradoxical to refer to shame as a "feeling," for while shame is initially painful, constant shaming leads to a deadening of feeling. Shame, like cold, is, in essence the absence of warmth. And when it reaches overwhelming intensity, shame is experienced, like cold, as a feeling of numbness and deadness. (In Dante's Inferno) the lowest circle of hell was a region not of flames, but of ice — absolute coldness."*

I do not claim to have regularly (if ever), experienced the depth of shame described above, but as I researched shame in examining my own life, I have been overwhelmed by the potential destructiveness of shame that many people shared with Ronson.

In his book, Ronson lays out vignette after vignette of men and women who have been publicly shamed, and those who have shamed others. In both scenarios, life has been hell for many people, including those who were so wracked with shame, or guilt for shaming others, that they took their own lives. It is not edifying reading but I believe it is essential for understanding this destructive behaviour of our time. I am grateful that I did not work in the shadow of public shaming that pervades our society today.

The quote by Ronson, from James Gilligan's book on violence particularly among men who choose to seriously harm and kill others rather than suffer shame, caused me to think deeply about my dad and what prompted him to direct such pain in my direction. It also sharpened my thinking and appreciation around the gifts and personality I have recently discovered and celebrate about myself.

In the pages that follow, I will explore more about identifying shame in our lives, including how to combat the false stories of shame we hear in our mind. Before I move on however, I mention one more significant reflection from Ronson. After all the people he met and interviewed for his book on shame and shaming, he notes that:

"...the cure for shame is empathy."

In my experience, this has been true and liberating. To offer empathy and to receive it are both transactions that have transformed my mind and healed my soul. With respect to the former, I woke one morning at 5.00 am with absolute clarity about the next section I had to include in these reflections; the fact that we actually learn shame.

Learning Shame

Since we have established that shame is a primitive emotion, it has to 'live' somewhere in us and our brain provides that space. In order to appreciate how shame exists in our brain, let's review how we learn. Briefly, all learning takes place as follows:

1. Sensory Memory where information enters our brain through our five senses; sight, smell, touch, sound, and taste. From here the information moves into our Working Memory, via a process of screening through paying attention and acknowledging (perceiving), the senses accordingly.

2. From our Sensory Memory, information is presented in our Working Memory where it is rehearsed or practiced until it is encoded as new knowledge in our Long-Term Memory. Incredibly, as we rehearse the 'new' information in our Working Memory, any prior knowledge associated with the new information is retrieved from the Long-Term Memory, to be processed and encoded as new knowledge. Therefore, if we are receiving new information via our senses relating to anything that 'reminds' us of past actions that brought us shame, our Long-Term Memory retrieves those past memories and experiences, so that they might be added to the new knowledge about shame being rehearsed in our Working Memory.

3. Long-term Memory is where our shame is stored indefinitely. [6]

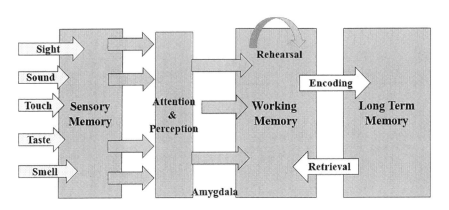

Figure 1. A model demonstrating how we store knowledge in our brain

As previously stated, our amazing brain is doing exactly what it is designed to do; process and store all information in our Long-Term Memory, which functions so until we die. Further, all new knowledge is stored in our Long-Term Memory as:

- Episode, story and/or parable (at least 70% of our knowledge is stored in this fashion). This allows us to access people and events associated with elements of shame stored in our Long-Term Memory.

- Facts, definitions, procedures and rules which help us to accurately report instances that may have caused us shame.

- Knowledge of how to perform tasks that allow us to record experiences of shame. This can include verbal reporting, acting out our experiences, presenting our knowledge in music, and using art to express our knowledge among others.

In short, we learn shame from information via our senses, and from prior knowledge of shame already stored in our brain; aka in our Long-Term Memory.

One other point is germane to our understanding here. All stored knowledge in our Long-Term Memory is associated with emotional responses such as joy, frustration, horror, sadness, satisfaction, celebration, revenge, awe, wonder, etc. In other words, all new knowledge we learn is associated with an emotional response. Since any instance of learning shame is accompanied by a faulty human emotion about ourselves (previously referred to by Brene Brown), it is imperative that we learn how to appropriately identify and express those emotions This helps us fully understand the nature of shame, including ways of effectively combating shame in our lives.

In addition, the biology of the learning process in our brain includes millions of cells (neurons) linked by dendrites (like branches of a tree) which transfer impulses throughout our brain. If damaged in any way, this process of transferring information via neural pathways can heal and begin operating effectively again. Thus, by identifying our emotional responses to shameful experiences, we are able to encode new knowledge in our Long-Term Memory that indicates we do not have to remain captive to past destructive experiences of shame. This phenomenon of healing neural pathways is now understood as neuroplasticity. [7]

Brain Biology and Shame

Having established a broad base understanding of how we learn, let's now turn our attention to the destructive emotion of shame. As I review my life and learning, including dealing with shame, I understand that we 'learn' and store shame in the Long-Term Memory of our brain. From our knowledge of adolescent brain research, [8] we understand that the immature brains of children and teenagers have 50% greater neuron connectedness than in adults.

Therefore, consider this with me; if we constantly hear the message as children such as we are useless, we don't belong, we are incompetent, we don't think and, we are stupid and cannot learn, these neural pathways are strengthened, and the profound impact of these messages is stored forever in our Long-Term Memory.

In addition, we know that neural pathways infrequently used actually die off. If messages such as we are special, we belong, we are loved, we are touched and held, we are told we are smart in particular ways, are not communicated to us, these messages of hope and affirmation are not as robustly present in our Long-Term Memory. Compounding this, as adolescents sleep, the brain actually prunes neural pathways that are not regularly accessed during our waking hours. In other words, any minimal positive messages about our competence and belonging may be pruned, and the messages of shame thrive and dominate our Long-Term memory.

A possible consequence of brain biology is that we hide in our shame. We learn we are useless and unwanted, and all the time our beautiful brain is just doing what it was designed for; to faithfully record and encode all messages it receives from our Working Memory. However, there is hope.

Norman Doidge [9] suggests, if we nip false messages we experience as children and teenagers in the bud, we potentially stand a strong chance the neural pathways conveying messages of shame will weaken and atrophy. I believe this would be especially true when we consistently reflect upon our progress in learning and the positive achievements we make in our lives. Further, as we reinforce learning in a positive emotional environment, we are reinforcing knowledge that we are capable, special, loved, unique, talented, etc. I always taught my education students an alternative to one of our well-known paradigms:

> *"Practice makes perfect,"* to: *"Practice makes progress."*

I believe that constantly examining our progress and reflecting upon our learning and changing behaviour is a key to combatting the neural pathways of shame to our brain. In other words, if we don't 'use' our 'shame pathways,' they will atrophy and die.

Of further interest in this regard is a special school in Toronto, Canada, called Arrowsmith School. [10] This School was established for children and some adults with severe brain damage and learning difficulties. The school recognises the brain as a muscle that can be strengthened through exercise, and that damaged or atrophied neural pathways can be renewed for acquiring and storing meaningful and edifying knowledge in our Long-Term Memory.

The exercise in the case of shame is constantly reinforcing ideas in our Working Memory, known as rehearsing, about our range of intelligence, our competence, our worth and belonging, and our overall dignity as a child, teenager and adult.

Reflections

Feeling unworthy of love and belonging were certainly among my predominant emotions as a child on the farm, although I did not have the language at the time to articulate those emotions. I also recall events where being left out and considered unworthy contributed to me eventually fermenting a resentment and ultimate hatred towards my dad. I recall a specific occasion where I felt left out and thought I was a burden and not important to dad.

He was using the tractor to till some land, with my brothers riding on the tractor. Henry and Rossco must have been around five and three years old, and I would have been eight. I wasn't allowed on the tractor. Rather, I had to pick up sticks and small shrub roots that had been disturbed by the tilling and stack them in piles. Every time they would go past me on the tractor, I felt so alone and sad that I wasn't counted worthy to ride on the tractor with my brothers.

Dad's constant barrage of criticism eventually found a home in my Long-Term Memory and it took me years of hard work to mitigate against the belief that I was useless and no good for anything. Meanwhile, my shame and belief that I was useless motivated me in later years to myriad success, albeit sometimes hollow in terms of eventual satisfaction. Unfortunately, it also drove me to push hard to prove myself to my dad, by engaging in wildly stupid and sometimes self-destructive behaviour.

Examples of the latter included being the crowd idiot through meaningless and attention-seeking behaviour, drunken behaviour that could have ended in disastrous consequences and an ongoing struggle to 'prove myself worthy.'

Key Learning Points

If you have travelled with me this far in my story, let me share my own specific learning about shame to date:

- We actually store shame knowledge in our brain. Therefore, **we learn about shame**, including what it is, what it is not, how to identify it in ourselves, how it influences our negative thinking about ourselves, and, how we can mitigate against the effect of shame in our lives. I believe this knowledge is paramount in living lives of hope and purpose. Knowledge *about* shame enables us to take the next step; knowledge *of* shame.

- As we gain knowledge of shame, we begin to **understand shame**, including how it works in our lives. Understanding therefore becomes vital towards taking steps to examine our own lives for clarity, regarding ways in which shame is potentially impinging upon our lives. In turn, we learn effective ways to love and care for ourselves, and others.

- From understanding we move to **being in action**, whereby we exhibit behaviours such as listening to others, expressing empathy for others, negotiating and collaborating with others, leading lives of generosity towards others, and hope in our future.

- Finally, we adopt a conscious and intentional habit of **examining our behaviours and beliefs**, in order that we meet the life-giving aspirations we set for ourselves. It is quite a journey.

I explore all these steps in following pages of my story. Thus, our focus will be based upon the ramifications of adopting the following simple steps:

- **L**earning about shame,

- **U**nderstanding the impacts of shame,

- **B**eing intentional and confident in adopting new ways of 'being'

- **E**xamining, or 'reflecting upon' people and events that have influenced us, including ways in which we have inspired and mentored others.

I deliberately chose the acronym **LUBE** since I suggest we all regularly need a good oil change, tune up and service, including panel beating from time to time.

Chapter 3

A Dog, a Pig, and a Cow

On the farm we had a Blue Healer dog named Bell, who was old and probably arthritic. I must have been five at the time when dad decided to put Bell out of her pain. He asked me to join him without explaining what he was going to do. He had Bell on a piece of rope, acting as a lead, and he was carrying his .22 rifle.

We walked about 1,000 metres up Ironstone Road to a small gravel pit in the forest behind the farm. Dad held Bell close and pointed the rifle at her head. I remember she had her ears pricked and was looking towards a log on the edge of the gravel pit when dad said:

"Poor Bell."

And he pulled the trigger.

I still remember the shock and sadness at seeing Bell collapse. I was numb from confusion as we walked away from Bell's exposed body in the gravel pit and back to the farmhouse. On that long walk back down the hill, not a word was exchanged between dad and I.

In later years I wondered how much this event affected my frustrating reluctance to initiate conversations with my own daughters as they were growing up, especially as teenagers. I am aware of many opportunities I had with each of my girls to engage in rich conversations about what might be happening in their lives, but I just couldn't do it. It still frustrates me as I reflect upon this in my later years, although I no longer 'beat myself up' for missing these potentially rich moments in time. But I know they were there.

On another occasion on the farm when I was probably around seven years old, dad had me accompany him to put down a boar that had become aggressive and was no longer safe in the pig pens. He took a shot at the pig with his .22 rifle but the boar's head was obviously really tough so the bullet bounced off. Now it was mad and it charged through a fence and into an adjoining paddock. Meanwhile, dad had one more shot that wounded the pig as it ran off. Dad told me to stay close to him as he followed the boar to get another shot.

Eventually he cornered it among some fallen tree branches and after a couple more shots, he finally put the pig down. I don't remember what I was thinking, except that it was a dry throat, scary experience. In hindsight, I think dad involved me in these incidents so I could 'learn by watching,' but I would have preferred on both occasions if he had just 'talked it through' with me as to why he had to put both animals down, and especially why it was so hard to kill the pig.

A third example of seeing, but not understanding, also deeply troubled me. We had a few excellent Jersey cows in the herd, well known for the quality of cream in their milk. One was named *Twinkle,* and another I remember well was *Patsy.* Both were a beautiful golden colour with black markings. They were so quiet that you could walk up to them any time in the paddock, and they would appreciate a cuddle. *Twinkle* had been retired, but *Patsy* was still milking, and was always the first cow to enter the shed and the first to enter the stall to be milked. When we started milking one Sunday morning, I realised *Patsy* was not there.

"Had my dad noticed," I wondered?

I reported that *Patsy* was missing, but there was no response from dad, which puzzled me. I can't remember what happened next, but during milking, I returned quickly to search for *Patsy*. Nothing. At the end of milking, I retraced my steps in a thorough search for her.

"She had to be somewhere," I thought.

There was a small, low-lying area by the river that always had rich grass. It was about the size of a major International Sports Stadium, but she wasn't there. By now I was worried and feeling a bit scared. The paddock was close to the river and was uncleared land. As I walked further into the paddock and towards the river, I felt quite nervous. Something didn't seem right. *Patsy* would not simply disappear.

I was increasingly scared and all kinds of horrible thoughts were invading my mind. The whole experience was so unreal for me. Then I saw her. The hair on the back of my head stood up, I felt a cold shiver through my body, and I had that terrible dread when you know something is wrong.

Patsy was lying on her side and flat on the ground. Not normal. As I drew closer, I saw she wasn't moving and then I saw a small round hole in her head. She had been shot dead. My body just went cold, and I couldn't go any closer. A feeling of deep sadness overwhelmed me and I just cried and cried. Eventually I went back to tell dad, but he didn't say anything, or seem to be surprised.

"Had he known Patsy was dead?"
"What had happened to Patsy?"
"What was my dad thinking?"
"Who killed her?"
"Why would they do that?"

I had so many questions running through my head and not one answer. To this day I do not know what happened to *Patsy*. I know she had been shot and I can only surmise some 'weekend hunters' had done this. It troubled me for days and years following.

The Influence of Dads

Upon reflection, with respect to my relationship with dad, I became used to 'not knowing' or 'understanding,' and to accept that was the way life worked. A dog and a pig don't matter anymore and a cow is dead. So what? I suspect my dad didn't know how to talk to me about these things, and that he was doing his best to teach me by having me with him as he performed these tasks that arise as part of life as a farmer. I am sure he never meant me any harm by his silence, and I do know it taught me respect for animals in pain or, as in the boar's case, they can potentially endanger lives. In terms of *Patsy*, I just don't know.

We know dads have an incredibly powerful impact upon the early learning of our children, a point stressed repeatedly in three invaluable books by Australian researchers and authors, Bruce Robinson [1] and Steve Biddulf, [2] which I wholeheartedly endorse. At this point, I caution anyone reading these books or consulting resources, to guard against shame endeavouring to convince you that it is too late for you to change. It is not. Be strong and courageous; you are worthy and you can do it.

Admittedly, it is easy for me to encourage in this regard, but I acknowledge that I constantly battle with intrusive thoughts about being a failure as a dad. Whereas I attribute the source of many of these thoughts to my early experiences of shame, I also acknowledge that, by sharing these struggles with mentors and receiving empathy and counsel accordingly, I am able to resist the temptations of shame that may lead me to lose total confidence in myself, and to berate myself for times I failed in my role as father and husband.

In reality, we all fall short of standards of behaviour and effort we know are reasonable. In these cases, it is not the fact that we know we have failed that is germane, rather it is the resources we have to help us regain our dignity and resolve to carry on, being mindful of the gifts we have. We have roles and responsibilities as fathers and 'father figures,' or 'tribal elders,' to encourage and affirm children, youth, and younger men and women in their own lives.

To this end, resources such as those listed above by Bruce Robinson and Steve Biddulf have been most helpful to me. There is also an excellent platform, *The Fathering Project,* that offers ideas and strategies for dads and 'father figures' to consider and adopt.

The Fathering Project

In conjunction with publishing two books, Bruce Robinson initiated *The Fathering Project,* [3] a program based in primary schools. The project contains a range of resources for fathers and 'father figures' and encompasses invaluable tips and strategies regarding our responsibilities apropos child rearing and embracing our roles as mentors and 'father figures' in our communities. A strategic aim of *The Fathering Project* is to have dads and father-figures engaged with children in an endeavour to role model adults offering respectful and loving teaching and care to children and teenagers, especially about their value and dignity in their communities.

Men involved in *The Fathering Project* receive training and support for spending time with children and teenagers, engage in all kinds of activities and 'live' a message that they belong to a community and have access to a network of support, encouragement and love. The message is community, where children can learn to trust themselves and to grow as confident learners and altruistic citizens. In my experience, this is an invaluable community initiative as a context for our children and teenagers to lay down strong messages of hope and trust in themselves for their futures. School and community are places where I found succour as a child on the family farm.

Chapter 4

School, Community, Rabbits and a Fire

We used to walk about two kilometres to school, often in the company of hostile magpies during spring, a flooded river in winter, snakes across the path in summer, cold rain in winter and stinking hot days in summer, and our neighbour Bob Slee's dog, *Doodah*. At times when we raided Bob's orchard on the way home from school, Bob used to call out:

"The Prout kids are in the orchard, Doodah."

But when *Doodah* saw who it was, he would wag his tail and forget about it. *Doodah* was awesome and we loved Bob!

At school we maxed out one year at 18 children, all in one room with one teacher, Standard (Grade) One to Seven. During winter, we took turns to bring a billy of milk each day so we could have hot cocoa for recess. There was a fireplace in the room, and we would be rostered to light and tend to the fire to boil the milk for our mug of hot cocoa. When I first started school in Standard One, my two classmates and I each had a special chalk board called a slate, about the size of an A5 sheet of paper, upon which we could write with a crayon.

Later, as we learned to print, we used paper and pencil, and then pen and ink. The pen had a wooden handle, like a small brush for a set of paints, and a steel nib. You had to dunk the nib in an ink well, which was a little clay container in a special hole in the desk, to be able to write. Before we could use ink, we had to mix the powder with water, sometimes with disastrous results – spilt ink. It was really hard to write with pen and ink. I preferred the chalk board. In retrospect, my early attempts at writing were abysmal.

School was a break from dad and the farm, but I struggled academically. I am sure my struggles were more to do with my deep shame of believing I was useless and no good for anything rather than the potential I had for learning in a safe environment. I certainly remember a fear of being caught out if I did anything wrong in class. I was petrified once when a man came to visit us – a Primary School Superintendent I presume – to test what we knew. Not much on my part. Our teachers were always kind and generous, but I just could not relax in school. I sometimes arrived late, having chores and work in the dairy before school, and rushing home to help milking after school.

I enjoyed sports days where I could excel. The school was on two hectares of land with a couple of huge gum trees, a clay tennis court, a creek with the occasional tiger snake, and a shelter shed if it was raining. Our teacher lived on the grounds so he would go home for lunch. I remember falling out of the red gum in the school ground and having the wind knocked out of me. How I didn't break anything I will never know; just all in a day's work for a kid, I guess. In addition, the Mountford and Ratcliffe kids would walk home with us and stop at home for a snack before they carried on. They also loved mums cooking. They lived four kilometres further on from our farm so they had a long walk each day.

Community

Christmas Tree and presents from Santa at the Ferguson Community Hall with the whole community was so special. After Santa's visit, we would all show our toys to each other, and enjoy cake and ice cream. We also had card nights. Euchar and Five Hundred were games I loved, and I was able to attend in my early teen years with mum, or our neighbours who offered to drive me. Any event at the Ferguson Hall was special because it brought the whole community together and I embraced the unity and safety of that. My dad rarely attended any of these events so they were places where I could relax and enjoy any affirmation adults offered.

Dad didn't have any time for neighbours in Ferguson, a fact I only understood years later. Once, during the year I turned fifteen on the farm, I drove the tractor to the Ferguson Hall for a community engagement to carry out maintenance on the building. When Dad arrived home after night milking, he queried me about spending that time, stating as he did that, I could have found better things to do on the farm. Even at that stage, his comment gave me some insight into how isolated he was from the local community. By contrast, I felt safe, appreciated, and respected by the men of the community, and I loved working alongside them in any collaborative event.

In later years my name was added to the Honour Role in the hall as someone from the Valley who had been in the military and engaged in a conflict zone. This experience of community was not lost on me. Again, I felt safe among the men and women of the district, and I am sure it was this experience that fostered my decision in later years to research Community Education in Canada. [1]

An Early Entrepreneur

A phenomenon of my childhood was the rabbit plague confronting farmers in the Ferguson Valley in the 1950s. Rabbits are not native to our country, and they breed rapidly. They were introduced into Australia in the Eighteenth Century by people migrating from the UK. Rabbits can begin breeding at four months old and a doe has around five rabbits per litter, with five or more litters in a year. That is a lot of bunnies! I remember looking out over the paddock closest to the house and it seemed like the whole hill was moving with rabbits, eating all the pasture in the process. Farmers had to utilise various strategies for dealing with this major problem.

Meanwhile, I was able to trap rabbits and sell them to the Dardanup Butcher for twenty shillings (20c) a pair. In those days we called rabbit meat 'underground mutton.' I was around ten – eleven years old when I started earning money from trapping rabbits. I began with twelve rabbit traps, a little hoe and a hemp bag I would carry to check my traps each morning.

I set the traps in the late afternoon, usually close to newly dug burrows or tracks rabbits were clearly using to go for food. The process of setting traps included scratching a small hole in the ground for a trap outside the burrow, or along the tracks. Once the trap was set, it was covered with dirt so it wasn't visible to the rabbits. In the morning I would go around and release the trapped rabbits and take them home to prepare them for the butcher.

I learned all the skills of trapping rabbits by accompanying and watching our neighbour, Keith Butcher. Keith also gave me my first set of traps, shaped the hessian bag for me and gave me the required small hoe. After following Keith a couple of times, I was ready to venture out on my own. This was one of my earliest memories of experiential learning, and what I would later understand as informal mentoring.

I learned so much from my rabbit trapping business, especially about being responsible and working hard to prove I could be trusted to deliver what I had agreed. I made a commitment to Mr Roy Kessel at Dardanup Butchers to supply him with rabbits and he, in turn, could promise his customers specific product they ordered for sale. I valued the chance to prove my worth in this way, and I appreciated the trust Mr Kessel placed in me, including his support to be accountable for my behaviour.

Mr Kessel was one of the early adults who mentored me through mutual trust and agreement. He also initiated a Junior Football Team from Dardanup and somehow managed to convince my dad to let me to play when I was fifteen. Mr Kessel's trust and support was a balm for my soul in combatting my dad's negativity and harassment.

The Ferguson/Wellington Mills Fire

I was five years old and Henry just two when a terrible fire roared through the Wellington Mills and Ferguson area. [2] The fire burned out the village and Saw Mill at Wellington Mills, but no one was badly hurt or injured. From there, it carried on to the Ferguson Valley and caused extensive damage to fencing and property.

The Anglican Community Church was burnt to the ground and has since been re-built on the same spot. The Ferguson Hall and School somehow survived the fire, but the railway bridge across the Ferguson River on our farm was burnt out. It left all the steel rails hanging across the river without any support which was an odd sight. The entire railway between Wellington Mills and Dardanup was now wrecked because all the wooden sleepers were burnt out.

The fire encircled our farmhouse, but fortunately for us and our neighbours Keith and Sheila Butcher, our homes and sheds were not damaged. I can still remember the amazing roar of the fire and watching it race through the trees along a fence on the farm. I can't remember where and how it was eventually stopped, but it was certainly a scary time for everyone involved. I also think all farms escaped major damage to homes and sheds; just fences were damaged.

Within months after the fire, my Uncle Bill obtained the contract to remove the rail lines between Wellington Mills and Dardanup. I am not sure what happened to all the steel, but I do remember being able to ride in Uncle Bill's truck when they were loading and carting railway lines from the tracks on the farm. That was special.

Reflections

With respect to understanding protection from shame in my life, the most significant impact to this point was seeing the grace extended by my mother to neighbouring children, the power of belonging in community, the interest and support towards me by our local butcher, and seeing the community recover from the shock of a major bushfire.

I also experienced the steadying voices of neighbours, Keith and Sheila, and the warmth and love in the gentle, strong, voice of our parish priest, Father Cunningham, as consoling my spirit and bathing my soul in healing balm. These experiences and memories were the harbingers for understanding the role of informal and formal mentors in my life.

Chapter 5

The Genesis of Mentors in my Life

My earliest memories of role models loving and encouraging me included our neighbours, Keith and Sheila Butcher, and Father Cunningham[1] who between 1947 – 1958 was our Parish Priest in Dardanup. Dardanup was the village closest to our farm. [2] We attended Sunday Mass every week and along with all the other kids, I would sit as close to the front of the church as possible. For his sermon, Father Cunningham would come down to our front seats and he would ask us questions and tell stories. I later adopted this 'best practice' in my teaching career.

Once, when I was around eight years old and the smallest kid in my year (if I had been a crayfish, they would have thrown me back as undersized), Father Cunningham asked me a question which I obviously missed, and I responded with something possibly quite heretical. Many in the church laughed at my response and I felt ashamed and embarrassed for getting the answer wrong. Father Cunningham was my hero and I never wanted to let him down. However, what he did next has influenced the way I have been a teacher all my life. He looked at me and he said:

> *"Peter, that is the first mistake you have ever made."*

I suddenly felt two metres tall, and all the laughing stopped. It was like I was surrounded by a warm light that mitigated my embarrassment. Of course, it wasn't the first mistake I had made, but he rescued me in a moment of shame and embarrassment. This was such a powerful contrast to the negative and hurtful mantra of my dad. In Father Cunningham's presence, I experienced firsthand the beauty and power of love and acceptance, despite my error.

I have repeated this story countless times to my education students, making the point that as teachers, we can have a powerfully transformative impact on a student's life, often without any knowledge of our influence. Years after this event, I made time as an adult to seek out Father Cunningham and remind him how significant that moment had been for me.

Father Cunningham had been Chaplain to the 2nd / 1st Infantry Battalion of the Australian Army during the horrific battles against the invading Japanese Army along the Kokoda Track during World War Two. He was awarded an MBE in 1947 for his service to troops at Eora Creek on the Kokoda Track in 1942.[3]

In 2012, my brother Ross and one of his son's walked the Kokoda Track and they vividly described the Eora Creek crossing. Rosco noted it would have been like a 'shooting gallery' as wounded troops were ferried across the creek under fire from Japanese troops higher up the valley.

I don't know how this experience affected Father Cunningham, but I do know, on one hand he was a strong, capable and courageous man, and on the other a gentle and loving person. He said in church one day:

"Dardanup needs a community hall, and I am going to build it. If anyone can help, they would be welcome."

In my life since, I have only rarely seen leadership quite like that. With community help, Father Cunningham built the hall that stands today. He kept bees and supplied the whole district with honey, regardless of anyone's faith or religious beliefs. Everyone in the district loved and respected Father Cunningham and he remains one of my all-time heroes. I had seen him in overalls laying bricks to build a community hall. I had been with him collecting honey from his hives. I had been at 'Bushy School' [4] where he taught and loved us all, and I saw him leading us in Mass every Sunday with such gentleness and love for God.

Neighbours and Mum

Keith Butcher was a man like Father Cunningham for me. I admired everything about Keith, and I loved Sheila, Keith's wife (I am sure almost every other kid and young man in the Valley loved Sheila). Keith and Sheila's farm was just over a kilometre past our farm on *Butcher Road*, which was the end of *Prout Road*. As stated earlier, Keith taught me how to trap and skin rabbits that I sold to Mr Roy Kessel.

Keith always encouraged me despite the fact I was little and skinny in frame. He worked hard and he was tough. He wore shorts 365 days of the year which I copied, and I always felt safe with Keith. He was my hero, role model and true mentor.

Mum was the first to model unconditional love for me. I agree with my brother Ross who says it is a pointless exercise 'comparing mothers.' Rather, we just rest in the understanding that our own mothers are precious to each of us in our own unique experiences of them. I like my brother's counsel and wisdom on this matter.

Every spring mum would remark on how beautiful the flowers were, how green the pasture was, how special each newborn calf was, and how valuable all the fruit we grew on the farm was. I thank God for mum teaching me to love and respect the land and for the experiences of (1) eating homemade fig jam and cream from the dairy, (2) fresh bottled fruit during the winter, (3) her homemade ice cream, (4) reading me stories every night, (5) chatting with me and my little dog Tippy until Henry was old enough to be my mate, (6) protecting me as best she could when I was in trouble with dad, (7) taking me to the Ferguson Hall for card nights with the adults, (8) teaching me to love and honour our Aboriginal people, and (9), for sharing her insights into what she was learning from all the reading she did.

Mum was a nurse so she always looked after us when we were sick. Neighbours would also often come to her for help with their own sick children. Mum was loved and respected throughout the district and I was always proud of her for that. She worked so hard in the dairy and on the farm, and was an amazing cook; her sponge cakes made with fresh farm eggs and covered with passionfruit icing were to die for. She did all this on an old wood stove that made the small house fiercely hot in the summer months. However, I never saw or heard her complain, but she endured some very hard times.

Farm Kid's Mothers Have Extraordinary Patience

I vividly recall a time when mum was going out on an important date and she was taking we three boys with her. She spent time dressing us in our best clothes to go to a special event and then needed time to take care of herself. Mum instructed us to go to the vehicle shed and wait in the truck for her. In the shed was an open bag of grey cement.

Grey cement feels so cool when you run fingers through it but grey cement also sticks to your best and only set of clothes. Three boys soon had distinctively grey tones to their bodies and clothes. Mum is now dressed and ready to go, until she gets to the shed... Mothers have huge hearts and an unbelievable capacity to resist what could have been justifiable infanticide.

Later, I remember feeling so bad that mum had to take us back inside to dress us in our second-best clothes and be late for her outing. I learned from this and many similar occasions just how hard it is to love unconditionally.

Almost Seriously Injuring our Mother

Henry and I were once faced with the possibility we had terminated our mother's life. Mum was pregnant with Di, although I didn't know that at the time, when I did something to upset Henry. In his furious response, Henry threw a three-pronged hoe in my direction from the third level landing of the house, and mum was standing alongside me on the veranda by the kitchen door. The hoe missed me, hit a veranda post, and veered off in mum's direction, striking her on her temple. Down she went like a sack of spuds.

Now we were terrified, believing mum was dead on the veranda. Dad and Bob Slee were working away in a paddock, so we raced off to get them, but when we arrived, we were too scared to say what happened. Bob eventually picked there was something wrong. Us saying we left mum lying on the back veranda may have been a clue! We all ran home to find mum alive and well, albeit a bit groggy. Whew, that was too close. Henry still says he can't remember what he was mad about!

Reflections Re: Mentors

I have mentioned mentors in my life to date, and in the next chapter, I will review this concept in detail, including discussion of similar terms and what they might mean and imply. In my story I make a number of distinctions, in relation to the following:

1. **Heroes:** Having a hero in our lives is, I believe, a significant first step in our process of maturing from childhood through teenage years, and into adulthood. Our heroes can be real or imagined, and their main influence can be as markers for our aspirational ideals. As childhood heroes for me, Father Cunningham and Keith Butcher were shafts of warm light, especially when things were really dark with my dad. They were men of character, love and hard work who offered me a light into the next week, and ultimately into a future that I had not yet comprehended.

2. **Role Models**: From being a hero, I identify special men and women in my life who morphed into role models from whom I learned many invaluable life skills and ways of behaving. Somehow, the hero for me was just that; a label for someone in whose presence I felt safe. A role model was the one whose behaviour and values I could appropriate and attempt to copy. Obviously, role models were people from whom I could seek advice and counsel, especially around farm work. In my early years on the farm, I had heroes and role models. Later in my story, I will expand upon the agency of these roles in my life.

3. **Mentors – Formal and Informal:** Gradually, I began to experience and understand the power of relationships that I now refer to as mentoring, where I was physically and emotionally safe, and where I learned so much about the people I loved dearly. Their teaching and counsel was invaluable in forming impressions about my own self-worth and value. In my experience, mentors are people who cared enough about me to give 'tough love' that included specific feedback for my benefit, albeit not always easy to hear.

- **Formal mentors** in my life have been academic advisors and lecturers, line managers, and those responsible for articulating work and performance expectations, including military personnel. In this regard, the mentoring process, which included outlining expectations and review of effort and outcomes, was well defined and unambiguous. Formal mentoring for me normally took place within defined work environments.

- **Informal mentors** were those with whom I established intentionally deep and meaningful relationships that led to significant intellectual, emotional and spiritual growth in my life. In some cases, my informal mentoring relationships have resulted from a conversation with someone I have admired or from the way they have taken an interest in my welfare. In other cases, they resulted from seeking out a particular person to 'pick their brain,' or just simply 'hang out.'

As adults, I see the profound difference we can make on our own children's lives, including the lives of their friends, classmates and other friends, simply by taking an interest in them, and by encouraging and expecting them to begin learning the vital skill of knowing and taking responsibility for their own actions.

4. **Coaches, Teachers, Siblings, Spiritual Directors, Work Colleagues, Significant Peers:** Individuals with whom we transact in these roles can have a huge influence upon our lives, both positive and negative. Unfortunately, I don't have anyone significant in the first two roles, but I have giants in my life, including my siblings, specific cousins, Spiritual Directors, work colleagues, and significant peers. When acting in what I term 'incidental relationships', I suggest these people are closer to acting as informal mentors than any of the other roles.

Finally, being raised in a church family was a place of refuge that would become a powerful foundation for my faith in later life. The intentional reflection and examination of my life as an adult in my seventies, leads me to identify and specifically define the form and function of mentors.

Chapter 6

Mentors: Champions Upon Whose Shoulders I Stand

There has been significant research around the principles and ideals of mentoring, mentors and protégés. I recommend two significant articles where mentoring has been reviewed, prosecuted and evaluated. The first is led by Catherine McLaughlan [1] writing for Health Services Research from the University of Michigan in the U.S. McLaughlan acknowledges that there is:

> *"An amazing range of uses and lack of consensus about what mentoring is."*

She adds that, after searching widely for a definition, she believes an original source of the term, and including processes of mentoring, can be found around the time of the Trojan War. Before Odysseus left for the war, he asked his elderly friend and counsellor Mentor to serve as a counsellor to his own son Telemachus. Thus, in McLaughlan's view, we have adopted Mentor's name as shorthand for "a wise and trusted teacher or counsellor."

I like this understanding because it has the implication of trust and a relationship between an older person (mentor), and a younger protégé. It is also more typical of the informal relationships in my experiences with older people or life-long peers and friends. I now have rich, mutually respectful and special relationships with the latter.

The second article is led by Lillian Eby [2] and published by the National Institute of Health in the U.S. Eby is from the University of Georgia, where she and colleagues distilled research from three main 'streams of mentoring.' These streams encompass:

1. Youth mentoring that; *"assumes supportive relationships for personal, emotional, cognitive and psychological growth."*

2. Academic mentoring for; *"imparting knowledge, providing support and offering guidance."*

3. Workplace mentoring for; *"personal and professional growth of protégés."*

I am familiar with the formal academic and workplace streams, and I have engaged informally with youth in the youth stream. I will refer to the benefits of all three in my life story. I add a fourth stream of mentoring to the three identified by Eby, namely 'Spiritual growth and understanding,' based upon and including my own mentoring experiences. I refer in detail to this stream in the final chapter of my story, including naming spiritual directors whom I love and honour. However, to be consistent throughout the rest of my story I will refer to mentors and protégés, rather than mentors and mentees. With respect to the efficacy of mentoring, I add a caveat on behalf of Eby and her colleagues. They caution not to:

1. *"Overestimate the potential effect of mentoring."*

2. *"It is unknown whether significant correlations between mentoring and outcomes reflect causal effect of mentoring,*

therefore we need to temper what are sometimes unrealistic expectations about what mentoring offers protégés."

3. *"In general the types of outcomes we can reasonably expect from mentoring are in:*

> *(a) general attitudes,*
> *(b) interpersonal relations, and,*
> *(c) motivation/involvement of protégés."*

In light of the numerous articles written on mentoring and the relationships between mentors and protégés, I believe these cautions by Eby and colleagues are most helpful. We should not expect too much from our mentoring efforts, or from what our mentors may or may not be able to successfully teach us. In my view, mentoring relationships are only as robust and efficacious as the commitment of the mentor to care about the well-being of their protégé and the protégé's desire to learn. We should therefore hold these relationships respectfully and lightly.

A third perspective on mentoring by Mary Abbajay [3] provides a concise and helpful summary of the key principles for successful, formal mentoring relationships. These principles encompass the need for (1) clear lines of communication in an organisation, and (2) expectations for assessing performance reviews. Clearly there is significant agency in the formal approaches to mentoring outlined by Abbajay, especially in large organisations. My work experiences include many enjoyable relationships that were formal and designed to help me succeed in my academic studies and in various workplaces.

However, my most valued experiences of mentoring are centred on the friendships I have with three long-term mates, plus a number of older men with whom I have established life-giving and authentic relationships. Further, there are numerous relationships I have with a wider circle of younger men and women that are mentor/protégé, characterised by counselling and listening to and learning from one another. With respect to the latter, my informal relationships are often characterised as 'short term goal-oriented agreements.'

On the other hand, some formal relationships lasted for the time of my specific academic pursuits or research efforts. In all these instances, I concur with Stephen Covey [4] that it seems pointless if you set out to learn something:

> *"...and then do nothing with your newfound knowledge."*

As I reflect upon my 'Lane Eight' journey of failure and success, I concur with Covey that what we learn from our mentors is only as valuable as our intention to listen and act. Here I refer back to the points made previously in this chapter in relation to the caveat on effective mentoring relationships by Eby.

Further, for the purposes of clarification in my story, my own definition of mentoring is:

An intentional relationship (either formal or informal) between two people that is mutually beneficial for the intellectual, social, emotional and spiritual growth of both parties, the latter normally identified as mentor and protégé.

Since there is a significant dependence upon effective relationships in mentoring, it is vitally important that we understand the importance of active listening in relationships.

Listening and Feedback

Listening is possibly the biggest challenge facing protégés in the mentoring process. Often the feedback, or counselling we receive from a mentor, can be hard, even painful, to hear. As Sheila Heen [5] says:

> *"I wish I could offer you a pain free learning environment."*

Heen also notes that the benefit of feedback is entirely dependent upon the attitude of the one receiving the feedback. The receiver has the power to accept or reject the feedback. In this respect, Heen acknowledges that the interaction of asking for and receiving feedback can be a tough process. Further, James Clawson [6] indicates feedback as:

> *"...neither moral nor immoral and neither right nor wrong until we respond to it, either accepting or rejecting it...the challenge is for the person who listens to remain non-defensive with ears and hearts open, listening carefully to what is being communicated."*

In my experience, Clawson's attitude towards feedback is critical for mentors and protégés to understand and embrace. I have certainly experienced the tough love of feedback, and I am now convinced that all feedback is invaluable, no matter how hard it is to hear. Heen's counsel in the process of seeking feedback, or reacting to negative unsolicited feedback that I would define as criticism, is to respond as follows:

> *"Thanks for the feedback. Can you give me one suggestion for improving my performance?"*

Over my career in teacher education, I taught this response to my students. It helps them in power differential situations when a mentor teacher gives what I call 'global feedback' which is effect quite useless and vague for the beginning teacher. The protégé, in this case the beginning teacher, needs to gather their emotions after what can be hurtful and deliberately demeaning feedback, and respond with:

> *"Thanks for the feedback. Can you give me one suggestion for improving my teaching?"*

The mentor must now respond with a constructive comment to at least save their own face, especially after initially giving a stinging and meaningless rebuke to their protégé. Sadly, there are many of these kinds of formal mentors 'out there.' Even in our treasured relationships, I think it is sometimes appropriate to respond sometimes with:

> *"Thanks for telling me this"*, or *"Thanks for sharing your insights"*, or, *"That gives me something to think about."*

This action stems from a sound EQ and it gives us a moment to process the feedback without cutting off the flow of counsel and learning with your mentor. I hasten to add that, in some of my primary relationships in the past, I was unable to get past the initial self-talk I heard:

> *"See, you are useless and stupid."*

I would then 'clam up' as a protective but ineffective mechanism. I am finding learning and growing a life-long process that I may never get right in this life. In this respect, I think my epitaph will read:

"He still hadn't figured it out."

With respect to mentors, my life has been enriched beyond measure. Mentors helped me work through the impacts of shame, and how those impacts can be ameliorated over time, and rendered less pervasive in our self-talk and ongoing relationships. Mentoring is a gift given and a gift received. Whether mentor or protégé, we are assured of quality of life that can be life-long in practice and emotional efficacy. There is a significant example of this assertion from a movie based upon events during World War Two.

Making Our Lives Count

The worse thing I can imagine is a man, facing his own mortality, and not being sure if his life has mattered. You might recall the following, powerful scene from the opening of the 1998 movie *Saving Private Ryan*. In the scene, an older James Ryan is walking through the U.S. Memorial Grounds in France, honouring the fallen soldiers at the Normandy Invasion. He turns to his family and asks:

"Have I been a good man?"

The motivation for this question was in relation to the last words spoken by Captain John Miller to Private Ryan:

"Make your life count."

Captain Miller and a small squad of soldiers had been commissioned to find Private Ryan and return him safely from the front line of the Allied Invasion in Normandy. In this endeavour, Captain Miller and most of the men in the squad were killed but Ryan survived, thus prompting his life-long question in relation to how he had lived his life.

I would like men and women who have blessed me in my life and helped make me a better man to know they made their lives count. We can never be 'good men.' After all, how do we measure 'good'? In relation to what standard or criterion? However, we can endeavour to make our lives count. I honour and thank the men and women I remember as significant peers and mentors in my life. With all my flaws and failings, I trust I have honoured them, notwithstanding the bad decisions and mistakes I have made along the way, and I endeavour to honour those people now as I resume my story from childhood to teenage years and adulthood.

Chapter 7

High School and Destiny

I distinctively remember how I felt the morning I turned ten years old. At this stage the physical beltings from my dad were less frequent but the constant harping about my uselessness and overall standing in the family was ongoing. I can honestly say the physical beatings did me no lasting harm, albeit some of them were painful at the time. I believe an occasional smack for good reason is part of us learning self-discipline. However, constant berating and criticism of our character takes root in our mind and spirit, thus saddling us with long term struggles and heartache. The old adage I heard as a kid which no longer rings true, if it ever did:

Sticks and stones may break my bones, but your silly words can't harm me.

As already indicated, the words we hear find their way into our brain and remain as markers of our worth and dignity or haunt us. Either way, positive emotional experiences aligned with words are our most effective pathway out of shame's impact and towards wholeness of mind and spirit.

Meanwhile, I was age ten and I felt older. I sensed that since I had reached double figures, I was no longer a child. After all, I could milk cows on my own and I could drive a team of two draft horses. More importantly, I was in love with Anne Gibbs, one of my primary school peers. Events between age ten and twelve that stick in my mind as potentially life threatening but 'best memories' include:

- Parents think they can hide stuff from farm boys – not so much. Hiding a .303 rifle and ammunition on top of a cupboard doesn't mean it won't be found. When you rest a .303 rifle against a small dead tree and pull the trigger, the kick back can shake that tree out of its mind.

- Contractors building power lines across the Ferguson Valley in 1959 thought it safe to park a bulldozer in the gravel pit behind the farm for the weekend – not so much. Farm boys love starting bulldozers. Once we had it started, why not push some stuff around? Now we need to put stuff back. It is difficult to replace a small tree that has been uprooted by a bulldozer and to replace gravel piled in a heap, and to cover bulldozer tracks. Farm boys live in the belief they got away with it, and sometimes adults have a sense of humour and let things pass.

- When knocked out of gear at the top of a long hill, a Massey Ferguson 35 tractor picks up speed at an alarming rate. Three brothers on a runaway tractor go deathly pale; they say nothing. Farm boys do not need to state the obvious; we were about to die. Sometimes farm boys escape death without knowing how. Farm boys tend to forget near death experiences until the next one comes along.

- A bottle of beer stolen from the fridge doesn't really get cold in the river, but is drinkable, nevertheless.

- When they reach their teenage years, farm boys believe they are invincible. At a later stage in life farm boys get to realise they are not invincible and they wonder how they are still alive.

- Mothers of three sons on a farm have a tough life but they maintain a sense of humour. Mothers of three sons on a farm get grey hair early in life.

Boarding School at New Norcia: 1957 - 1959

I was twelve when I left Ferguson School at the end of Grade Six to go to St Ildephonses Marist College at New Norcia, around 350 kms from the family farm for Grade Seven and High School. As a point of interest, New Norcia is the only monastic town in Australia. [1] I never got to say good bye to Anne. I was still the smallest kid in my class, and I was scared and lonely at Boarding School.

The Principal, Brother Oliver, was a fair man, but the rest of the brothers were cruel and unkind. In Grade Six, we were taught by Mr Bumstead (his real name) from the U.K. I was in Brother Richard's dorm for Grade Seven and Brother Raymond's for Grade Eight and Nine. Every Saturday afternoon we had sport which I loved, and then two movies that I also loved, in the college theatre after dinner. We also had Tuck Shop on Saturday so we could buy Chew Chew bars, Red Skins, and other awesome lollies for the movies. That was my high school years.

I was definitely not an academic. Not yet. My school reports detailed my daydreaming in class, uninspiring Latin homework, and generally a hopeless all-round academic aptitude. We were forbidden to talk in class. I didn't understand stuff, but I wasn't allowed to ask in class. I couldn't do my homework at night. I found myself bending over every morning before class in Grade Nine for a whack on the bum with Brother Raymond's strap which he called Little Bertha, or the big one, Big Bertha. So, I just took the Bertha treatment every morning when Latin homework was checked.

Up to Grade Nine, I was still the smallest and skinniest kid in my class. I was always unsure of myself and I generally hated school. I wasn't good at making friends, mostly because I didn't think anyone would consider me worthy of being their friend. Daydreaming was an 'opt out' in class, but it is an art form for me today. I do some of my best thinking when I am 'daydreaming.' I recall vividly one day in Grade Nine when I was distracted by something Brother Oliver, our English teacher had said. I was processing it by looking out of the window. Our classroom was on the second story of the building and our window overlooked the Monastery across the road. Brother Oliver interrupted what could have been a Nobel Prize in Literature by declaring:

"There goes Prout, skipping over the hills of Ferguson."

In an instant the prize in literature vanished. Just like that. I still daydream and I encouraged my student teachers to respect students who do so. Some of our best ideas come from just drifting. We need to take time and space to just be still and wonder, and it became another beautiful strategy in combatting shame in my life.

On the other hand, there was my involvement in athletics and sport generally. In my reflections about my future unrealistic striving to excel at sport after leaving school, I harkened back to a comment dad made to me during a term break in my second year at New Norcia. He was asking about my sporting prowess and teams in which I had been selected. I said I was playing in teams in my age group when he asked:

"If you are good enough, are you eligible to be selected in teams above your age range?"

I admitted I would be eligible, and as I did, I felt like I was hit with a huge shirt front, [2] accompanied with a deep sense of failure. Dad made no further comment about my athletic and sporting ability. He didn't need to. I experienced the tone of his voice and non-verbal judgement on my skill.

In later years I learned he had been competent in many sporting areas. I also realised excelling in sport had been another motivation to convince myself I could do it. I loved all kinds of sport. I can't remember participating to actually 'prove' something to dad, but I never sought his counsel or advice about it. However, later in my life I pushed myself to extremes to prove my academic and intellectual worth. After all, this was an area he had not entered.

A Champion Senior Student

One of my best memories from New Norcia was when I was in Grade Seven, regarding an interaction I had with a Grade Twelve boy. Murray Ghatti was a House Captain of Torres House, when he gave me a great gift of assurance through a comment he made for my benefit. He was lacing his footy boots and I worked up the courage to go over and say: *"g'day."* Murray knew my name and although I have completely forgotten what we talked about, just as he finished lacing his boots, he said to me:

"Peter, one day you will be a House Captain."

I have no idea what prompted this senior student who looked like a man to me to say those words. I was skinny and insecure, and I couldn't believe what Murray said would happen. But we will see later that, although I wasn't at school to be a House Captain, when I was seventeen, I was running the dairy farm by myself. Sometimes we have an instinct about a person's qualities that they don't see in themselves. I was fortunate in later years to meet Murray at a campground and tell him how much his words meant to me that day.

We call this inability in our own mind 'blind spots.' They include the good things about us that we may not perceive, plus some annoying habits others always see that we sometimes deny. The phenomenon of blind spots is covered brilliantly by Sheila Heen [3] in her TED Talk and is listed in the 'notes' section of my story.

The Power of Peer Mentoring

My most important 'take away' from High School happened when I was in Grade Eight on our way home for school holidays. A bus would take us to Perth where we would catch the train to Bunbury or Brunswick Junction, where some boys alighted. As we were waiting for the train in the city, I was with Michael O'Neil and two other boys who for the life of me I cannot remember their names. The two boys wanted to go to an 'adult' movie in the Savoy Theatre on Hay Street, basically a porn movie. Quite possibly we would not have been admitted, but they insisted we go.

There is no way I wanted to go but I was too scared to say anything. Michael said he wouldn't go but we could. The two boys pestered Michael and I was silently praying he would resist, which he did. I was so relieved. We didn't go to the movie. I will never forget Michael for that day. Notice, I cannot remember the other two. Michael was the strong one I needed to stand up on my behalf in that moment.

While I was at New Norcia, I remember the whole school sitting on a bank in the early evening of October 4, 1957, to watch the first artificial satellite launched by Russia, cross the night sky. This was Sputnik. [4] It was amazing to be able to look up and see this tiny space craft speed across the sky. It represented the beginning of the Space Race that eventually led to Neil Armstrong landing on the moon on July 16, 1969.

Back to leaving school. I believed I was a failure at school. I wasn't happy at New Norcia and now I was heading home to the farm, where I was considered by my dad an even worse failure. My school reports make funny reading now but at age fourteen, I was still in the habit of reacting to criticism and shame generally by 'emotionally hiding' and mentally agreeing I was useless and without any rights. I pretended that it wasn't happening but inside, it hurt like mad. It was like living under dark clouds and being denied any sunlight. In later life, this practice of refusing to address the pain or issue at hand proved counterproductive and caused me great pain and distress accordingly.

How Were My Brothers, Sister and Mother Faring?

During my school years, especially before I went to New Norcia, it never occurred to me to consider the impact of my dad's behaviour and attitude towards me on my mother, my brothers, and sister. However, as adults my siblings and I have prosecuted these events in conversations, a process that has been profound and inspirational for each one of us. I know mum's faith carried her through years of pain and heartache, although I could never estimate just how much she endured.

One scary, vivid memory of mum's pain was after dad left the farm one particular New Year, to go to Perth we assumed. As he walked out the back door of the house, mum said:

"Have a nice New Year," to which he replied:
"Why do you think I am leaving here?"

I was standing there with my brothers and as he left, I vividly recall mum turning to us and saying:

"If I knew you boys were going to treat your
wives like this, I would slit your throats right now."

I confess it was an unnerving moment although I didn't believe for a moment that mum would harm us. Nevertheless, her pain was patently obvious to me at that time. During most of my childhood, I recall feeling lonely in the family. Although I have memories of certain unique experiences with my brothers, I don't think I was ever totally relaxed with them simply because I was always waiting for the next episode of abuse and criticism from dad. I also left the farm when I was twelve years old to go to boarding school and never really spent any more substantial childhood, or teenage years with them.

As I examine events of my life, I now see clearly that due to my lack of belief and confidence in myself, I was estranged from my brothers. This was not because of anything they did or failed to do, but because I was constantly on alert for dad calling me to carry out a task or to help him with something, both of which filled me with dread.

It was an event spent with my brothers years later that crystallised these reflections about my childhood and my relationship with my sibling. I travelled with Rossco and Henry for four weeks through inland Australia and it was during this time that I finally felt like I was the brother who belonged with the other two. Interestingly, with respect to my relationship with my sister, Di, I never felt the same intensity of regret, loss and loneliness as I did with Henry and Rossco.

Reflection

I now believe that behaviours I unconsciously appropriated to live through the shame I experienced in my pre-school years were imprinted in my DNA. I am convinced I was born with a gentle and teachable spirit which was foundational to my overall well-being. For example, I recall feeling the awe and wonder in cold winters, including when the cattle water trough froze over or in the early morning when the frost was thick enough on the ground to make the grass brittle underfoot, and I recall it at sunrise in seeing the beautiful low mist over the ground as the sun gradually melted the frost.

It was fun to make paths through the frosty ground and pretend I was building a road, or to find a fresh warm cow pat in the morning to warm my cold feet. No, not gross, just warm and sensuous on cold feet. The river would flood, creeks would rush along to join the river and we could wade through parts of the river that overflowed onto paddocks.

Other phenomena of wonder for me included springtime with fresh growth, the smell of freshly cut hay, wildflowers and bees buzzing, warm sun and birds singing; all welcome harbingers of a break from winter. Tadpoles became frogs and cows birthed calves. I never stopped wondering at the miracle of a brand-new calf being dropped on the ground by their mother and almost immediately standing up and 'walking.'

Feeding weaned calves and feeling their tongues wrap around my fingers as they sought to suckle was special. As I grew older, I learned how to lead them from sucking my fingers to drinking from a bucket. Awesome. The majesty of these experiences helped me forget about my own world of fear and unworthiness.

Later in my adult life, I believe these 'simple' delights served me well in maintaining an emotional homeostatic balance, albeit thrown off balance on many occasions. I hasten to add I haven't continued walking in fresh, warm cow dung as a regular strategy to soothe my soul. Rather, I appreciated later teaching that altruism, and appreciating and accepting what is before me at the time, are all balms for overcoming the messages of shame I hear.

Chapter 8

1960: A Fork in the Road

At age fifteen, having completed Grade Seven, Eight and Nine, I found myself back on the family farm and unsure of what would happen next. For the first few weeks of the year, when I knew my peers would be back at school at New Norcia, I felt sad and wishing I could be with them, even though I knew I wasn't flash academically, or in most sports. Working with my dad was also hard, although not as brutal as my time in primary school. I was less afraid of him and of making mistakes; he never encouraged me, rather he was always criticising me for things I didn't know. He wasn't able to teach me because he was so angry all the time.

On reflection I am amazed that he was living in what I now label 'a cauldron of hostility.' I mean, how can anyone stay that angry for so long? He must have had many unresolved issues locked away. Meanwhile, I managed to find some rhythm in the days and weeks, and to stay out of dad's 'anger zone.' Upon reflection, I am amazed that despite all the abuse I still sought my dad's love and approval. As an example, one evening after milking, when I was walking behind dad as we returned to the house, I felt an overwhelming urge to say:

"I love you dad."

I have no idea what prompted this. I just know I felt it in that instance. I also know I didn't say it. The feeling was there, but the words would not cooperate. I recall being momentarily conflicted between having that sense of love and being afraid to say it. I was scared of what might have happened if I had said it. I still haven't figured this out, but I know in my first marriage I always struggled to say the words 'I love you' to my wife, and to my three daughters. My daughters assure me they knew that I loved them, based upon the way I treated them, but I am cognizant of the fact that I was never spontaneous in *telling* them I loved them. I know I loved, and was most protective of my sister, but I didn't tell her either.

Being a Teenager

My social life during this year was again influenced greatly by Keith Butcher who was my lifeline. He took me in to Bunbury to play hockey every Saturday morning. I scored a goal in my first game, thus prompting additional encouragement from Keith. I was thrilled and I quickly excelled at hockey that winter. I broke my collar bone in a social game of footy one Sunday afternoon and I had to milk the cows that night with my arm in a sling. No problem. Mum took me in to have it set next morning after milking.

Keith also took me to Junior Farmers where his brother-in-law joined in taking care of me. Both men worked hard to talk my dad into letting me go to Junior Farmers activities and social dances. I also joined Young Catholic Workers and mum would drive me to Dardanup while others would take me to socials and dances.

Among these people from church who looked after me were young men in their twenties who took an interest in me, and by watching them, I learned how to be around girls and with everyone in the group. I especially loved watching the older boys and young men dancing and I determined one day I would be able to dance with their confidence. Dancing then meant taking a girl lightly in your arms and following specific dance steps and moves around the perimeter of the dance floor. There would be a band with drums, brass, piano and maybe strings. The process for dancing was you would go up to a girl and ask her if she would like to dance. Fortunately, I never received a 'no' for an answer. After the set, you were expected to walk her back to her seat and thank her.

You could at that point ask her for the next dance, or if you were really game you could 'book her' for the last dance. This was an indication to her that you liked her and if she agreed to save you the last dance, you were made. When these socials were at night, mum would drive me to Dardanup and then visit my Aunty Lorna and Uncle Bill before waiting in the car to drive me home. What a loving saint my mother was. All these people made life bearable in the midst of constant criticism from my dad.

Change Was Coming

Eventually, I couldn't stand the abuse from my dad and after yet another confrontation in March 1961, I stood up to him and said I wasn't taking it anymore. There had been way too many incidents of his abuse and disregard for me to go on accepting. For example, after Mass one Sunday, Mr Wells commented, in reference to me:

"Peter is growing up, Dick."

To which my dad replied:

"The bigger they are, the harder they fall."

I was in the back of the car and I was horribly embarrassed at my dad's reply to a compliment about me. From an early age I remember the phrase 'such a shame' being applied to someone who failed to do what the community believed they should; they allegedly 'wasted a talent' or they didn't meet a particular standard of behaviour. In some way I understood that shame was the community standard against which we were measured at school, work ethic, athletic success or not, behaviour, and more. My experiences of shame had become what Brene Brown [1] identifies as:

> *"...self-created stories we develop that may not be accurate, or gremlins in our brains."*

In other words, we encode in our Long-Term Memory, stories or episodes about not being a champion. As noted in Chapter Two, this is the result of the amazing biological functioning of our brain.

After the incident with Mr Wells, I began to experience resentment and hate towards my dad. I had wondered about love, but I now felt a hardening of my heart towards him. The previous Christmas I had asked mum, if I bought dad a dressing gown, did she think he would love me? She simply advised me to buy a less dramatic gift. There were just too many ongoing 'put downs' and ridicule from dad to continue ignoring, especially as an almost sixteen year old battling face acne and a growing interest in girls.

A moment of physical 'assault' after lunch one day was a trigger that almost ended in chaos in the farmhouse kitchen. Dad had been berating me about something over lunch, and as he rose to leave the table, I said:

> *"Oh, shut up!"*

At this, he threw what was left of a hot cup of tea at my bare chest. I exploded out of my chair and leapt towards him around the edge of the table. Providentially, mum was at hand, and she jumped between us. I was shaking with fury and I know it could have been a horrible mess if mum had not been there to 'cool the heat' I was feeling. In her advocacy role between us mum declared that:

> *"You shouldn't speak disrespectfully to your father,"* to which I responded:

> *"He shouldn't throw hot tea at me!"*

What a pathetic situation for my poor mother to handle. Not long after this incident, I was called to my sister's bedroom where my parents had obviously been talking about me. Dad said I should go for an apprenticeship which mum dismissed because I was too old along the fact that I needed a Junior Certificate, indicating I had successfully passed exams at the end of Grade Ten. Dad then suggested the army and that was as far as I recall the discussion advancing. No decision. More uncertainty for me.

Ironically, with respect to the army, dad got his wish later, albeit under controversial circumstances. Meanwhile, I was sick of living with a constant mixture of dread and fear in my guts and it all came to a head one Saturday afternoon just before milking. My relationship with dad was now toxic and in the words of my brother Ross:

> *"There had to be a circuit breaker, or someone would get seriously hurt, either mum or you."*

With respect to a circuit breaker, I love the famous saying by Yogi Berra:

"When you come to a fork in the road, take it."

Rossco was right, a fuse was burning on a time bomb in our family. The circuit breaker eventually came one Saturday afternoon after Henry and Rossco had taken hay out on the tractor and trailer to a paddock for the cows after milking. As Henry drove back to the house along the gravel road, he was zig zagging along the way. Nothing harmful, but the tractor wheel marks were obvious on the road. Dad had been in town, probably gambling on horses and drinking at the Dardanup Hotel, as was his habit.

I was outside the dairy preparing for milking when dad drove home and saw the tractor marks. Instead of taking the driveway up to the farmhouse, he drove another 100 metres to the dairy, jumped out of the car, picked up a piece of metal strapping that was lying on the ground, and strode towards me saying he had enough of me being stupid on the tractor. My blood boiled and I backed away saying:

"Give me a piece of metal and see how you go."

Naturally this took him by surprise. He stopped momentarily, then advanced towards me saying:

"Come here, Peter."

"No way," I replied, with a couple of nasty expletives for good measure.

I mean, if you are going to go; go all out! Basically, I was motivated in that moment by potential freedom from the ongoing abuse. I also feared if he hit me, I would retaliate and that I might not stop. I could feel the fury rising in me. So much pent-up anger aligned with my mistreatment, humiliation, ridicule and physical and mental abuse exploded and I knew I had to get away. I believed my only option was to turn and run. Years later I discovered Brene Brown, [2] quoting Linda Hartling's research that, in these kinds of situations, we can:

1. *move away and hide,*
2. *move toward and seek to appease, or*
3. *move against and confront.*

In this case I had exhausted myself trying to appease and I believed confrontation could have ended in disaster. According to Brown, I had chosen to 'move away'. In this tense standoff, the fury I felt rising in me was scary and powerful. I kept backing away from dad until he stopped. I then walked away up to the house, and asked mum for an old suitcase in which I packed all I had, including £15 (approximately $30.00).

I kept watching as I was packing since I knew dad would come up to the house for afternoon tea before he would have to milk the cows. When I saw him walking towards the house, I went outside and hid among some trees in the bush behind the house. Later in the army I learned I was practicing:

"Observing without being observed."

Eventually he left the house to walk on his own down the hill to the dairy to milk. As I watched him, I recall being struck by the lonely figure he was. Around fifty-four years later I was to experience that same lonely walk as a father. Meanwhile, I went back to the house to say goodbye to mum. As I was about to leave, she held me in a powerful hug in the kitchen and said:

"I know you have to leave, and you go with my blessing."

I walked out the door numb, but with a sense of freedom and adventure. I will never forget the love and care of my mother in that moment. Importantly, she understood that I had to go. How that moment must have torn her heart. She was also uncertain about where I was going, which made two of us.

Earlier, while dad was milking, I visited our neighbour Bob and as fortune would have it, Bob said he was going into Bunbury after milking. Awesome. After I left mum at the farmhouse, I walked back to Bob who was cleaning up after milking. With the benefit of hindsight, I have no idea how I would have 'escaped' if Bob wasn't going into Bunbury. I waited for him, but I didn't disclose why I needed a ride.

Bob didn't question as we drove out of his farm when I asked him to stop at the bridge across the Ferguson River. I had hidden my case under the bridge and I simply placed it in the back of his ute. No questions were asked. Years later Bob said he would not have taken me if he knew I was running away from home. I had just turned sixteen at the time.

It was after dark when Bob dropped me in Bunbury. I was hungry and I staved off the hunger pains by going to a movie, always an escape for me. After the movie I slept on a park bench in the Memorial Gardens. It was a tad chilly so I didn't sleep much, but the night passed without incident.

Two Personality Traits

As I reflected upon this experience, I appreciate I tend towards impulsive behaviour. When I recently shared this insight with university colleagues who knew me well, I noticed the group knowingly 'rolling their eyes,' and expressing disbelief that it had taken all this time to acknowledge this quirk of nature in my personality. I honestly hadn't seen this in myself – a classic blind spot. I mention this because some of my behaviours that I considered a response to shame were indeed due to my propensity to 'act first and consider the consequences later.' These factors became more evident as I examined behaviour in my later life.

How Do Mothers Do It?

I have since reflected upon the powerful role mothers play in their sons' lives. During my Camino de Santiago walk in Spain in 2015, I spent a great deal of time wondering about the strategic and unheralded role mothers' play in shaping the character of their sons and have come to the conclusion that this influence is profound. A mother's love is something I believe is imprinted on the souls of boys becoming men. We sons seem to be the reflection of all that is noble, just, honourable, soft, gentle and kind in our mothers. What we do then with this beauty is our responsibility.

During my fifteenth year, I was an unpaid farm hand happy to be out of school where I was a dismal failure academically, socially, and in sport and athletics, but equally unhappy under the tyrannical domination of my dad. I recall many times my mother attempting to advocate on my behalf with dad, but also suffering in their relationship.

My gentle light during this year was the love of my mum and the encouragement of Keith and Sheila Butcher. Father Cunningham had since been replaced in the Dardanup Parish by a man who was the antithesis to him who had no interpersonal skills and was an alcoholic. However, Father Cunningham's presence in my life had been imprinted forever.

When I was a child, mum would always be in the dairy helping out, and every morning after the last cow was milked and just before the shed was cleaned and milking ended, she would rush back to the house and have a sizzling cooked breakfast on the table for dad as he walked in the door. All this prepared on an old wood stove she managed to light before milking and somehow kept burning although I never saw her go back to the house to check that it would be hot for cooking when she returned from the dairy. As I recall, mum always did this with grace and dignity and without any help from dad or I.

Only after being a parent myself, I reflected upon how a mother's heart could stand such pain and simultaneously be so loaded with love to set me free. Sadly, I never asked mum about this and how she really felt at the time I left home. So much love we sons potentially take for granted.

What About Dads?

I have since wondered about the torment my father must have endured. I wonder what happened before he came home that fateful day. He was a gambler. After he died, we discovered there was nothing left for mum; dad had gambled it all away. Maybe he lost a lot of money at the races that afternoon? Maybe he had been at the Dardanup Pub and had a few drinks too many? Whatever. He didn't stop to check who had driven the tractor; he just went for me. I could never please him. A person with balanced emotional intelligence doesn't handle life with the degree of irrational behaviour that I saw in my dad.

I now understand from Brene Brown's extensive research that this is the logical consequence of not dealing with feelings of shame. We eventually push back and blame others for our feelings. I found this phenomenon to be true as I later committed to try and understand my dad's life and forgive him. Extending empathy towards him and myself became a healing factor. Dad had no one in his life to confide in and talk with about the things that may have been bothering him. It is too easy in instances like that for people to lash out at those closest to them. I suffered a great deal under his moods and temper, but it didn't last forever. I also know that it is upon the anvil of pain that our character is hammered out. To paraphrase Carl Jung:

> *"I was not going to be a result of what was happening to me, rather I wanted to choose who I was going to become."*

So, I took the fork.

Reflections

I harken back to my decision to, in the words of Brene Brown, 'move away' from my dad. At the time of his final threat to belt me with a length of flexible steel, I refused to simply take the grossly unfair and unjust punishment for something I had not committed. It has been most helpful in the process of writing my story, reading research on shame, and discussing some of these events with my brothers and sister, to reflect with a dispassionate lens upon that day outside the dairy on the family farm.

I appreciate Brown's review of Hartling's research, but I also found it to be missing something. This was especially true as I wondered years later what it must have been like for Henry, Rosco and Di to witness my relationship with dad, and what impact it had upon them. I wondered how they coped and what it must have been like when they found one evening that I was no longer at the family dinner table. Did they feel safe without me being there? Which of the three options articulated by Brown from Hartling's research would they adopt? Were there other options for them? Or, were any of these options necessary?

In light of the abovementioned options, Pete Walker [3] suggests we have four responses to any confrontation, namely:

1. *fight, when we respond aggressively,*

2. *flight, when we respond to a perceived threat by fleeing,*

3. *freeze, when we 'give up' and accept the inevitability of being hurt, and*

4. *fawn, when we respond to threat by trying to appease an attacker.*

I recognise 'moving away,' or 'fleeing' as my reactions to emotional and physical danger. I have since discussed these phenomena at length with my brothers and sister and, out of love and respect for them, it is not for me to reveal details of their responses to dad's behaviour. However, I will re-examine these options in more detail in the final chapters of my story, including the possibility of traits of the four responses being accessed by people in trauma.

I am convinced, however, that there is a fifth option to Walker's framework which is in fact, no option at all. I think of many girls caught in abusive relationships in families and I am not convinced that escaping the situation is an option for them. As a sixteen-year-old boy, I could leave, find work, survive and thrive. Upon hearing stories from women I know well, the option I exercised was definitely not there for them, albeit they could leave under extreme duress and pressure from their family, most often their father. In many cultures, there is simply no option for girls to escape family abuse. They are, in fact, left with no choice.

The Future

The morning after my 'sleep' on the park bench in Bunbury, I caught the 6.30 am train to Perth to stay overnight at my Aunty Ruth's place in Wembley. The following day, my cousin Alec and I travelled to Dalwallinu on Alec's ex-police motor bike. We had another cousin farming in the Dalwallinu area out on the Kalannie Road just past the Rabbit Proof Fence, and I appreciate the fact he gave me shelter and work.

Chapter 9

1961-1962: Transformative Experiences

On the farm in the Dalwallinu Shire, I met two men, Ross Harvey and Jeff Eldridge, who initially were role models and later informal mentors. Under Ross and Jeff's supervision I grew up quickly, including physically. Ross and Jeff were men in their late twenties who expected me to work hard and keep up with them. I thrived under their teaching, expectations and encouragement.

If I made a mistake, they helped me learn from it. They expected me to drive the trucks carting seed, and later grain to the wheat bins at harvest. I got to operate a massive John Deere tractor, a Cat D4, a large self-propelled header and other machinery and farm equipment. All exciting 'boy stuff' that helped me on my journey to manhood.

During this time of physical growth, I was also beginning to feel better about myself emotionally. In retrospect, I was obviously seeking identity, or was it ways of finding my way through the shadows of shame cast by my dad's words and behaviour? I am now convinced that shining light upon shame is a trigger for finding ways out of emotional entrapment towards wholeness and emotional maturity.

Ross and Jeff became strategic mentors for me. They both accepted and invited me into a special relationship of hard work and camaraderie with them. Everything I learned through Ross and Jeff's tutelage, or being their protégé, was accompanied by joy, satisfaction, learning and progress. Emotionally, I felt safe, included and worthy. This special phenomenon of emotion in learning deserves deeper analysis.

Emotions in Learning

From all my years teaching beginning teachers the art and science of teaching, I understand that nothing we learn, be it rewarding or demeaning, is devoid of emotion. This is why around 70% of knowledge and understanding in our Long-Term Memory is encoded as story, or parable, or episode. [1] In my case, I was being taught by men who cared for me and whom I respected.

Everything I was learning was in the context of success, encouragement, affirmation and commendation. Having Ross and Jeff as mentors, I was learning new skills and experiencing progress and success. I acquired a sense of worthiness that I believe helped me along my journey towards becoming a man, unafraid of vulnerability.

My knowledge and understanding were encoded in a rich bed of positive emotional well-being. In contrast to my 'story of learning' with my dad, which was accompanied by pain, terror, fear, ridicule and criticism, my learning now was in the context of safety and respect. In terms of emotions and learning, I recommend a powerful example of emotions in learning in Matthew McConaughey's story. [2]

For now, being with Ross and Jeff was healing for me, but I missed growing up with boys my own age. I experienced a massive physical growth spurt during this year, but another much deeper growth took hold and has continued to flourish ever since. I share this experience in the final chapter of my story.

1962: Managing the Family Farm

Meanwhile, for Christmas 1961, I was welcomed back to the family farm when dad requested that I take care of the farm while he and mum enjoyed a three-month cruise to Japan. The same dad who used to say I was useless and no good for anything was now asking me to look after the farm on my own for three months. Amazing. I was seventeen and ready for my next learning curve.

By now I was most interested in girls. My acne was healing and I was strong and fit, and much more confident in myself. Every Saturday night there was a dance at the Bunbury Rowing Club and I would attend as often as I could. I could usually get to Dardanup in the farm truck and catch a ride from there with my cousin Keith and another mate, Mick Twomey.

Horses Can't Dance

One particular Saturday night I had the luxury of the use of the family car to go to the Rowing Club, picking up Keith and Mick along the way. As I left the house and drove just 400 meters down the road, I noticed one of our farm horses, a scatty colt, on the side of the road. It was dark, and he seemed spooked by the headlights of the car. Unfortunately, I didn't have the presence of mind to turn them off. I realised the horse was rattled and not sure of himself. I also knew he was unpredictable, so I was a tad worried.

I had stopped the car just in time for him to figure out he could jump over the lights shining in his eyes. Almost in slow motion, a full-grown horse launched itself towards the car. Sitting behind the wheel, it felt time stood still, as a full-size horse landed on the bonnet of my dad's new car. Once he landed, he was obviously quite surprised:

> *"So that's what those lights were about,"* I am
> sure he thought.

I sat there helplessly as he kicked the sun visor right off the windscreen. Any moment I was expecting him to smash through the windscreen and join me on the front seat. Fortunately, the latter didn't eventuate; he just did a couple of dance moves, then rolled off to the side of the car and galloped back up the road. I sat there thinking:

> *"Did that just happen? Why me?"*

I reluctantly drove back to the house and reported the incident to dad. Amazingly, he didn't react in any hostile way but I bet he was dying to laugh. I mean, you can't make up a story like that, right? Anyway, he told me to go on into town and without any further encouragement, I did, minus the sun visor and a few dents on the bonnet. When I met Keith and Mick for a ride to the dance, they paid out on me big time; funniest thing they had ever heard, they said. Next morning at mass there were many laughs at my expense:

> *"How did your dance with the horse go last*
> *night Prouty? Did you ask him for a dance, etc.?"*

It was one of the very few occasions I noticed dad seeing the funny side of something, especially where I was concerned.

Dancing

As mentioned earlier, at around age fifteen, I learned how to go about being a gentleman at dances. By seventeen, I was a totally relaxed dancer. I knew all the moves. I could confidently walk into a dance, see what was happening, find a girl, and go straight into the right moves. This was a dream I had back at fifteen and now I could do it. Awesome. Speaking of right moves, if the music was right and the girl was willing you could gradually move to the centre of the dance hall where the slower dancing was happening. Here you could almost stop and just sway to the music. Even kiss your girl, right there in the middle of the dance floor. I loved dancing and I found out in later years, dad had actually ridden a horse through the doors of the Dardanup Hall and on to the dance floor. Now, I never thought of that.

On another one of those rare evenings when I could take dad's car, Keith, Mick and I decided to go to a little place called Noggerup where we heard they were having some great Saturday night dances. Mick and Keith came to the farm and we headed off, with Mick driving as I had a rotten headache, but nothing a good dance wouldn't fix. I was sitting next to Mick, and Keith was at the passenger door, thus three across the front seat. Mick approached a corner on the gravel road, way too quickly. Quite possibly he touched the brakes, I don't know. However, I do recall we were suddenly travelling sideways around a corner on a gravel road It was not unlike driving on small ball bearings.

I don't remember much detail after that, except, as we flipped over and before we landed back on all four wheels, I saw my fingers through the overhead light in the roof of the car, indicating that, during the 'roll over,' at least one door had sprung open. No seat belts in those days, but we all landed back in our same seats after the rollover. The back window had popped out and the car sustained some obvious dents, but we were OK. Amazing.

Once we gathered our senses, we started walking back to the farm, having no idea really where we were. We had decided to take a back road through the bush to the dance. Eventually, we were picked up by a farmer and driven back to my place. Mick and Keith hurriedly left, and I was left to face the music. To protect Mick, I said I was driving, since I knew dad had no regard for Mick's dad, or for Mick himself. I have no idea why. It was just how dad worked. At 5.15 am next morning dad was uncommunicative in the milking shed and I was wondering when it would come to a head. It didn't really. Keith Butcher came down and they drove off to retrieve the car, which they towed home. It looked very sad.

In Charge

This was bad timing since my parents were due to head off across the Nullarbor in four weeks to begin their return cruise from Sydney to Japan. Dad cashed in insurance and bought another Falcon, a red one this time. Without further significant incidents my parents drove to Sydney to meet their ship for their cruise. I always wondered what went through dad's mind as they drove away. I know what went through mine:

"You beauty, I am free at last!"

While our parents were away, Henry went to board with family friends and Rosco and Di went to Aunty Jean and Uncle Ron, both close by in Dardanup. Now I had the farm to myself. Keith and Sheila were incredibly kind during this time. Every night I would go to their place for dinner. Not only was this such a kind and generous gesture, but I just loved spending every evening meal with them and learning from them.

This is an example of mentoring that I believe begins with having heroes, then role models and then a relationship that becomes reciprocal and mutually beneficial. Thus, I acknowledge Keith and Sheila among my first mentors, following Ross and Jeff the previous year.

I cooked for myself on weekends. We had an electric fry pan, *Sunbeam* brand. They were all the rage in the 1960s. Anyway, when the main pan went beyond clean to gross, I discovered I could flip it over and cook eggs in the round hollow on the back. The white of the eggs came out with *Sunbeam* printed on them. Gold. Some weekends my cousin Keith would come to the farm and we would have fun cooking up a storm, mainly huge chunks of steak on the hot plate of the slow cooking, wood fired oven.

A Barricade on *Butcher Road*

A temporary fence across *Butcher Road*, from *Prout Road* to Keith and Sheila's farm, caused some consternation for a neighbour one afternoon. I was milking seventy plus cows and I had to break in some new heifers who had birthed their first calves. This went OK, except for one I couldn't coax into the dairy. The dairy was close to *Butcher Road*, and in order to get the new heifer into the dairy for milking, I strung a piece of wring lock netting across the road so she would be guided into the yards. It worked and I quickly went in to begin milking, forgetting the netting for the moment.

In our neighbourhood lived John Gardiner who knew two speeds when driving his car; stop and flat out. In the moment I erected the temporary fence across Butcher Road, John had decided to come and visit the Butchers. At his normal speed. John saw the netting too late to stop, and I saw him just before he hit it. I quickly ducked down pretending to be taking teat cups off one cow and on to the next, but out of the corner of my eye I saw a huge cloud of gravel dust in the air and the wire netting explode across the front of John's car.

"This is not going to end well," I thought.

In my peripheral vision, I saw John storming towards the dairy. Now I was convinced it was not going to end well. I had no place to hide; but the cows needed me. No more time to think. John was in the dairy.

"Peter Prout, what did you think you were doing; stringing wire netting across a public road?"

"What netting?" I innocently asked.

Fortunately, John understood my predicament and reminded me that main roads were not places for stringing wire netting. I dodged a bullet there. He was gracious enough to keep the whole episode quiet, including freeing me of any debt towards fixing a couple of scratches on his dad's car.

Alone, but Never Lonely

There were times on cold, dark, winter nights in a big house, alone on the farm that I experienced moments of, well, fear. One cold stormy night our dog, *Doodah* (son of Bob Slee's *Doodah!*), climbed into the kitchen through the wood box that opened to the outside. I woke up with a cold wet nose touching my neck. I almost leapt right out of bed in fright. Now we were both scared of the storm.

A revelation to me during this year was appreciating it was OK to be alone at times, especially to just 'be' and to enjoy the moments. I never felt lonely, just at peace being alone. I did not process anything radical or of significant depth of learning and knowledge during this time on the farm, but I am sure it was significant for my emotional and spiritual strength development.

The routine of milking each day, including other necessary chores, kept me physically occupied and engaged in meaningful work. Meanwhile, there were times when I was conscious of this as an apprenticeship for the next stages of my life. Without my parents at home, I made no effort to go to Mass each Sunday. The priest was an alcoholic and, in my view, a disgrace to the memory of Father Cunningham.

Instead, I always marvelled at each newborn calf, the glow of the sun as it came up each morning to warm the dairy and the sense of awe that I was running the farm on my own. I wasn't reading, but I loved listening to radio news and current affairs programs on the Australian Broadcasting Commission (ABC), network. Overall, I was at peace with myself.

Community

I decided once I would bake a sponge cake as I was missing mum's cooking. I did all I remember her doing to mix the sponge cake and I placed it in the wood fired, slow cooking oven, which I had just lit. Apparently, you must wait for the oven to reach a certain temperature before trying to bake a cake, or anything else for that matter. Whatever. The sponge turned out like vulcanised rubber; even *Doodah* wouldn't eat it. I phoned Jenny Gibbs, Anne's mother, and asked her how to bake a cake. Jenny told me the oven had to be hot before doing so. Made sense to me.

Jenny also operated the local telephone exchange which you had to call to be connected to any number you wanted. She also knew Syd Gardiner who ran the milk truck morning and evening collecting milk cans from dairies in Ferguson. When Syd arrived at the farm for the evening run, he handed me a cardboard box full of cakes and biscuits. Jenny had called the neighbours and Doodah and I ate cake for weeks.

Community. You can't live without it. Nor can we fully grasp the form and function of mentoring without experiencing community. The farmers, should I say, their wives, of the Ferguson Valley became my community that night when they gave selflessly to me. I have never forgotten their generosity and, if I dwell upon it, I can still recall the sense of awe and 'belonging and connectedness' I felt that night as I opened the cardboard box in the dairy and found all the cakes and bickies.

As previously stated, I was alone on the farm, but not lonely. In my view this is the unique gift and wonder of community. We are not lonely in a true, caring, community. Later in my life as I wrestled with my shame demons in confronting, but healing group therapy sessions, I appreciated that giving and receiving empathy is a significant part of our journey of emotional healing.

Transport

I had the farm truck for a vehicle while my parents were away and once when I went to pick up a girl to go to a dance, she refused to get in. Some girls have no sense of humour or adventure. By contrast, another of my dates, years later at university, was in my Volkswagen when the running board on the driver's side of the car fell off on the Mitchell Freeway. She didn't mind. She had class! Anyway, the truck broke down while my parents were away so, on one occasion, I decided to drive the tractor twelve kilometres into Dardanup to meet my mates for a Saturday night out. It was freezing cold coming home from a dance after midnight on a Massey Ferguson 35 tractor. I only did that once!

A Lamb for a Girl

Keith and Sheila let me borrow their car for another date with a girl who said she would love a pet lamb. John Gardiner had sheep and sure enough he had an orphan lamb. I raced over to his farm on the tractor to pick it up. Now what do I do with it while milking? I know. Let it run loose in the house, which I did. I was a hit with the girl when I took the lamb into Bunbury after milking.

A few days later Sheila came down to clean the house. Sweep floors and things like that. All I had done was cook on weekends and wash my dishes. Anyway, Sheila found these little black pellets through the house and, upon closer inspection, she realised what they were. Sheep shit. She was not happy finding lamb shit inside the house and she firmly reminded me you don't keep sheep in the house. At the time, I thought it had been a great idea.

While I was on the farm, I was fortunate that the local garage in Dardanup was run by Harry Wallace who also ran a 'gym' a couple of nights in a shed on the Italiano farm. Harry was kind enough to teach a few of us how to train using weights. I eagerly accepted the opportunity to train, and I began to build muscle bulk and strength that would prepare me for more hard work ahead.

Providence

On a more sombre note, I almost cut myself in two on a circular saw, which was driven by a belt off a pulley attached to the power-take-off on the tractor. We used the saw to cut dead wood and old fence posts into lengths to fit the wood stove in the farm kitchen. On this particular day, it had been raining, the wooden bench holding the saw was slippery, and there was saw dust piling up under the bench making sure footing difficult. In these unsafe conditions, I slipped forward as I was pushing a log through the saw.

Fortunately, I managed to regain my balance, but it was another one of those moments when time seems to momentarily stand still and you appreciate just how close you were to something really serious happen. In my case, the 'serious happening' would have involved me falling forward on to an exposed saw that cut wood like butter. I still marvel how I was spared on that occasion. Being cut open by a fairly large saw would not be my preferred way to go.

Times Up

My parents eventually arrived home safely from their cruise, and my brothers and sister came home for us to be a family again. I recall the warmth of the experience in this short period, especially being back with Henry, Rosco and Di. However, it wasn't long before dad started finding fault with things I hadn't done while he was away, including what I had done that was wrong. I can honestly say this didn't bother me because I had grown so much, and I reaped untold benefits from having the responsibility to successfully keep the farm ticking over while my family was away. I also overheard dad telling a neighbour he was planning to sell the farm.

"No future for me here then," I thought.

I left home again in November and worked on a farm in Dardanup until I entered into the next stage of my informal education.

Reflections

- In terms of mentoring, most of my learning that year was 'experiential' and informal in nature. Keith and Sheila were wonderful neighbours. Keith helped me with any problems on the farm and Sheila had a warm, tasty and nutritious dinner for me every night. There is no substitute for feeling loved and 'embraced,' especially when you are seventeen and you get a nutritious hot meal every night!

- I also appreciate the significant impact of being included in community and having been extended grace and understanding by John Gardiner, especially after he crashed through my temporary wire fence across the main road. Belonging in community is where we find healing and purpose. These can include extended family, sporting teams, performing arts groups, music ensembles, community aid, SES, church, AID organisations, schools, advocacy and environmental groups, to name just a few.

- Above all, during this period of my life, being embraced, undeservedly, by 'salt of the earth people' in the Ferguson Valley farming community was the source of my greatest comfort, teaching and counsel.

It has been helpful for me in examining my life and behaviour, to appreciate actions influenced by my impulsivity, my personality, and those prompted by messages of shame. I will amplify these reflections further in my story. For now, however, the next phase of my education was in a less nurturing community, rather more a 'learn or burn' environment, and definitely experiential.

Chapter 10

The University of Hard Knocks

I remember 1963 as a period of specific classes at the 'University of Hard Knocks.' I was now eighteen and full of confidence. I joined a school for two weeks in Fremantle where I learned to shear sheep, after which I found a job with a shearing team traveling through the Goldfields to stations in Kalgoorlie, Leonora, Laverton and Wiluna. We were away from February until the end of May. Stinking hot most of the time.

I was given a learner's pen for shearing and at other times, I was a roustabout. A roustabout's work on the shearing shed floor included picking up fleeces and throwing them on the table for the wool classer to decide into which bale the fleece would go. It was hard work, but I loved it. We had a cook for the team and we slept in rough quarters with iron beds and thin mattresses.

One night, at a station in Leonora, I pulled my bed outside for some cool, and I woke with a station horse examining me at close range. I am not sure who jumped in fright first, but I can confirm that waking up peering into the nostrils of a horse is a tad discombobulating.

Lessons Learned: The Memorable Way

An incident in a wool press leads me to believe I should come clean with how naive I was among this team of shearers. Remember, I thought I had really grown up and that I was on top of my game now? Well, not so much. The wool presser added to my education one day after shearing.

The wool presser's job on the team was to compact the wool in a special box that contained a bale for the wool. He would compress the wool as much as possible in the bale by stamping it down with his feet after which he would use the handles and spear mechanism on the wool press for extra compression. Once he was satisfied the bale was full, he would push two steel rods through the top of the box and under the spear. This allowed him to open a door of the wool press to release the spear. Next, the wool presser could stich the bale closed, release the steel rods, and pull the full bale out of the box.

OK. One day the wool presser told me he was worried that the spear was coming down crooked and he was having trouble getting it to fit snugly into the top of the wool press. He asked if I would get inside the wool press and watch it come down to see where it was possibly malfunctioning:

"Sure," I said.

At the end of the day, I was sitting inside the wool press watching the spear come down, which it did. And there I was. Locked inside the press. The team all went off for their beers after work and I was left in the wool press for a while. Eventually I was released and was mortified. You just have to grow up smart, I guess. The other occasion was even more embarrassing, but I should tell you.

I will call my next class 'Shades of Blue.' You see, Merv Smith was the ringer of the shed; i.e. the fastest shearer, so Merv's word was law. He told me you could catch small ticks from shearing and working in the pens, especially with feral goats that would come in with the sheep. After shearing one day, I can't remember when in relation to checking the spear on the wool press, he said I should check if I had any of these ticks. The best place to spot them was on your testicles, and by holding a mirror under your balls, you could see them jumping on to the mirror, thinking it was another home for them. I know. How dumb can you get? Right. I was convinced to lower my dacks and hold the mirror.

Sure enough, Merv and the other shearers could see these ticks jumping off my balls onto the mirror. I reluctantly agreed I could see them, even though I had no idea what I was looking for. Of course, Merv had the cure available. He would paint my balls with special blue stuff and that would fix them. And so, it was. I had my balls painted with blue stuff. Next day the cry all day throughout the shed was:

"Hey blue balls. How are they hanging?"

Sometimes we need a sense of humour. We also need to learn how to spot when we are being taken in. My naturally trusting spirit meant it took me longer than others to wise up. All experiences in our life are cumulative and they add to the richness of who we bring to every following event, career, relationship and responsibility. In other words, they shape us. It is just up to us to figure out how they will shape us.

If the latter is true, we always need to look inside our heart before we react and not seek to blame others for our actions or behaviour. We can become stronger in character, or weaker, due to split second decisions we sometimes make. All is never lost. If we do make dumb decisions, we can learn from them. I should know. I made plenty. I will say more about this later, especially in relation to getting feedback from people. All kinds of people.

One weekend, at our last shed at Cunya Station outside Wiluna, I was invited by the Station Manager, Frank Green to accompany him on a mill run. A mill-run comprised checking that water was flowing into drinking troughs for the sheep. The journey was an unforgettable experience for me and such a privilege. Sleeping in a swag under the brilliant stars was just awesome. The night sky was spectacular and inspiring, and the howling of dingoes added to the awe of the moment. I confess I was a tad jumpy during some of the latter noise.

As we travelled between windmills during the day, we saw dingoes, goats, emus and roos, plus a tree full of budgerigars, which are tiny indigenous Australian parrots. Their main characteristic is their brilliant, multi coloured plumage. At first, I thought it was the most amazing tree full of spectacular blossoms, until we got closer and the 'blossoms' flew away.

Another weekend I was taken into Wiluna by Bob Hodder, one of the team, to meet his mum and sister. Bob hoped I would be interested in his sister to get her away from the loser she was with. That didn't happen, but we did have fun at the pub that night. When we got back to Bob's place there wasn't really anywhere for me to sleep. Good planning Bob. Since I had consumed a few beers, I wasn't fussy so with a blanket for warmth, I managed to fit into the bath in the outside bathroom.

I had my head down the tap end and my legs over the other end and I slept fairly well until Bob's mother entered the bathroom in the morning and screamed because there was a man in her bath. I mean, did she have to scream? I woke up forgetting where I was, and that there was a hot and cold tap just above my head. From experience I can tell you two brass taps really make a mess of your head when you jump up from the bath in fright in the morning, especially if you had a tad more than you needed to drink the night before.

Overall, my experience on the shearing team was amazing. I met great people, including many of the Aboriginal stockmen and women working on the stations. I left the shearing team in May to return to Perth. I don't suggest that my above-mentioned education at the University of Hard Knocks could be classed as mentoring, but it continued later in 1963 in a different context.

Town Life and New Skills

Following my time on the shearing team, I was offered a job at Pederick Engineering, in the Great Southern town of Wagin. I appreciated this opportunity and grasped it with both hands. I saw this as a chance to learn new skills from other men at Pederick's, including from Bob Haymes, the foreman of the enterprise. As a first experience working in a sizeable factory that included many facets of engineering and production, I thrived.

Men were valued for their unique skills and creativity, and there was a positive culture of mutual respect and teamwork among everyone involved, including Mr Pederick and his two sons. It was like working with Ross and Jeff on the farm when I was sixteen, but among men in a factory. There was a great diversity of building unique farm equipment, repairing farm machinery, and a wide range of other repairs and production. The work environment was based around teamwork, high energy and fun, and pride in what was being created and built at Pederick Engineering.

Based upon my experience with dad, I understood the privilege of working in such an environment, and I appreciated the patience extended to me as I learned new skills. I was taught and assessed in a formal supervisory network of development, trial and production. Upon reflection, I was most fortunate to be in the right place at the right time. The farm economy was strong and Pederick Engineering machinery could be found across a wide spectrum of our broad acre farming of grain growing and harvesting in Western Australia.

The other benefits were the girls in Wagin, and many opportunities to play sport and enjoy living in this vibrant town. In particular, I enjoyed mixing with blokes my own age and learning a new skill, welding. This was also my first experience living in a town. Overall, my time in Wagin was full of new learning experiences and opportunities to meet many new and kind people. I joined a local basketball team for summer evening's competition and the local Fire Brigade where I quickly became involved in the Volunteer Fire Brigade competitions. I was part of the team to travel to Albany and Kalgoorlie and twice to Fremantle for memorable competitions.

It was awesome being among blokes my own age and to have the opportunity to engage in all kinds of community sport, including football in the Upper Great Southern Football League. Community in Wagin was alive, vibrant and inclusive, with one exception that I will highlight shortly. In the meantime, I joined the Federal Football Club and enjoyed getting back into playing footy. I turned nineteen in February 1964 and, since I was now physically big and strong, I loved the physical body contact of footy. I was particularly proud to win the Club's Most Improved Player that year. I recall hearing my coach at three-quarter time once saying in his address:

"Shift something out of the way like Peter Prout does."

The coach's words alluded to my willingness to play hard and to, well, crash opponents aside to win the ball. I played with and against many talented Aboriginal footballers, including one of our coaches who was a fine Noongar man. After our home games, we would go to the Federal Hotel in Wagin for drinks and for announcing best player awards from the game. However, none of the Aboriginal players joined us.

During my youth, this didn't occur to me as strange and I was unaware at the time that once sundown came to towns around the state, most Aboriginal people had to 'leave town' and go to their designated 'communities' for the night. Some years later, one Aboriginal man told me the police would ask him:

"Do you play chess?" "Well, it is your move – out of town."

A deep regret I have is that I was living in a town where this attitude towards Aboriginal people took place, and I was totally unaware. Accordingly, a question for myself has been how would I have acted if I had known? As a white male, I took membership of various community groups in the town as 'given.' But this was not so for Aboriginal people throughout Australia living in similar towns to Wagin. I hasten to add the latter, because I am sure most citizens of Wagin were as ignorant of the plight of Aboriginal people in regional towns as myself.

Meanwhile, on November 22, I was driving into Wagin and had just turned off the Albany Highway when I heard the news of President Kennedy's [1] assassination. I was so shocked, I had to pull over and weep in sadness and loss. Like many of my generation I believed Kennedy and his wife Jacqui were the leaders of a new Camelot where everything seemed good and noble. I was passionate about leaders and justice and I thought JFK represented so much hope to the world.

On another occasion driving into Wagin, I heard my hero Ray Sorrell won his second Sandover Medal [2] as best player in the West Australian Football League. I was a fan of Aussie Rules Football and I loved playing the game. Ray was my hero and in future was to become a role model, mentor and dear friend.

The Socio-Political Horizon

The years 1963 – 1964 were also times of great social upheaval around the world, especially in the U.S. and in Australia. Australian troops first became involved in the Southeast Asian (SEA) Region in 1955. This conflict initially included confronting a growing acceptance of Communism in Malaya (later Malaysia), Laos and Cambodia, and extended into Vietnam in 1961. The Vietnam conflict began when U.S. troops landed in the south of the country to stop a so-called communist force advancing from the north. At the time there was fear in the West about communism taking over 'the free world,' and that they must be stopped in Vietnam. Australian troops were first engaged in Vietnam in 1962.[3]

Borneo [4] was also a conflict zone in the campaign by President Sukarno of Indonesia to take Brunei from what was then known as Malaya and add it to the Republic of Indonesia. Most of the island of Borneo is Kalimantan, which is part of the Indonesian Archipelago. The Malayan conflict had seen Australian troop involvement since 1955, but Vietnam was now considered far more urgent. However, troops from the Royal Australian Engineers were being posted to Brunei in support of British Battalions engaged in fighting Indonesian troops along the border of Brunei and Kalimantan.

In 1964, the Prime Minister of Australia, Bob Menzies, declared that we needed an enlarged military to support the war in Vietnam, so a 'lottery' system was instituted to recruit men aged twenty into the army. [5] Every young man turning twenty in 1965 had to register in June 1964 for the National Service 'ballot.' This was literally a lottery using marbles with dates on them; if your birth date came up, you were instructed to go for a medical. My birth date was picked, so in October 1964, I had to go for a medical exam in Katanning. Back to my home of birth. I was informed that I passed and that later in early 1965, I would be instructed as to where to report.

During my time in Wagin, I used to travel back to the farm to visit family. I knew that whenever I visited, my 'little sister,' now twelve, was always happy to see me, as I was to see her. On one of these occasions, I was returning to Wagin after a hectic weekend, including some energetic dancing at the Bunbury Rowing Club, when I went to sleep at the wheel – not such a good idea. Since it was unable to steer itself, my little Austin Lancer decided to park in a creek, until I could take over again. I woke up immediately to find myself next to a bridge and indeed parked in the sandy creek bed. It was evening on Sunday night and not much traffic. However, along came a bus load of blokes from a footy match. They stopped, got out of the bus and chorused:

"Strange place to park!" Smart buggers.

Anyway, they gave me a ride. I can't remember if it was all the way to Wagin, but I eventually arrived home. Next morning, I had to work, but I managed to get a mate from the local Ampol Service Station to retrieve my car. Fortunately, there was no damage since it had landed in soft sand in the creek bed. So lucky. At about the same time, I received official word that the family farm was to be sold, so the remote possibility of going back to that career was closed. It was time to let go of the dream of being a dairy farmer.

In August 1965 I was given a terrific farewell by my Wagin mates at Pederick's, the Footy Club and the Fire Brigade, before reporting to Karrakatta Army Barracks in Perth to begin the next major turning point of my life. My farewell party in Wagin was in a gravel pit with kegs of beer and a huge pile of old tyres. During the evening someone lit the pile of tyres and at some stage Jimmy Weare staggered up to me and asked:

"Can you smell rubber burning?"

"Nah, Jimmy," I said, *"don't worry about it"*

Great party.

Reflections

During these years on the shearing team, and at Pederick Engineering, I was generally content in my spirit and free of any self-doubts. I attribute this state of mind and heart to learning among men and being free of any sarcasm and criticism from dad, or any other adult. On the contrary, I appreciated the adventure and opportunities to learn new skills and to explore numerous work options.

In retrospect, I grasped times alone to think, and 'in the moment' wonder about what was happening around me. I cannot recall any time where I was worried about my future or my intellectual, social and spiritual well-being. As I think about this time, it appears it was a time of preparation, for what I did not know. However, one moment stands. Just before I heard I had drawn the ballot for National Service, Bob, the foreman at Pederick's, had given me more time on a routine and mind-numbing activity. I indicated I was tired of the role and I wanted to know when I could take on more challenging work. I recall saying I didn't want to be doing this work for the rest of my life.

Bob was gracious in his response and I distinctly remember him saying he would find more challenging work and skills development for me in the future. Something was obviously stirring in my spirit, and possibly for the first time since I had left the family farm, I was thinking about my future prospects. Little did Bob and I know that a whole new career change was imminent.

Thus, I graduated from the University of Hard Knocks and I was ready for my next adventure. Apart from Bob, the foreman, my football coach and men in the fire brigade, not much formal, or informal mentoring occurred during my time in the 'University of Hard Knocks.' I always listened carefully to instructions and counsel from workmen at Pederick's and my coaches, but after that I just enjoyed living and working in a fair-sized regional town, playing all sport on offer and travelling to dances and sundry other activities one enjoys in late teen years.

PART TWO

A Second Chance

Chapter 11

On becoming a Man

Having 'won' the conscription lottery, the next significant life changing event was induction into the Australian Defence Force (ADF). I was twenty years old and in the second intake of men from the 1965 ballot. On September 29, I reported to Karrakatta Barracks in Perth where I received my ADF Regimental # 571, similar to all men from WA, plus my ID, 3929. Thereafter, 571 3929 was inscribed on dog tags I was issued later for posting in Borneo.

As we assembled at Karrakatta Barracks, the mixture of excitement and nervous energy among twenty-year-old men from all walks of life in WA was palpable. We were instructed to report to the barracks with a small suitcase of personal belongings and casual clothes. As we were issued boarding passes for our flight to Melbourne, we experienced some taste of the life of a soldier. I recall some army personnel at Karrakatta Barracks trying to order us into line in their best 'official commands,' but, when compared to what was to come, they paled into insignificance.

From Karrakatta Barracks, we flew to 2nd Recruit Training Battalion at Puckapunyal in Victoria, the coldest place in Australia. I was placed in 19 Platoon, C Company. My Platoon Sergeant, Sartorius, was a real character and we soon learned you did not mess with our Sergeant Sartorius. Upon reflection I don't believe our sergeant knew or cared about engaging in any formal mentoring relationship with any of us.

On Becoming a Soldier

There were thirty men in 19 Platoon living in multiple Barracks housing sixteen men with four men each in of four cubicles. Our toilets and showers were 50 metres away and the Mess Hall about the same distance. We had to be out of bed and ready for hut inspection each morning at 6.30 am. Hut inspection included a corporal or the dreaded sergeant checking that our bed was made perfectly and that all our clothes were folded in our lockers, exactly as stipulated. If anything was out of order, the bed and locker would be tipped up and we would have to do it again, without holding up our Barrack for breakfast. In early days this frequently happened.

Becoming a soldier was a process I loved. I enthusiastically engaged in everything about our introduction to army life. The more Sergeant Sartorius abused us, the more amusing I found it. He could never match the ways my dad had yelled at me, so I would smile inwardly, but I dare not let him think it was funny. We had to march all day, learn to carry our rifle, how to accurately fire the rifle, how to throw a live hand grenade, and generally how to act like soldiers.

I distinctly remember a day when we went out on parade (line up for whatever we would be doing that day) and no longer thinking of myself as an individual, but as a member of an invincible fighting unit. I was among men my own age and I was about to excel in many ways. As a result, I rapidly grew in self-confidence and self-belief; a sure tonic for combatting the effects of shame.

Years later, as I thought about these events, I am amazed that the army could turn thirty boys into men who would do anything when commanded, and all this was achieved in approximately twelve weeks. I wasn't scared of the way sergeants and corporals yelled at us, and as a result, I quickly became a leader in our platoon. I was strong, athletic and ready for anything among men of my own age, and no longer the skinny and scared kid. No longer the undersized crayfish.

My relationship with my Platoon Sergeant was a fascinating one. There were many strategies employed by our sergeant to teach us the importance of discipline, including learning to instinctively obey an order. For example, when standing at attention we had to be stock still with eyes fixed on something in front and not move a muscle, especially when our sergeant peered into your face. My first experience of learning this discipline of looking ahead without wavering was when Sergeant Sartorius focussed on me and I met his eyes. Big mistake.

"Are you in love with me Recruit Prout?"

"No Sergeant!" (Wrong answer!)

"Why are you looking at me, do you want to date me Recruit Prout?

"No Sergeant!"

"So, you don't like me Recruit Prout?"

"Yes Sergeant!"

"So, you are not in love with me Recruit Prout!"

And it could go on. I dare not laugh.

'About turn' was normally a 'shoe in' command to undertake. Not so much this time. One day at drill exercises which involved learning how to march, I had one of my 'daydreaming' moments where I probably figuring out how to bring about world peace, ands this resulted in being 'blessed' again by our platoon sergeant.

Among the many drills we learned and practiced was turning left and right at 90 degrees and a 180 degree about turn. I can't remember which one we were doing, but at the end of the action I realised twenty-nine of my mates were facing the opposite direction to me. I woke from my daydream to realise I was in the wrong position. *"Shit,"* I thought to myself. And I waited. Nothing. Then I felt Sergeant Sartorius' warm breath behind my left ear. Remember I cannot move, but inside I am almost pissing myself, smiling inwardly and wondering what was to follow:

"Are you stupid, Recruit Prout?"

"No Sergeant."

"Then are you deaf, Recruit Prout?"

"No Sergeant."

"Then why are you facing the wrong way?"

"I have no idea, Sergeant."

"So, you are stupid, Recruit Prout."

I can't remember the exact details of this little conversation, but I did feel a tad stupid and it must have looked funny to an onlooker. Meanwhile, twenty-nine other men had to remain stock still until sergeant sorted me out!

Testing the system of dress code in recruit training was not a good idea. One day John Cross, who I knew from Bunbury, and I turned out for PT in our black footy shorts and not the daggy khaki army issue gear for PT. it was an interesting decision. Our Platoon PT Instructor said nothing at first, but eventually called out:

"Recruit Prout and Cross, fall out!" this meant "Get here to me – now!"

"Do you see this log?" he asked, pointing to a reasonably sized log on the exercise area.

"Yes corporal," we answered.

"Well, take my log to the top of Cairn Hill!"

"Yes corporal," we replied, delighted as we were to get out of boring PT work.

Cairn Hill was a hill about two kilometres away and had a stone cairn on top although I can't remember what the cairn was for. Anyway, off we go, one at each end of the log, and delighted for another challenge. We made it to the top of the hill and came running back to report to the corporal.

"Where is my log, Recruit Prout and Cross?" he asked.

"On Cairn Hill, corporal," we replied.

"Who told you to leave my log there, go back and get it!"

Off we went to bring his log back. We loved the whole idea, but we didn't wear our black footy shorts to PT sessions again.

Towards the end of our training, we did a fifty-five-kilometre forced march with rifles and a full pack each. It turned out to be an overcast day with occasional rain and a cold wind. We marched in groups of three men wide and ten deep, known as a rank of soldiers. I loved the challenge and towards the end of the march, I broke from our rank to encourage other recruits who were getting tired and struggling to keep going.

I finished up carrying two other men's rifles along with my own, and another's battle pack. We were never to break rank, but on this day, I knew it would be OK. We finally made it back to Barracks. Together. It was another moment of deep satisfaction for me. Next day our Platoon Lieutenant quietly said to me:

"We saw you, Recruit Prout!"

I was thrilled and proud to be able to help some mates make it. This was awesome because now I was excelling in something, including being designated as point soldier for our platoon.

Unfortunately, one of the disturbing things I recall about Recruit Training was a five-day leave we were granted in Melbourne. We had been instructed about STDs and safe sex, but when we were all ready to board a train from Puckapunyal to Melbourne, our CO roared *"God help the girls in Melbourne"*, to which hundreds of twenty-year-old men roared with delight.

I was not impressed. I was looking forward to staying with family friends and exploring Melbourne, so the comment by our CO didn't measure with me. However, in recent years as a witness to the *#Me Too Movement* and other calls for more respect by men towards women, I appreciate how hard it can be to shift cultural thinking in this country, especially as I reflect upon the lack of respect for women I saw in the army.

Upon reflection on my teenage years, I realise that until this point in my life, I only knew how to talk *about girls* and not *with, or to them*. The culture in which I lived and worked to this point was bleak in terms of teaching respect for the beauty of dignified relationships with girls and women. Significant personal learning in this area was still to come.

Graduation

Eventually, around mid-December, we had our March Out Graduation, and I was delighted that special family friends from Melbourne, Mr and Mrs Swan and their daughter Paula and son Doug, met Henry from boarding school at Wangaratta and came to see me on the day. I was able to spend some special time with them after the Parade. I also appreciated having my bro there on the day. There are a number of significant reflections I have from this time of Recruit Training:

- It is powerful how a group of boys can become men, who then believe they are invincible, especially when armed with a rifle. I can distinctly remember the day on parade where I no longer thought of 'me as an individual,' but as a cog in an indestructible machine that was the army.

- From this experience it has never been difficult for me to understand how cult leaders can make people do all kinds of weird and sometimes shocking things. Nor is it hard for me to look at our world now and to understand how politicians and other so called 'interest groups' can use propaganda to turn people against one another.

- I do believe discipline is important, to forgo what you would choose for the sake of a whole group. For example, everyone in the army needs to learn that discipline to obey an order might save your life, and the lives of your mates. On the other hand, discipline can also help you decide in life when you need to take a stand against a mob.

- The Army was a transformative experience for me. The option my dad laid out when I was fifteen had become a reality at the right time of my life. It was time for me to become a man, although throughout my entire time in the army, I didn't experience any 'shame attacks.' Rather, I was 'in the zone' of challenge and learning where I was completely absorbed and engaged.

Success Among My Peers

After graduating from Recruit Training Battalion, I was posted for my Corps Training to the School of Military Engineering (SME), Casula, just outside Liverpool in Sydney. I was now Sapper Prout, Royal Australian Engineers. Before we began training at SME, we were all given leave to go home for Christmas. I spent Christmas 1965 with my family. Dad had sold the farm towards the end of 1964 and in early 1965 the family had moved to a new house in Bunbury.

Early in the New Year, 1966 I returned to SME to begin Corps Training. I was one of thirty men in 6th Troop and part of a Squadron of two hundred and fifty men which was a full complement for an RAE Squadron. We all turned twenty-one that year so wherever possible, we had many parties. We trained in building component bridges for armies to cross rivers or bays, transporting supplies in various sized boats or rafts along rivers, getting vehicles across rivers on wire ropes, planting anti-personnel mines, learning how to disable a mine, building barricades, and exploring caves and tunnels, the latter of which I hated due to claustrophobia.

A major personal success was winning our Army cross country and helping 6th Squadron win our Sports Day. The cross-country distance was about ten kilometres, and I knew I was one of the favourites to win. I had been training for the race, along with my Bunbury mate, John Cross. I was also good mates with Des Mayo, a fantastic aboriginal bloke from the Northern Territory. I have since tried to contact Des, but no luck to date. On race day we were part of a huge mob so I needed to be near the front to avoid getting boxed in.

Crossy and I paced each other for all of the race with another group of three blokes always in front of us. Towards the finish, Crossy and I ran up to the lead group and with about 800 metres to go I dropped to the back of the five. They thought I was gone, but with about 400 to go, I kicked away and as I ran past the lead group, I heard Crossy say:

"Prouty, you bastard!"

I had too much speed by then for any of them to catch me. Yeah. It was a great thrill to win again among men my own age.

Posted For Action

At the end of our training at SME, I was treated to a visit from Sergeant Sartorius. We had a March Out Parade to honour the end of our Corps Training, during which I was called out to receive the Cross-Country Trophy from our Unit CO. As I marched out and halted to attention, I saw Sergeant Sartorius behind our CO. Sure enough, at the end of the Parade, I was called over to the official party to be met by my former sergeant. I smiled and made eye contact.

He reciprocated, or at least I think he did. He then pointed out my step to attention was slack and not how he taught me. I agreed, but I was now a soldier with permission for a bit of flair in my dress and marching. I didn't articulate that thought, but we had a brief and wonderful catch up. I would have volunteered for any outfit Sergeant Sartorius led.

I was posted back to Perth to join 22nd Construction Squadron based at Karrakatta Barracks. I had applied to go to 17th Construction Squadron in Sydney but was sent to Perth since it was my home state; 17th Construction Squadron had been due to go to Vietnam and I thought it would be my duty to apply. In retrospect, I am glad I didn't go since I would have been reckless enough to get my head blown off.

Speaking of reckless behaviour, which I now admit is part of my DNA, we travelled back to Perth by train. In those days, you had to change trains at Kalgoorlie to accommodate the different rail gauges in WA. We were accompanied on the train by Lieutenant Casey who had been my SME Troop Commander. He was a good man and we respected him, and I presume he was on the train to ensure we arrived safely back in WA.

There was a two-hour stopover in Kalgoorlie and some of us might have visited a local pub and had a few beers. Around 11.00 pm, once we got underway again on the train, Crossy and I became a bit restless and thought we needed to do some exploring. The roof of the train seemed to be a good place to start. And so, it turned out to be. We walked all the way to the engine and then back to the last van. The only problem was that people complained to a conductor that they could hear footsteps on the roof of their carriages.

"How could this be," wondered Lt. Casey, so he stuck his head up to investigate.

Sure enough, two of his sappers were indeed jogging along the roof of carriages.

"Sapper Prout and Sapper Cross, get down immediately," he ordered, but not all that convincingly.

He disappeared, so we explored a tad more. It turned out you could climb outside each carriage and shuffle along a narrow board to peer in each cabin of a carriage. This was fun because we could knock on a window and then piss ourselves laughing as kids would grab their parents' arms and point to the window. How could two blokes be outside the window of a moving train? The next morning when we pulled into Perth, we had a chance to examine in daylight the narrow board and minimalist things to hold on to as we rode along. We agreed we had dodged another bullet, but we had the best trip ever from Kalgoorlie to Perth. And Lt. Casey didn't say a word. A good man indeed.

Reflections

At this period of time, I felt like a competent young man who could be relied upon and who could tackle any challenge posed. I thoroughly enjoyed the company of all the other men in my unit; I felt equal to all and more competent than most along with an incredible sense of personal value, coupled with loyalty to my peers. It is not until I undertook the journey of examining my experiences and writing my story that I appreciate these concepts to be true of my physical and emotional growth age twenty-one. Later in my story, I will share more about the power of writing down our thoughts and reflections, especially including what we were learning at the time.

Despite this growing self-confidence, I was still naive to any depth of understanding and wisdom about political and social issues, and I entered wholeheartedly, without any intentional reflection, into all aspects of army training and challenges. It was a full-on game for me and a time of challenge, learning and physical growth that temporarily at least served as a highly effective defence against any negative feelings, experiences, or inadequacies typically associated with shame.

At this point, I believe it important to acknowledge that I now understand a good deal of my behaviour was attributed to my impulsive approach to life. Looking back, I don't recall reading any book of substance; I was just 'going with the moment.'

This cavalier and impulsive approach to life was about to be stretched.

Chapter 12

A Depression in the Ground

Following our arrival at Karrakatta Barracks, we were notified that we were to be posted to complete the construction of a road from Keningau to Sapulot in Brunei, a Province in Borneo. In preparation for going to this conflict area, we undertook weeks of training at the army base outside Bindoon and this included firing live rounds as we practiced crawling along the ground to avoid machine gun fire. I was also introduced to the M60 machine gun which is a terrifying weapon. It has such destructive power, and even then, I wondered how I could possibly aim this deadly weapon at people.

In early May, members of 22nd Construction Squadron eventually flew out of Sydney on a Qantas flight to Singapore. Before departure, we were given our dog tags and we had to carry the breach blocks for our rifles in our carry-on baggage. The reason for this was we were flying over Indonesian territory, so we had to avoid any acts of aggression against their sovereignty. This was somewhat ironic, since our rifles were in the baggage of the plane and we were going to be in a disputed territory with Indonesia in Borneo.

Years later, after I was discharged from the army, I read Joseph Heller's book *Catch 22* which describes the U.S. Army Airforce occupation in Italy during World War Two. I laughed all the way through the book because it validated all the quirks and occasional mind-blowingly stupidity I experienced during my time in the Australian Army.

Our brief stay-over in Singapore was at Changi Barracks which Australian soldiers were forced to build during the Japanese occupation of Singapore in World War Two. I found our stay in the barracks to be deeply moving and emotional, especially since I had taken time to read about the fall of Singapore in February, 1942, just 24 years prior to us occupying the same barracks.

In preparation for our posting to Borneo, we were aware that we were not confronting an enemy like the situation in Vietnam, but I was conscious of the fact that young men my age were, and I felt that deeply as I walked around the barracks. Further, I smiled inwardly at the larrikin nature of the men my age who had been forced to build the barracks as Japanese prisoners a short time previously. Legend has it the Aussie soldiers deliberately constructed the barracks on the side of a steep hill and, on many occasions, took great delight in watching inebriated Japanese soldiers staggering back to their quarters after dark. I felt proud to be a small part of that legend.

From Singapore, we were flown to Jesselton, the capital city of Brunei, now called Bandar Seri Begawan. From Jesselton, we travelled by train on open, flat bogies to a region in Sabah called Keningau. During this part of our journey, we traversed the Sook Plain where Aussie troops were still remembered fondly by the Dayak people as their liberators from the Japanese. The train travelled at walking speed – literally.

On one occasion as we passed through a village, I noted on the side of the tracks a set of wheels on an axle for a bogie. I jumped off our open bogie and, after much gesticulating and smiles with locals watching us pass through, heaved the wheels onto our bogie. Nobody objected to my 'borrowing' the wheels as they made an ideal set of barbells for weight training at our base camp.

At some stage, just beyond the Sook Plain, we disembarked from the train and piled into trucks to complete the journey to our base camp. Our task from base camp was to complete construction of a road and thus provide easy access to the capital for Dayak people living in the ranges, rather than having to cross the border to Kalimantan in Indonesian Borneo. This was part of an appeasement process to keep the Dayaks well served as Malaysian citizens. The Dayaks were such gentle and loving people. Once I gave some children a small cake of soap, and they immediately ran down to the river and washed until it was all gone.

The people lived in large, thatched-roof homes made of bamboo and set on posts about two metres off the ground. This was to keep animals such as leopards and various monkeys out. Big pythons too I suspect. Speaking of the latter, one day one of our men came back to camp in a Land Rover and reported seeing a python crossing the road. He couldn't see the head or tail, just the body as it was crossing. I am glad I didn't see it. I hate snakes.

The jungle was amazing. Monkeys in the trees and so many snakes. One day I went to put my hand on a log to jump over and a green snake reared up at me. Flight took over from fight and I jumped back to avoid any confrontation. Another day, while I was on patrol, I took off my boots for a break and my ankles were covered in leeches. The jungle floor is so wet they can live right among the leaves. You dare not lie down on the ground as leeches soon seek a home in your ears. However, once we cleared any trees, the land would soon become dry and dusty. It would rain without fail at 3.00 pm every day but we would still work and be perspiring in the rain. As soon as it stopped, steam would be rising off our shirts as they dried in the baking sun. Amazing.

A Tree Fell in the Jungle

On June 9, I was out helping some other sappers clear trees when a tree fell on me and smashed me up. I have the official army report which is handy because I don't remember with any clarity what actually happened. On August 4, when I was in the British Military Hospital in Singapore, I reported my recollection of the accident to Captain Berry, the investigating Officer for the accident. In my recollection:

> *"I had cut down two trees which had caught up by vines to a third tree, so I had to cut the third tree to release them. As the three trees started to fall, I walked away in the opposite direction, but one tree hit me after it must have swung around, but on this I am not clear."*

After later visiting the accident site, Captain Berry added in his report that there was a depression in the ground where the tree hit me, therefore falling on me but not pinning me to the ground and completely crushing me. When I was recently granted access to these reports, I confess it was sobering reading. I understood the tree had grazed me and knocked me forward, not into the ground. I thank God for a small depression in the ground at exactly the right place. The following witness account by Sergeant Jim Nixon, our terrific leader and man, offers more clarity:

> *"At 3.45 pm 9th July Sapper Prout had finished sawing three individual trees which would not fall, in this clump of trees was one approximately 50 cm thick which we had not touched, as in normal*

practice we left these specific trees and tried to work from another angle. I instructed Sapper Prout to leave the chain saw and for Sapper Hall to try and cut a 25 cm tree that was leaning into the foliage of the earlier mentioned trees. Sapper Prout and myself took a position behind a tree that was safe, providing all things worked out equal. As Sapper Hall cut the 25 cm tree, the unexpected happened and next the whole stand of trees were falling onto us. I called Sapper Prout to get out and as I dodged to the side Sapper Prout ran down the hill and was doing so when hit."

Sapper Hall was sent to notify Squadron HQ of the accident. Meanwhile, Sergeant Nixon administered morphine and when help arrived, I was carried by stretcher to a suitable area to be winched into the helicopter. I remember blokes making a stretcher out of their army belts and clothes, but I couldn't stand the pain as they lifted me. Six of my ribs and my pelvis on my left side had been fractured, so as they lifted me, the stretcher closed around my broken bones. It was crazy.

They fixed the problem of the stretcher and began carrying me out. I have no idea how far I was carried but I remember trying to sit up because I felt like I was drowning. The men would push me back down, unaware that broken ribs had punctured my left lung and I was bleeding in my lungs, thus the feeling of drowning. From the accident site, Sapper John Harris reported:

"The stump blowing party of Taffy Excel, Butch Bradshaw, Trevor Hughes and myself had prepared for a blast and the 'fire on' call had been given. Immediately after that warning, I saw movement at the top of an opposite ridge above a steep incline

and gully. A shout to 'stop', 'abort' or whatever was given, and Butch had to scramble back through the forest debris and cut the fuse with a machete. He had a few words, needless to say. As it turned out it was a stretcher party carrying Peter on a makeshift litter of belts and shirts. Sgt Jim Nixon was administrating a pain killing injection and the track was being cleared of branches in the way."

Meanwhile, I was panicking at the thought of dying in the jungle. Sergeant Nixon administered morphine and I vividly recall clinging to his arm and crying:

"Don't let me die Jim!"

So much for the brave Aussie digger in battle. My behaviour must have been terrible for Jim, especially since I know he respected me, and he had often complimented my hard work. Eventually, the party arrived at a spot where a helicopter could lower a stretcher and, at 6.25 that evening I was evacuated to a Medical Centre in Brunei. Basically, it was a small hospital run by the British Army.

As I was being winched into the helicopter, I could feel my life slipping away; it was a really weird and terrifying feeling for someone age twenty-one. My overriding fear was that I was going to die, and I didn't know where I stood with God. I also remembered thinking I would never run again, or play footy, or see my mum again. I definitely didn't feel ready to die, but through the 'lovely haze' of the pain killer I was given, I think I just accepted it.

I regained consciousness next day in hospital and battled in awful pain for a few days. I was comforted every time I woke by a nurse by my side. What angels they were. They also contacted my parents with the news, which was encouraging to me. The one thing I didn't look forward to however, was nurses turning me to wash me and change the sheets. I also learned to watch the clock in my room and to indicate when it was time for my next painkilling injection.

Eventually, one of the nurses informed me I was getting to like my injections too much; it was time to wean me off whatever it was. It was also scary because, for a few days, I couldn't move or feel my feet. In my pain haze I thought I was now a paraplegic, but it turned out I was only severely bruised from my shoulders to my backside. I still have a slight superficial numbness to touch my skin on my right thigh, but otherwise I recovered reasonably well.

Military Hospitals

After five days at the small emergency Army Hospital in Brunei, doctors decided to air lift me to the British Military Hospital (BMH) in Singapore. Consequently, on July 14, I was strapped in the bulkhead of a military plane bound for Singapore. As we took off and gained altitude I panicked as I suddenly struggled to breathe. I remember thinking:

"This is just great, I made it this far and now I am going to die strapped to the bulkhead of a plane!"

Luckily the nurse traveling with me looked up to see my arm hanging over the bulkhead and my face going grey. I understand she strapped an oxygen mask on, just like the announcements in commercial aircraft when we travel, and we arrived without further incident at Changi Airport. I have since developed further issues with claustrophobia, especially being in top bunks or similar enclosed sleeping areas, and I wonder whether being stuck in a bulkhead of a plane as I felt I was 'out of oxygen,' may have been a contributing factor.

After landing, I was waiting on a stretcher in the warm sun for an ambulance to take us to hospital, and I looked over and saw the barracks where we had been posted just over a month ago. I recall a deep sense of sadness and failure at that point. As I felt my energy slipping, I again felt I was going to die right there in the sun as I was overcome by a melancholic sense of a great deal of effort for nothing. After all the preparation in recruit and corps training, in those fleeting moments, I now believed it had all been pointless.

It is difficult all these years latter to accurately access those fleeting memories, but the experience has since given me a deep respect for the process of dying, including no fear for myself now, and the confidence to sit in a relaxed, respectful, and comforting way with people who are dying.

Finally, I was admitted to the hospital, and I was immediately given blood. Records show I had been given a litre at the Brunei Hospital and another one and a half litres on arrival at BMH. Next morning, I felt like I could jump up and get back to the jungle. Amazing what a boost of blood can do. I can easily understand why Lance Armstrong [1] chose being re-fuelled with his own blood every night after a day's racing. It works a treat. During that first night I woke in my new surroundings to hear what I thought was a tap running:

"Strange," I thought to myself.

However, it wasn't a tap, I was pissing over the bed and on to the floor. The freaky thing was I couldn't feel it happening. Since I couldn't pee on my own in the Brunei hospital, I had endured a catheter all the time. Obviously, the catheter had been withdrawn and I was pissing in my bed, not being able to feel it happening although I could see it. It was a weird experience. The nurses were pleased because this meant some feeling was coming back to my legs. I was just too tired to be embarrassed or care at that point.

Recovering in BMH

Life for a sapper in BMH had its moments. I gradually recovered and had lots of fun with the staff. All staff were military personnel, including the doctors and nurses. I am told by another mate from our Unit, Murray Schroder, who had been injured on the first day we arrived in Brunei, that initially I wasn't too pleasant to a British doctor who castigated me for not having a shirt on and for not saluting him in bed. Murray informed me that, to be polite in re-telling this part of my story, I expressed disdain towards the doctor, and said that I said I didn't have a shirt on because I was too hot, and how was I supposed to salute lying down.

Nothing more said, but I was lucky because the British Military doctors could be nasty about protocols like that. Murray also told me years later that all Australian Army personnel in hospital were given a can of beer a day, but because he thought I was so sick, he drank mine for me. Great mate.

Another amazing thing about the ward was that there were great chips out of the plaster in the wall behind our beds. The holes had been painted over, but you could clearly see big chunks missing. It transpired that they dated back to the Fall of Singapore during World War Two, when Japanese soldiers shot patients in their beds. Not very comforting.

Many of the nurses at the hospital were Irish and fun to hassle. One day one of them gave me the bed bottle as I was having to pee lying in bed. I let rip when suddenly I felt something warm and soft on my thighs and looking down, purple froth was pouring out of the mouth of the bed bottle. Of course, I freaked out, and nurses came from everywhere. It was all a set up and great consultations took place between all of them concerning a diagnosis. Meanwhile, I had purple foam all over my crotch from the chemical they put in the empty bottle.

I don't remember how long I had been in the hospital before they would permit me to get mobile but I do remember the first time I saw myself in the mirror in the bathroom. I honestly thought I was looking at someone else. I didn't recognise myself from all the lost weight; I was literally skin and bone. My ribs were sticking out and my pants would fall off my hips. However, I was lucky to have been so fit and strong when I was injured since it helped in terms of a quicker recovery once back in Perth.

In hindsight I was disappointed I was left lying in bed for so long. However, I would have been charged with insubordination if I had ventured out of bed without permission. So much better now when we are encouraged to get moving as soon as possible after surgery.

I spent seven weeks in BMH before being transferred to the RAAF Base Hospital in Butterworth, Malaysia. I arrived at Butterworth on August 9 and stayed for about ten days. To my delight, I could now walk around, and I discovered a pool in the hospital grounds. I was desperately keen to get in the pool and begin swimming. After some research, I managed to get a pair of bathers, and in I went.

My last memory of swimming was back in Perth at City Beach in the surf when I was fit and strong. Now I could hardly move my limbs and I had dived into the middle of the pool. My body refused to do anything, including dog paddle.

"This is lovely;" I thought, "I have come this far to drown in a bloody swimming pool!"

Somehow, I made it to the side of the pool and was determined to get fit on land before trying swimming again.

Repatriated Back to Perth

I was flown back to Pearce Air Force Base in Bullsbrook, WA, on September 1, 1966, and transferred to Hollywood Repatriation Hospital in Perth. My parents soon came from Bunbury to visit me, and I was discharged a few days later. I was given leave to go back to Bunbury, but I was only there a few days when I felt sick and noticed my urine was orange in colour. I asked mum to come and have a look and she immediately said I had to get back to hospital.

It transpired the blood I had been given in Borneo was infected and now I had Serum Hepatitis – Hep B. My skin went yellow along with the whites of my eyes, my fingernails blue and my urine orange. Great. I was in a ward at Hollywood Repatriation Hospital with blokes from World War Two. One man died in bed alongside me on my first night there. This hospital stay lasted for at least six weeks before my liver function tests were reasonable enough for me to be discharged into my mother's care, until I fully recovered, in Bunbury.

I experienced serious injuries in Borneo, but it never ceases to amaze me how we recover from physical trauma, just as we can from emotional trauma. However, in both instances I believe we need to decide we want to recover. I can honestly say that every day since that event in Borneo, I have thanked God for the gift of each new day, the next breath, and beat of my heart. When confronted with believing you are going to die it really does clear your mind of everything that does not matter as well as sharpened your mind towards things that do matter. Gradually.

Chapter 13

Recovery

A major highlight in Hollywood Hospital was meeting a man named Fred Jackson, who was in the bed next to me. Fred had a brother, Ernie who used to visit, and I immediately bonded with Ernie, thereafter known as Jacko. After my discharge from hospital, Jacko became a father-figure to me. It was the beginning of a wonderful friendship. I was developing a loving reciprocal relationship with Jacko, like nothing I had previously experienced between myself and another man.

I used to love wandering around to Jacko's place just to sit and listen to his lived experiences. Jacko was the one who paved the way for me to seek out and listen to other older men for their counsel and friendship. I was now moving more into the realm of relationships with important mentors who would guide me through post army experiences.

Discharged From Hospital

In January 1967 I still had almost ten months of service left in the army until I was to be officially discharged. I was living in the Barracks at Karrakatta with the rest of the men from WA who had also been in Borneo with 22nd Construction Squadron. While I had only been in Borneo for just over four weeks until I was injured, the rest had stayed on a further five months. Because I was officially on rest and recuperation leave, I didn't have to return immediately to army duties, and so I was able to enrol in education courses run by the Army Education Centre which allowed me to work towards possible university entrance in 1968. This was a golden opportunity to explore further career possibilities after I was discharged.

It was also about this time that my disenchantment with army life began. Eventually, my recuperation leave expired and I had to re-join the squadron. By now my peers were sick of sitting around with nothing to do, and all kinds of devious ways were invented to evade 'work duties.' Duties included laying some curbing on the driveway into the barracks, a job that could have been completed in a few days However, they made it last well beyond our due date for discharge. Other duties included sweeping the said driveway, trimming trees, cleaning vehicles, and occasionally having a parade.

The latter caught me out. I had mastered the art of skipping parades by hiding out in an unused classroom and studying for my exams, but the day came when I was busted. Since arriving home from Borneo, our trusty Self-Loading Rifles (SLR), had been exchanged for another weapon which I had never seen before. However, I was about to go on parade and go through the drill routines with a weapon I knew nothing about. My mates had no mercy for me, so I made sure I was in the back rank, and in true army style, I fudged it. Successfully. And I managed to avoid all future parades.

Every Friday afternoon, Perth would have been ripe for conquering because we were all missing from work and could usually be found at the Ocean Beach Hotel in Cottesloe. This is a good time for another segue into a minor personal crisis. During my studies in the army, I met a beautiful blonde. It turned out her dad was the C.O. of Campbell Barracks in Swanbourne where the really tough soldiers live and train. All soldiers know when you see a vehicle carrying Regimental Colours on a little flag on the bonnet of the car, you stand to attention and salute. One day a group of us, just a couple of weeks away from being discharged, were sitting around outside our Karrakatta Barracks in the sun, just hanging out.

We noticed an official car drive through, but we just carried on 'hanging out.' Later that day we had an order to attend a parade. We wondered what this was about. It transpired my beautiful friend's dad was in the car and he had complained to our C.O. concerning the slack behaviour of 22nd Construction Squadron. In keeping with usual army practice, our C.O. blasted our Sergeant, and our Sergeant made us practice saluting for twenty minutes on parade. Next time I went to meet my girlfriend at her home I was very sheepish, but I don't think her dad knew I ignored him in his flash car when he came to visit us at Karrakatta.

I managed to stay out of further trouble in the army until I was finally officially honourably discharged on September 29, 1967, exactly two years to the day from when I was recruited. I celebrated that day for quite a while at The Ocean Beach Hotel with Dave Regan, who had also been in the army. Meanwhile, Brian Brand whom I recently met, was a terrific mate in helping me work out a career path to become a Physical Education Teacher.

This option appealed since I loved sport and I reasoned that I would also like teaching. In addition, I was eligible for a Returned Soldiers Re-training Scholarship that meant the first three years of my university fees would be paid by the Department of Veterans Affairs. Gold. However, I still had to pay rent and living expenses so I needed work whenever I could get it.

A Mature Age Student

In December 1967, I successfully passed exams in Geography and English, thus earning Provisional Entrance to The University of Western Australia (UWA), to study for a Bachelor of Education with a Physical Education Major, and Geography and Anthropology minors. In preparation for my university entrance exams, I bought a book called *Word Power Made Easy*, and by studying this I was able to increase my vocabulary exponentially. Mum was amazing in helping me prepare for my exams. Whenever going on a home visit home to Bunbury, mum would test me on words until I was exhausted. She was so supportive of my goal to succeed at university.

Before university classes began in 1968, I enrolled in an intensive two-week course called *Speed Reading*. This was an important skill for being able to read numerous texts and other information for my studies. Before starting the speed-reading course, I was reading around 300 plus words per minute with approximately 30% comprehension but by the end of the two weeks, I could read 1100 plus words per minute with over 80% comprehension. I still practice this skill for my recreational reading, although I can slow down if I need to concentrate more on reading to learn.

During the Christmas break of 1967-1968 I stayed in my parents in order to save for university, I worked as a night orderly at the Bunbury Regional Hospital where I met nurses Gale, Zoe and Georgie. I was unable to drink alcohol because of my hepatitis, so I had a year of watching my mates drink and think it was funny, which it often was. Once in the Highway Hotel in Bunbury, I was sitting with a bunch of mates and girls. They had jugs of beer on the tables and some cooked crabs. Someone dropped a crab in a jug of beer and it was the funniest thing I had seen in a long time. When another bloke went to pour himself a beer, I could see his puzzled look:

"I am sure that crab wasn't there before!"

I thought that was funny!

In The Company of Champions

I was fortunate to be invited to join the two-week Bunbury Summer School in January 1968. This was a course run by the Department of Physical Education. Brian also attended and I met many other awesome men and women who were already P.E. teachers. They were fantastic people who further inspired me in my career choice. It was also one of the best two-week periods of learning and fun I had experienced to date as we participated in numerous activities and sports to sharpen skills for teaching.

I was further blessed during this time to be mentored by two great men, Jim Davies who was Superintendent of Physical Education for High Schools, and Len Pavey who was teaching P.E. Studies at Teachers College. I respected and loved both these great men, from whom I learned a great deal. Len in particular did me a huge favour during Summer School when he took me aside and said:

"Prouty, stop being an idiot."

I knew immediately what he meant. In the company of these people, I was inappropriate at times in my behaviour, saying asinine things as we were being taught something new. It was all to get attention, although I didn't realise it at the time because after all of my experiences to date, I was still very unsure of myself, thus some of the ongoing reckless behaviour. Len did me a great favour in pointing out this blind spot, which made me more aware of my behaviour and actions in the future.

This is not to say I never did anything stupid again. Far from it, but at least I was now aware of the need to learn more appropriate ways to behave so people would respect me and not shrug me off as immature, or unsuitable as a prospective teacher. I remain ever grateful to Len for caring enough to point out an obvious blind spot.

Finally, as I was preparing to enter university, I experienced another moment of grace relating to my mother. As I drove with her down Thomas Street towards university one day, she mentioned how proud she was of me, and how she had always dreamed of attending university herself. Although she was a highly respected and capable Registered Nurse, she was thrilled for me to be able to fulfil this dream for myself. In later years, I became aware of so many cases of parents resenting their son or daughter when their child achieved an unfulfilled dream the parent had harboured for themselves. How blessed I was to have such a giving and empowering mother.

Mothers and Sons

I am a passionate believer in the power of mothers in their sons' lives. My mother was the softness in my life. She was the model of service and patience. As I grew physically and gained more self-confidence, mum's influence reminded me to use my strength with respect and restraint. Only now do I appreciate just how 'powerful' her gentle strength was. Mum encouraged me through the process of applying for university, when many others would have written me off, and with good cause I must admit. No formal education, very poor literacy and numeracy skills with the latter still not flash, but an intrinsic motivation that stemmed from watching mum read, and always discussing with me events going on around the world, as well as local social justice issues.

Mum had such a bright mind and a heart for justice. Her faith and her reading to me as a kid imprinted me in ways I only realised later as profound. I credit her with any strong character traits I have, and any good things I have done. I take full responsibility for my failures and less than wise decisions, and at this point, I want to share a story about another powerful mother from First Century Palestine.

Her name was Mary. She experienced an amazing life changing event when she was possibly as young as fifteen and was informed that she was pregnant with a special child. History shows this child was born in a stable in Bethlehem. Soon after the birth, the parents and newborn son became refugees in Egypt, and when they returned to Nazareth in Galilee, Mary and her husband Joseph raised their son, Jesus, and his brothers and at least two sisters.

Jesus was an apprentice carpenter to his father until an event that literally changed the world. Jesus was thirty years old at the time, and therefore Mary would have been around forty-five. We don't know how many family members were present at a wedding in Cana, but we know Mary was there with her first-born son. At the wedding Mary became aware of a possible social catastrophe; the groom had run out of wine at the wedding. This had the potential for great shame and embarrassment for the groom. Mary notified Jesus of the problem to which he replied, in effect:

"It's not my issue."

At this point the profound belief of a mother in her son is demonstrated. The son was 'introduced' to the world. He is declared ready by his mother for the mission for which he was miraculously born. Her response to the wait staff was simple; she directed them to her son and simply declared:

"Do whatever he tells you."

Accordingly, Jesus instructed the staff to fill six large water jugs with water, which, as it was poured out for guests, became wine of excellent quality. In fact, it was the best the Master of Ceremonies had ever tasted. Thus began the public ministry of this remarkable man instigated as it were by his mother. Mary bore this man as her fist born son. She fed him at her breast and protected him in a dash to freedom in Egypt; she nurtured him as he grew in Galilee into manhood as a carpenter and a scholar of academic excellence and she calmly knew when it was time to promote him into a career that changed the world forever.

This 'ordinary' mother was the first to recognise the potential of her son. I know of so many mothers who have been the first to recognise the potential of their sons and whose hearts have in turn soared with pride and, sometimes, been broken with despair. Mothers have seen their sons off to war and they have seen them achieve great acts of altruism and heroism, and they have wept as their sons turned to crime and despicable acts of violence.

Military historians record countless young men who died in battle on the beaches of Normandy, the jungles of Vietnam or the bitter cold of Korea, crying for their mothers as they lay mangled and in pain waiting for death. Notorious inmates in Sing Sing Maximum Security Prison in New York State reputedly asked for cards to write notes to their mothers on Mother's Day, but never to anyone else, including their fathers.

After a six-year battle with dementia, my mother died in 2009. Although I loved and admired her, it is only now that I am beginning to fully appreciate her imprint upon my heart and soul. Mothers indeed have a unique place in our lives as boys and as men.

Chapter 14

1968: A Year of Profound Change

In 1968, the world experienced a litany of social, political and sporting shocks that left us numb and wondering if all this could be possible. Meanwhile, I was feeling embarrassed, and a tad threatened during the first few weeks of my university course. In retrospect, I was battling 'shame attacks,' especially the imposter syndrome of 'you are not worthy or good enough.' I was twenty-three-years-old and all my classmates were all aged seventeen – eighteen and just out of High School.

Since I had missed so many years of formal education, I knew I was academically way behind them. However, although I had low scores for my university entrance, you cannot measure a person's determination and motivation to succeed. I had an excess of both. I was looking forward to this marvellous opportunity to study and to learn, and highly attuned to the events unfolding in that year, 1968.

In later years I saw a film titled; *1968: A Crack in Time.* The documentary presented a timeline of events in 1968 that were overwhelming at the time, and equally so in retrospection. Among many of the key events that shook the world was the 'Tet Offensive' [1] of the Vietnam War. On January 30, 1968, North Vietnamese troops surprised U.S. and South Vietnamese troops in an ambush that inflicted heavy casualties. It was a turning point in a war that had been raging since 1963. Every evening, in homes of almost sixty million people in the U.S. and Australia, media coverage brought horrific and graphic images of war casualties into living rooms.

This was the first major conflict in history to be broadcast on colour TV, and these 'real time clips of war,' precipitated widespread student and community protests throughout the world which ultimately led to the end of the conflict when in April 1975, North Vietnamese tanks stormed the capital of South Vietnam.

After repeatedly denying in March, that he would challenge U.S. President Johnson for the Democratic nomination, Senator Robert F. Kennedy announced he would enter the presidential race. On the same day, although it would not be revealed until the following year, U.S. ground troops killed more than five hundred Vietnamese civilians in the My Lai massacre in South Vietnam. [2] **This** shocking event further inflamed peoples' opposition to the Vietnam War. There were anti-war protests in France, the U.K., Germany, Mexico and our own country. We also witnessed demonstrations for Aboriginal rights in Australia and the move for equality for women in careers, including fair remuneration for work.

Then, on April 4 one of my heroes, Dr Martin Luther King, was assassinated while standing on the balcony outside his room at a Memphis motel. Tragically, on June 6 in a hotel in Los Angeles, after he was all but assured of winning the Democratic vote to run for President, another of my heroes, Bobby Kennedy was also assassinated. Previously Kennedy had spoken so eloquently and sincerely to a gathering at Indianapolis, advising them of Dr King's death. [3]

Kennedy had been calm and convincing in asking the mainly African American crowd to return home peacefully, just as Dr King would have wanted, and those who had gathered to hear Kennedy did return home quietly. Alas, thousands of others in cities all over the U.S. marched in anger and grief, burning cities as they did so.

August heralded the 'Prague Spring' [4] in Soviet controlled Czechoslovakia, led by Alexander Dubcek who had been elected by the people as the First Secretary of the country's Communist Party. The victory marked a brief period of reform in Czechoslovakia. I remember watching TV news of Russian tanks rolling into Prague in August to crush this cry for freedom by the Czech people. In later years Czech citizens gained their independence from Russia, including the freedom to govern themselves.

Later, in October we witnessed the turmoil of student riots and deaths around the Mexico City Olympic Games. From an Australian perspective, these games were memorable because of the amazing 200 metre men's final, won by Tommy Smith of the U.S., with Australia's Peter Norman second and John Carlos of the U.S. third. At the medal ceremony for this event, the two U.S. athletes gave one arm salutes while wearing a black glove each, while Peter Norman stood still, but wearing a badge in support of black athletes. The two U.S. athletes were sent home immediately after the medal ceremony, and Peter Norman was banned by the Australian Olympic Committee from ever representing Australia again.

Ironically Norman's 200 metre time of 20.06 seconds is still an Australian record. Further, Smith and Carlos invited Norman as their guest at the Sydney 2000 Olympics, and after his untimely death, were pall bearers at his funeral. [5] There is a gripping DVD entitled, *Salute,* about these games, including Peter Norman's feat and support of his former US opponents.

Closer to home, on Monday, October 14, an earthquake shook the regional town of Meckering in the wheatbelt area of WA. [6] At that time, I was in an exercise physiology lab at the university working on a stationary bicycle to test my heart rate. As I was pedalling furiously, I looked up to see a skeleton in a glass case beginning to sway about. I recall thinking:

"That can't be good."

Meanwhile, our professor was telling us to stand in a doorway.

"Bugger that," I thought. *"I am out of here!"*

I joined fellow students in scampering outside the building. It was a weird sensation in the moments following the tremor. An eerie silence and foreboding sense engulfed the campus, before birds returned to their chatter, and we humans processed what must have happened. The earthquake didn't last long, but it was an exceptional experience to all of us born and raised in WA. Students in the university library felt the building move significantly, and that is a big building.

Many stories emanated from this event, some sad and others quite funny. For example, a farmer's wife in Meckering said to her husband whom she thought was working in a basement workshop of the house:

"Whatever you are doing down there, stop it.
You are shaking the house."

Meanwhile, in Perth a man called a local radio station and said he was about to get out of bed after a hard Sunday night partying.

When his feet hit the floor and it was moving, he thought he should withdraw the idea and stay in bed!

Finally, on Christmas Eve, Apollo 8 with Jim Lovell, later of Apollo 13 fame, Bill Anders and Frank Borman became the first humans to orbit the moon. [7] Apollo 8 circled the moon ten times and we held our breath with each orbit as the craft was out of radio contact every time it was on the far side of the moon.

Apollo 8 was ultimately another triumph for NASA and the U.S., and a major step towards fulfilling the late President Kennedy's vision to launch a man to the moon, and return him safely to earth, before the end of the decade.

Meanwhile...

Nurses, whom I met at Bunbury Regional Hospital, had moved to Perth to work in early 1968, and they invited me to join them in a shared house in Lillian Street, Cottesloe, which I duly did. It was convenient and fun for a while, but I needed a quiet place to study, and so with people coming and going on night duty, I bailed mid-year.

Many of my mates thought I was mad, but it was a dog's breakfast living with these women as it included all kinds of their mates dropping around for visits. Most nights I had to wash a pile of dishes before I could cook something to eat. The nurses generally ate junk food at home, unbelievable for people who should have known better. However, they were awesome women, and they did throw some memorable parties.

Fortunately, my mate Jamie who was an ex-scholar at Scotch College, recommended me for a job as House Master for the second half of the year. I gladly accepted and moved into 'Keys

House' to supervise boys after school for their homework. I had occasional weekend work, but generally the duties for free board and meals, were minimal.

I played footy for University Football Club during the winter and joined the University Athletic Club for summer track meets. I had tried out for selection at East Fremantle Football Club during pre-season 1967. What was I thinking?! I had just recovered from a fractured pelvis and I was deemed by the Department of Veterans' Affairs to have lost thirty percent efficiency in my left leg. Although I was selected for scratch matches in the Reserves Team, I was never destined to go much further with football at the highest level.

However, it was during this time I was introduced to one of my teenage heroes, Ray Sorrell. Ray was a fantastic bloke and already a legend in football circles He was ultimately inducted into the Australian Football League Hall of Fame in 2004. At the time, I was just thrilled to be running around on the training track with such a great man. I was blessed by his genuine interest in me as a person, and he soon became a role model. He also helped me purchase a VW 'beetle' that served me faithfully before I passed it on six years later to another proud owner.

In essence, I was finally beginning to grow up and mature. I was reading all kinds of literature, engaging in deep and meaningful conversations, seeking counsel and advice from my professors and teachers at university, and reflecting upon my time in the army and the ramifications of the ongoing Vietnam War.

However, fate was about to deal a different hand.

Chapter 15

The Black Dog

My first day at university for registration was a blur. I had been quite at home in the army and in my prior work experiences, but this was a huge 'change of gears.' Further, I was twenty-three, I had no idea of school life, and I felt totally awkward among all the recent High School graduates. A fish out of water would have trumped me. Having experienced a 'high' of achievement in the army and the previous P.E. Summer School, this was a place of learning where the highest priority was upon academic excellence and competence. What was I doing here?

I also found making friends in the city daunting at times. After all, leading up to my conscription I had always lived in rural areas and towns, and was still conscious of being on the back of the grid in terms of my formal education. My 'informal education at the university of hard knocks' didn't carry much agency among many of the city folk I was meeting. I was conscious of being a boy from the country who was trying to communicate with other young men who had been to high end private schools.

City mates who welcomed me included Robbie Young, Ken Venables, Jamie Lutz, and John Haslehurst. These peers were a blessing to me, especially as I learned how to live in a city and negotiate social gatherings. I worked hard at appearing relaxed on each of these occasions, but I distinctly recall questioning my worthiness. On the other hand, I was 100% focussed upon the learning opportunities I faced, and to work and to learn. With the above mentioned in mind, let me share my four year's experiences as an undergraduate student.

First year - 1968

I passed three of my four required First Year units, with a supplementary exam in English for the summer, which I failed. During the summer of 1968-1969, I taught swimming to earn pocket money, and I had been dumped by my girlfriend. Ouch. Then, after the tumultuous year of 1968, I prepared for my second year of university.

I took the whole of first year to feel marginally at home among the other young people at university, and to gain a sense of belonging. My P.E. professors and lecturers were fantastic; generous, understanding, respectful (with one exception) and awesome role models. So, second year had to be better than this.

Second year - 1969

For this year, I shared a one-bedroom flat in Cooke Street Nedlands. My mate Rod Lewis and I occupied the only bedroom, and Ken Venables slept on a sofa in the main room. We had fun times together, but three blokes living next door to the manager of the flats was never going to work. She and her elderly mother complained about everything we did, including laughing! I recall this time with Ken and Rod as highly significant in shoring up my self-confidence and belief in myself.

A memorable event on July 20 was Neil Armstrong's [1] landing on the moon. All over Perth, people were glued to TV sets wherever they could find them, including many shop windows in the city. It was a profound experience, especially since President Kennedy had cast the vision in 1962 at a speech in Soldiers Field Stadium in Chicago. Sadly, President Kennedy did not live to see his vision realised.

During winter break, I travelled in my VW to Exmouth Gulf with Rosco. Along the way, we spent a week in Carnarvon, first working for a builder and then a market gardener, before travelling on to Exmouth for a week to visit Jacko and his wife, Betty. Since Jacko had a serious lung complaint from being gassed during his time in the Pacific Islands during World War Two, he was permanently incapacitated for work. Jacko and Betty used to travel north every winter to exchange the cold for the tropical warmth of the north. I loved and admired Jacko for the way he overcame adversity and made the most of life.

It was awesome being with Jacko and Betty. Rosco and I hunted for a goat to roast for dinner, and I borrowed a Land Rover to do some exploring in the canyons with Jacko and Rosco. The break was more balm for my soul, especially being with Jacko. I missed him a great deal when they travelled north each year, and it was good to be with my Bro for this adventure.

A Home Owner

Buying a house was another major turning point during my second year at university. Since our manager kicked us out of the flat, I decided to buy a house. I had saved some money while in hospital in the army, and mum agreed to support an application for a loan from the bank. I looked for a house close to university, the beach and the river, and with these criteria in mind, I found 6 Morgan Street, in Shenton Park.

I had my friend Dave Andrich, and later another important mentor, living with me along with others from time to time. Eventually, we had all kinds of people dropping by Morgan Street. Some slept on a bed on the veranda, and on summer nights, others could be found sleeping on the back lawn. In between amazing parties and visitors, I managed to pass second year studies; I was halfway there.

In the summer of 1969-1970, I taught swimming again. In addition, I worked as a night orderly at one of our major hospitals. By the time I was ready to start university again, I was exhausted. I was hardly getting any sleep between my two jobs, so something had to give, which it eventually did. I didn't see it coming, but I was heading in the wrong direction in just about every aspect of my life at this time.

These two years tough for several reasons. To begin with, there were constant marches and demonstrations on campus against our troops in Vietnam. I knew of men my age who had already died there and students fresh out of High School were calling them murderers. Consequently, I found the Vietnam Moratoriums tough at first.

Gradually, however, I came to see how shocking our engagement in Southeast Asia was. I saw the horror of Vietnam each night on TV, and I started listening to the demonstrators. I was also battling the Department of Veterans Affairs regarding my ongoing pain and recovery from Borneo. Further, I came across doctors in Perth who treated me like a leper. When I was sent to one orthopaedic surgeon in particular, he held my substantial medical file in front of me, and then dropped it on the floor at my feet. His comment was:

"What is a healthy young man doing with a file like this?"

He made it sound as if I was complaining over nothing and did not deserve this treatment. I was immediately hit with the unhealthy message of being 'unworthy'. This was 1969 and I was still of the belief that you don't argue; you just accept whatever comes your way. Knowing what I know now, I would have, ever so respectfully, but forcefully, challenged this surgeon's behaviour.

In hindsight, it was clear later that Brene Brown's 'gremlins' were hard at work in my head. I was actively seeking the sense of belonging and worthiness that John Powel [2] identifies when we are seeking authenticity. I was the 'clown' who was always seeking to belong by being the 'fun of the party'. This conflictual reality of my mind and heart was building pressure at a rapid speed. I was 100% committed to full recovery from my injuries so I was overdoing all kinds of fitness and recuperative regimes. In turn, I was wearing myself out, working part time, and taking full time study.

By adopting the attitude that I was alone in my pain and that I had to work it out myself, I also did myself no favours. This attitude persisted despite meeting special friends, male and female, who would have understood my circumstances. Unfortunately, as yet I had no idea about the concept of being vulnerable and 'real' with my peers.

Third Year - 1970

My third year, which proved to be a bit of a blur, ticked over. I would spend every day on campus and every night in the library, studying until closing time at 10.00 pm. I was still passionate about learning, and I valued every opportunity to soak it up. At the same time, I was working hard to pay my living expenses, including working as a fitness instructor at a local health club. It was here one evening, when I was conducting a stress test on a gentleman, that I collapsed on the floor. Not a good look for the poor man on the bike taking the stress test.

I had been teaching swimming, working nights at the hospital, attending classes and helping out at the health club. As mentioned previously, something had to give. The owner sacked me, but he allowed me to continue attending the club for my own training.

Final Year - 1971

My final year, and this proved to be my toughest at university. My parents spent most of the year traveling by caravan around Australia, just at the time I began losing self-confidence to finish my degree. I confess, if my parents had been home, I would have wanted to confront my father with the rage and anger I felt building inside me. I identified him as the source of my loss of confidence, but I didn't yet have the emotional skills to deal with my feelings of rage. I could 'hear' his voice making all those negative, hurtful and demeaning comments, and I was emotionally and mentally weak enough to give them 'full volume' in my mind.

The Black Dog Hits...Hard

During this year, I gradually withdrew from friends and began to consider myself a nobody. Again. As I approached the end of the academic year and final exams, I was experiencing the genesis of a major emotional breakdown, which we sometimes call 'the black dog.' Ultimately, a major breakdown of all systems was the hallmark of my final year at university. It began with feeling like ants were constantly chewing away in my gut, and when they took a break, they were replaced by an empty feeling of dread heralding something bad was going to happen. I couldn't sleep and I wasn't hungry. Every day was a battle.

I felt like I was literally falling apart. I went from regular exercise each day to not being able to get out of bed in the morning. I would try to study, but the words would 'swim' on the page, and I knew I wasn't understanding anything. Attending lectures also became increasingly hopeless since I couldn't take notes or remember anything. Eventually, I was home one day, trying to study, when I looked at a bottle of prescription pain killing pills on my desk. They were powerful and designed to help me when pain from my hip became too tough to ignore. A thought flashed through my mind that I could just take all those pills and all would be OK. At that point I knew I was in trouble, and I literally ran out of the house to get help.

I sought out Jim Davies from Bunbury Summer School and I just broke down and wept at his desk, even though I had no idea what was wrong with me. Jim was shocked, which was the reaction of everyone who knew me. I can't remember much of the detail from those few days. They still remain a blur. I visited my GP who was also shocked to see me in such distress, especially since I always presented as the happy and fit bloke little troubled by anything.

Fortunately, I was blessed that my good mate Dave Andrich was still living with me. I understand my GP sought assurance from Dave that he would 'keep an eye out' for me, and I am forever indebted to Dave for his generous care. Over the time Dave and I shared the house together, he was my friend, then teacher, and a special mentor in my life. Prior to my breakdown, I recall many hours of deep and rich conversations with Dave and other men in the house, whereby after our often juvenile and late night, liquor fuelled, random thoughts, we would ultimately defer to Dave's wisdom and patience. Dave was at least four years older than any of us and I benefitted immeasurably from his knowledge and wisdom.

I was also grateful to my professor, and hero, Dr John Bloomfield who assured me I would complete the course. I went to John's house and just being in his home helped settle my spirit. His empathy was somewhat reassuring. Throughout the four-year course, John had been a source of inspiration and in later years, I modelled some of my teaching on what John said and did. Other lecturers were also kind and helpful, and I managed to get through my final exams.

Before exams, I sought permission from John for a week's leave from university, which he granted. I called my Aunty Jean and Uncle Ron in Bunbury and asked if I could come and stay with them for a week. They welcomed me, asking no questions, but somehow understanding my need for their care. I had no idea what I wanted, other than to be somewhere safe and familiar. Uncle Ron was my dad's elder brother, and such a gentle and kind man. Empathy was their soul food I needed. I spent time painting my VW, walking on the beach and welding legs onto an old steel bedframe that I found at the local rubbish tip. I just felt totally empty and incapable of anything more than simply 'staying alive'. After the week, I drove back to Perth with the bedframe tied precariously onto the roof on the VW.

Reflections

My main learning point from this breakdown experience revolved around trying to convince my dad I was not useless, even though he wasn't currently present and expressing those assertions. My Long-Term Memory was 'releasing' all the negative phrases in my mind, just as I would think about what a potential failure I was. This is not dissimilar to the "self-created stories" alluded to by Brene Brown, which noted in chapter eight.

It is not unlike having a recording in the brain that plays back all the negative things people have said about us, or what we believe they think about us. Shame 101. I had worn myself out physically and now my wrecked emotional self was taking over. I was ashamed, embarrassed, humbled, and totally out of ideas and energy.

I can't remember how long it took after exams to recover enough to function effectively after my emotional train wreck. However, one of the things that helped me recover was going to see a wonderful woman and counsellor, Dr Patrice Cook. Patrice was a nun with a degree in Clinical Psychology and had been recommended to me by a friend. It turned out to be a great suggestion. I can't recall much of the detail when seeing Patrice, but visits were strategic and timely. I saw Patrice a few times and whatever she did and said was enough to get me somewhat back on track.

The Power of Culture

Before concluding my university experiences, I want to share some of my thoughts about girls and women during this period of my life. In 1972, I met another father-figure friend who was the dad of one of my students at Churchlands Senior High School. This man, Bob Horseman, was a U.S. citizen practicing dentistry in Perth. Bob was also a former World War Two U.S. fighter pilot, although he didn't speak much about his experiences.

I would often go around to Bob's house just to chat and learn from him. This was in stark contrast to working among shearers, farm workers, welders and soldiers who would always talk *about* girls, often disrespectfully, but didn't really know how to talk *with*, or, *to* them.

In my past, I used to be part of these 'conversations,' *about* girls, although deep down I knew they were not respectful or honouring of girls and women. I also still remember saying to my mates at the end of university that if I had to go to a school where a woman was head of the P.E. Department, I would not go. As I write, I cannot believe I was so serious about this. I learned a few years later in Canada, and throughout my later life, just how powerful my Australian culture had been to lead me to seriously entertain such a dishonouring and disrespectful view of women.

There was also the subconscious belief in my mind that I could not trust myself to commit to a long-term relationship, especially marriage. This was partially due to seeing how bad marriage was for my parents and to my faulty belief that I would not be capable of maintaining a long-term relationship with any one particular girl.

In contrast with my academic success, the terrible 'systems' breakdown during my final year of study was my most traumatic and dramatic learning experience from my four years of undergraduate studies. It was embarrassing, humiliating, scary, lonely, enervating, and often dark. I had not yet really learned to use the four-letter word – help. However, I at least temporarily embraced a less frenetic lifestyle, which was influenced by a beautiful transformative experience by a lake in Tasmania.

Peace Over Lake St Claire

Many of us who had completed our studies in 1971 had applied to attend the National P.E. Conference in Hobart, commencing the day after Boxing Day. Additional to our conference experience, Richard Lockwood, one of our university lecturers, had planned a group hike in Tasmania from Cradle Mountain to Lake St Claire. I accepted Richard's invitation and I deeply appreciated the whole experience.

There were about twelve of us in the group, carrying our own backpacks with food, tents, sleeping bag and clothes. We began at the huts at Cradle Mountain National Park and walked west towards Lake St Claire. The hike was stunning, and nothing like I had previously experienced. Climbing Cradle Mountain was the first gift of the walk, and as we followed the trail, I was filled with wonder and awe as I beheld the beauty of the unique Australian landscape in Tasmania. It was hard going in parts, especially after rain, but it was a totally memorable experience.

On our second to last day, we arrived at overnight huts on the shores of Lake St Claire. Each of us was able to find a comfortable bunk inside and we settled down for the night. I was in a top bunk not far from the front door. Sometime during the night, I could not get back to sleep. After midnight, I heard a little shuffling noise, and a possum crept into the hut and began opening a backpack. In no time it found some biscuits and began happily munching on them.

I just lay there quietly and watched this cute little fella having a good nosh up. I remember thinking how fortunate I was to be seeing and enjoying it. The possum finally shuffled off, and around 4.00 am I sprang out of bed and climbed out on a fallen tree in the water over the lake. As I settled back on the log my heart was a tad disturbed, but nothing serious, just awe at the beauty of the early morning quiet.

I have since found these times of quiet, intentional, or serendipitous, to be most effective in restoring my heart and mind to a peaceful homeostasis. As I was reflecting upon the past year and wondering what was in store for me as a teacher, I experienced an incredible peace flowing through my body. It was calming, cleansing, warm and sensuous. It was the deepest feeling of joy and satisfaction that I could imagine. It felt like I was just where I was supposed to be. Compared to the events of the past year this was an extraordinary experience. It was also a harbinger of what was so come.

In the morning we walked out of the National Park and a bus took us back to Hobart. I really enjoyed our conference, including meeting P.E. teachers from all across Australia, and some from Canada. One of the Canadian presenters was a Professor from The University of Alberta in Edmonton. During his presentation he showed us slides of Alberta. That stroke of genius on his part convinced me to aim for Alberta for my next stint of studying!

After the conference I flew back to Perth and travelled down to Bunbury for the Summer School where I reported on what we had learned at the conference. My summer experience in Tasmania, plus catching up with friends and mentors at the Bunbury Summer School was enough to inspire my next steps as a beginning teacher.

Chapter 16

Teaching: With a Spice of Adventure

Although I had a university degree focussing upon anatomy, biology, physiology, kinesiology and sport science, our focus on actual teaching practice in my degree was woefully inadequate. Consequently, I started teaching at Churchlands Senior High School in 1972 with sound knowledge about our bodies, but very little about how to actually teach. Fortunately, by now I was twenty-seven so students thought I must have been an experienced teacher, and I was in no rush to set that record straight.

Despite the lack of preparation for teaching, two years in the army and a varied range of life experiences boosted my confidence for the task ahead. I had no problem relating to students, and I was easily able to establish good relationships with them. Subjects I taught included P.E. and Year Eleven Biology.

Thinking Laterally

In the absence of any content in my degree on how to teach, there were some teaching strategies I invented on the job. For example, I was about to start a unit of teaching hockey with Year Nine boys who hastily informed me:

"Hockey, that's a girl's game sir'"

"Oops," I thought, how do I motivate them here?

I had a lesson all planned with particular skill-based activities, including a modified game. Based upon the overall response from the boys, I quickly realised I needed to change my plan, so I sent the class to the bike racks with the directive to bring their bike or borrow one as bikes were not chained up in those days and return to the oval. As they returned, their curiosity and motivation were high. Meanwhile, I went back inside and grabbed some softballs and we had a 'game' of hockey on bikes, using hockey sticks and a soft ball. A bit like polo but without the horses. The boys loved it.

There were quite a few crashes and a bit of blood here and there. One boy gashed his leg when he fell off his bike, but he refused to go to the school nurse and get it attended to. He was proud of his wound. Thanks to an idea I remembered from another P.E. teacher, I had no more problems with motivation for playing hockey, although with hockey sticks and balls, not bikes, for the rest of the unit.

Discipline

Similarly, some discipline strategies I adopted were uniquely my own. I had a group of Year Ten students in a Health Education class who were testing my patience. I don't recall any lectures we had at university on gaining and maintaining discipline in the classroom, but I had learned a great deal about getting folks' attention in the army. One boy was particularly giving me grief so in frustration I reached over the desk and lifted him under his shoulders right out of his seat. He looked at me and said:

"You need to put me down."

I thought:

"Yes, I do need to do that."

Luckily nothing more was said. However, next class I apologised to the boy and the class.

Meanwhile, it was still difficult to get students settled first thing for class, and that's when I remembered my machete. When I was injured in Borneo my kit was packed and sent back to WA, and it include a rather mean looking machete that should have stayed in Borneo.

My mode of transport to and from school was a Yamaha 250 road/trail motor bike, with a backpack for carrying lunch and other bits and pieces. So, for the next class with this group, I brought my machete in my backpack, riding an off-road motor bike through the Western Suburbs of Perth. I walked into the class and, without a word, slammed the machete down on the teacher's desk. Silence. No more discipline problems in starting classes. Towards the end of the class, some of the students admitted they were momentarily frightened and wondered:

"What next?"

However, they added that they loved the moment including the opportunity, once the class settled down, to inspect the machete, and to pump me for more background regarding the said weapon.

At this stage I also developed an interest in photography, including developing film. Bob Horseman taught me how to do all kinds of cool things with developing, so I began taking photos of boys during P.E., including training for baseball, and posting them on the school notice board. Almost all the boys in the school would be watching each week to see what new photos were posted. It was gratifying walking past the notice board and hearing them speak enthusiastically about their P.E. classes. Sadly, teachers are not as free to do that sort of neat stuff anymore.

Out of the Classroom

Camps and excursions were other modes of challenging the students and providing them with memorable experiences. Stemming from my time in the army and various camps I had experienced during my university years, I was passionate about getting students out of the classroom and school, in exchange for insights gained from active learning and community living.

I was single and loved taking weekend residential camps and getting to know my students. I organised all kinds of such activities in my first year at Churchlands. I would recruit friends from university who were not teachers, to come on the camp site and talk to students about their careers, and life aspirations. The camps were heavily oriented towards activities and utilisation of the surrounding environment, either ocean or bush.

At one coastal camp, two Year Eleven boys found a small oil slick in a bay and then decided to 'swim in it.' It was a bit of a worry later as the oil had cut air flow into their skin and they began shivering really badly. Fortunately, we scraped off the worst of the oil and washed them carefully with detergent to get them clean. A robust discussion on human biology ensued followed by a sigh of relief for me.

A disastrous canoe trip for Year Twelve's was yet another of those experiences where fear ruled for a while, but later the students recalled the scary experience as:

"I was so scared, but it was the best time ever!"

When I scouted before the trip, the river was flowing quite benignly, but we had received some serious rain since then. Therefore, by the time we were ready to launch the canoes, the river was angry. However, I gave the OK to launch, all against my better judgment. We had taken water and control skills in relatively benign conditions, and it wasn't long before canoes began capsizing and inexperienced paddlers were beginning to panic, including me as I could see from behind just how fast the water was now flowing. Inevitably, students were in the water.

Thankfully, they were all wearing life jackets. One canoe became wedged in a branch of a tree and the force of the water turned the canoe, snapping off the front as it did so and making it not so easy to control. Following from behind I came across one of the students, Bev, clinging to a tree in the middle of the river. No canoe, or mates in sight. Actually, they were on the bank, terrified for Bev in the tree. I managed to pull into the bank and then swim across to Bev and bring her to shore.

Quite possibly the craziest idea I had in this first year of teaching took place in the May School Holidays. I was always thinking of experiences that might help students 'grow up,' and this was another brainchild along those lines. I set out on the Australind, the train from Perth to Bunbury, with a group of sixteen Year Tens and Elevens, with backpacks, tents and food. We were picked up by bus at Bunbury Railway Station by a friend who drove us out to Keith and Sheila's farm where Keith took us on a 'hayride' around the farm.

Later we set out to walk through the valley to a drop off point where Keith had taken our backpacks for our first night camping in the Wellington Forest. Next morning, we hiked to a spot in the bush not far from the Collie River, then our final camp site on the banks of the Collie River. On our final morning, we hiked to Wellington Dam where my same contact was waiting to drive us to a former school mate's dairy farm in Brunswick Junction. At the farm we had a huge barbecue that the campers demolished in record time.

Our ride to Brunswick Junction to catch the train back to Perth was in the back of a farm truck, complete with a cattle crate and lots of cow dung all around. The students rated this the highlight of our hike. From there, we returned by train to Perth where I had booked us into a Youth Hostel. Our city clothes were already at the hostel, and we settled in for a shower, dinner that I cooked, and a good night's sleep.

Over the next couple of days, I had organised for us to meet the Premier, the Lord Mayor, and visit the WA Printing Works, Daily News and Sunday Times where we met reporters and editors. We shopped for and cooked our own meals at the Hostel, and capped it off by staying up one night to visit a Night Shelter, where we had a meal with residents, followed by visits to the WA Police Station, Royal Perth Hospital ICU, and to Kings Park to watch the sun rise.

My overall vision for the rural/city experience was for my students to learn how to take care of themselves, to learn to cooperate, to experience something of life outside the city and to meet farmers in the stunning Ferguson Valley. In Perth, I wanted them to get an appreciation of 'who's who in the jungle,' and to experience what goes on at night in a city. Feedback from the students who took part was highly positive, and I appreciated the parental support for the idea.

Play

During all this time I also ran various other camps with no major mishaps, and I managed to learn to become a better teacher. I was still living in Morgan Street with my brother Ross and one of his mates. Rosco and his mate had off-road motor bikes so on many weekends, when I was not running camps and planning lessons, we would be off exploring. Everything inland and north of North Beach was bushlands for riding our bikes, jumping over logs, and generally pushing our luck. We always maintained we hadn't enjoyed a good ride if we didn't 'lay it down' at least once.

One particular Saturday I was racing Rosco along a beach south of Rockingham. We had heard people were stringing wire across tracks at head height to dissuade people from doing just that so we went down to investigate. After all, I knew about stringing wire across roads. Anyway, we were racing along the beach when I looked back to see where Rosco was. Big mistake.

I hit a wash in the beach with my front wheel, which stuck in the wet sand, and I was launched. According to Rosco, I did a complete front flip and landed on my back just in time to see my bike about to land on top of me. I managed to put both arms up, and with enough force and the bike's momentum, push it away from me. I jumped up and said:

"I'm OK, just broken my collar bone."
"Right," said Rosco: *"look down at your right leg."*

I looked. There was a huge flap of meat hanging from my right shin. It did not look good. A further complication was, I and three helpers had fifteen days before leading thirty students in, what transpired to be an amazing four-week camping tour of both Islands of New Zealand.

We managed to find a local who took me into Fremantle Hospital where I had surgery to repair the massive gash in my leg. This required a skin graft from inside my left thigh to cover the scar on my leg, which I still carry today. Now I had to be patient and wait for healing. I had been good at that in Singapore, so I figured I could do it again.

I appreciated my brother's support during this time. Somehow, he rescued my bike and brought it back to Morgan Street. Rosco claims he cannot remember how he achieved that.

Reflections

In retrospect, I attacked my first year of teaching with what I believed was my major asset, an inexhaustible supply of energy and passion. This frenetic approach to life was one of my dysfunctional and ineffective strategies for keeping shame at bay. By keeping busy and burning myself out for my students, I think I believed I could avoid confronting the 'shame demons' lurking in the shadows of my mind.

Towards the end of the year, however, I began experiencing some of the same emptiness and sadness from the previous year. I had not fully grasped the power of 'being still' accompanied by intentional reflective practice as strategies for combatting shame. Consequently, I went back to see Dr Patrice Cooke. Visiting Patrice again was enough to help regain much of my mental strength and self-confidence. Patrice asked me what I still wanted to do with my life, and at that stage, I had my heart set on going to Canada for further study at some stage in the future. Basically, all the advice Patrice gave was:

"Go ahead and do that!"

Second Year Teaching

I began the academic year of 1973 with an awesome Year Eleven Biology class of eleven students. What a gift. They were the best class ever. The class was small due to a timetable clash, and I mapped out how to approach the biology course almost as an individual learning journey. I asked each student what grade they were aiming for, and how they thought they would achieve it. There were six boys and five girls in the class. One week we knew the girls would be missing for our ninety-minute double period. As we were about to begin a unit in the course on Marine Biology, I suggested to the boys we should go down to City Beach for that day's lesson:

"No problem, sir," they said.

On the day in question, I brought my VW to school. To fit everyone in, we figured it would be best to take out the actual back seat to create more room. Wayne Loxley climbed into the tiny space above the engine. Being the tallest, Zane McDonald sat in the front seat and the other four sat on the floor. We had the best biology lesson I ever taught, at least according to a poll taken when we got back to school. Sadly, teachers can't offer these kinds of memorable learning experience now. Taking risks is part of who I am, and I appreciate that about myself. I am just grateful I didn't have any students hurt in some of my 'extra-curriculum' activities.

The rest of the school year went relatively smoothly. I had booked to resign at the end of Second Term – three term school years then – to move to Alberta, Canada. I was passionate about teaching, but I knew I still wasn't good at it. I had no problem relating to students, but I just wasn't happy. Without appreciating it at the time, I was still being driven to prove I was not useless. I also appreciated in later years I was too focused on trying to rescue some students from situations I thought were unfair to them. So much projection from my own teenage years. Both of these factors weighed heavily on my heart and soul, and after seeing Patrice another couple of times, I knew I had to get away.

School arranged for my replacement to come two weeks before I was due to leave to help him get to know my classes and the programme I was following. My replacement turned out to be Robbie Langer, who later played cricket for WA and Australia. Rob was a hard-hitting batsman who was exciting to watch when he was in form. I thought it was magic that the students had someone like that to replace me.

Nevertheless, it was a wrenching thing to say goodbye to my classes. I struggled to hold back tears and that didn't help them. I felt so bad leaving students I had come to know and love, but I also knew I still had a lot to fix within myself to become a more effective teacher.

Reflections

I had been on warp speed learning during this time. I knew I was far from sorting out my emotional turmoil, and would often get butterflies and periods of anxiety before classes, along with feelings of dread in the pit of my stomach. I didn't know when and where it would come, but I was able to function somehow. I was way too focused on some of my students, and I tried to 'take care' of them, instead of just being their teacher.

I was wearing myself out and not experiencing a balanced life. I was enjoying teaching, but it was exhausting. I would still be there most afternoons until 5.30 preparing for next day, and I was beginning to doubt myself again. Was I good enough for this? I was on a crusade to be a great teacher and to rescue any student who appeared to be struggling or doubting themselves. I had a gift for teaching, and I loved seeing the 'light go on' in students' eyes when they 'got it.'

Further, I was ignoring what could have been positive friendships with some women; scared mostly that I would get 'too close' to them. And love them? And then have to break up because I was convinced, I was not capable of engaging in a long-term relationship. I was looking forward to getting to Canada where I knew deep down, I would find the time and energy to look into my heart and soul and find out who I really was. I also felt I needed to get out of Perth and away from my received influence and criticism of dad.

Where Were my Mentors?

When I reflect upon my first years of teaching, I realise I was strongly motivated by what I now perceive to have been the 'deficit' of my teenage years. This 'deficit' was a longing to know that I was OK and that someone cared about me. I was also trying to find answers to my own emptiness. At this stage I should have been far more intentional about seeking counsel from mentors, especially Jacko, Bob, and Dave, but as yet, I hadn't grasped the power of mentoring, including what to ask for and how to be authentic and transparent with my mentors. To be perfectly honest, I was also far too ashamed to seek help.

I was single at the time, and I later realised some teachers resented me because they perceived I only offered all these activities to be 'popular' with the students. If Jacko, Bob, or Dave had queried me about my frenetic lifestyle as a beginning teacher, I believe I would I have listened. On the other hand, my good friend and mentor Dave advised me to wait until I had a few more years of teaching experience before embarking upon further studies. Of course, Dave was right, but the urge to push on was strong. This was not the only time I ignored good advice from a friend and mentor.

Interestingly, Dave had been accepted at The University of Chicago to complete his PhD. He was already a highly respected scholar at UWA and was a worthy candidate to extend his research in a reputable university in the U.S. Farewelling Dave was a tough and empty time. However, without planning on our part, we were to meet again in the U.S.

PART THREE

Canada: And Graduate Studies

Chapter 17

Searching My Outer Limits

Throughout my studies to date, I developed a real passion and love for learning, especially about best practice in teaching and managing schools. I sought out places for further study in Canada and the U.S., and finally settled on The University of Alberta (UA), mainly because Canada was a Commonwealth Country and, with oil money 'flowing everywhere' in Alberta, UA was offering amazing scholarships for international students.

A Process of Exposing Shame

Soon after I arrived in Edmonton, I purchased a ruled exercise book and began writing down all my memories, from childhood through to my arrival in Edmonton. I am not 100% sure what motivated me to do this; it was just a gut instinct that proved really helpful. In the following years, I read research by James Pennebaker and Josh Smyth, [1] and Pete Walker [2] who note that:

> *"...writing about past traumatic experiences is*
> *a positive step that has emotional health benefits,*
> *and is part of our recovery process."*

From my experience, I concur with the assertions of the above-mentioned authors. I had no immediate goal in mind as I started writing in Edmonton, but the process helped me later, as I sought counselling, to gain clarity in identifying constructive steps towards healing. Immediate positive outcomes gained from journaling included an unexpected clarity of events and people that had impacted my life to date, a sense of relief from the clarity and a feeling of a 'fresh start' in Canada. Upon reflection, I believe the last point was about stamping my personal authority upon my future behaviour and academic efforts.

Five years later, after completing my studies and arriving back in Australia, I experienced a tsunami of shame, after which I appreciated how important it had been to take time to 'write my story.' The process gave me confidence, especially during counselling sessions, to admit and articulate my past traumas, including figuring out reasons for leaving home to escape my dad's negative influence, what contributed to my breakdown and why I was so driven to want to be liked and accepted by people, including many of the students I taught at Churchlands. This was the temperature of my emotional state as I began my course in Graduate Studies.

Let the Learning Begin

With my P.E. background, I decided to take units in P.E. for my Masters and this included an invitation to the annual P.E. camp at Slave Lake, north of Edmonton. It was October and nature's colours were still stunningly brilliant, but it was getting colder. When I asked someone if October was as cold as it gets, they looked at me strangely. Little did I know what was still to come. We arrived at the camp late on a Friday night for introductions and an explanation for the plan of the weekend.

I met a Canadian on the camp who took me fishing in the lake on Saturday afternoon. I had never previously caught any fish.

Ever. Nor did my strike rate improve from this attempt. While we were fishing, he told me about ice fishing on the lake. I couldn't believe it and asked:

> *"Do you mean the whole bloody lake freezes over?"*

My new friend thought that was the funniest thing he had ever heard and, of course he relayed my shock to his friends. Worse was to come.

The whole camp team was sitting around a campfire that evening when I saw green lights dancing in the northern sky. I honestly thought someone had dropped a bomb, and that we were about to die. Having been caught once this day, I said nothing. I just waited quietly, to die. Of course, nothing happened. It was the Northern Lights, one of the most spectacular phenomena I had seen to date in my life.

Graduate Studies

I can't remember the exact dates when semester began, but I was nervous. I was vulnerable and 'on the edge' again. I had only two years of teaching experience, and I was entering a Graduate Program with men and women far more experienced in education than me. Imposter syndrome hit me, for a few weeks, but I managed to 'deal with it,' mainly by embracing the change of culture and the beauty of the colours in the Fall season. I also felt a powerful sense that I was in the right place, and I had way more confidence in my academic ability than when I started first year studies at UWA in 1968.

Before official classes, we had a social meeting of all the thirty men and women in the Masters Program, including people from various Canadian Provinces, a woman from France, two other Aussies, and an amazing man named Theo Ume, from Biafra. Biafra is within Nigeria, but Biafrans seeking independence fought a civil war against Nigeria from 1967 to 1970. It was a horrible war with millions of Biafrans dying from starvation. As I came to know Theo, I couldn't get over how jovial he always was, especially as a former officer in the army of resistance. I knew of some of the horrors of this time, but to have Theo share his experience was heart wrenching. This was also part of the richness of the Masters Program, having men and women from all over the world in class together.

One of the Canadians I was drawn to immediately was another Peter. He was a tall man and was carrying a bit of weight. He was married to Gail and they had a mongrel dog I loved. I had arrived in Alberta very fit and strong, and was running every day and loving the long summer evenings. After our informal meeting, we were asked on our first day of classes what we wished to achieve by the end of Semester. I was sitting next to Pete and when his turn came, he said:

"To fit into Prout's trousers!"

This had a nice relaxing impact on the assembled group and it was kind of Pete to help me break into the group.

As classes got underway, I knew I was out of my depth in terms of work experience in education. But how many of these people had been locked in a wool press? Or slept sitting upright on the ground in the jungle to avoid leeches crawling into your ears? I could do this. We were all in the same compulsory classes for every unit, so bonds of support and friendship quickly formed. I enjoyed the company of everybody on the course, especially listening to their teaching experiences and in their leadership roles. I was learning a great deal and absorbing it with pleasure.

Being among thinking and creative people was stimulating and encouraging. Here my background didn't matter. I was accepted on face value and, as I listened and asked questions, I quickly gained increased confidence and motivation to succeed. I discovered Canadians have a strong 'can do' attitude mixed with a degree of humility and innate desire towards collaboration, the latter almost instinctive. Further, their tendency to always seek to negotiate and take a neutral stance in order to enhance a group idea was in sharp contrast to the Australian way of immediately finding ten reasons why your idea would not work.

In late October, I was invited to be part of a group of our class attending a National Conference in Educational Administration and Leadership at the Banff Springs Hotel, and I graciously accepted. In lieu of paying the Conference Registration Fee, we had to work at administrative tasks at the conference. I was asked to help out on the sound desk. What I knew about a sound desk could be engraved on the head of a pin, but surely it couldn't be that hard? However, I still managed to convince our French colleague Elise to swap jobs. I just had to sit in the front row from the speaker, just in case they needed anything. I could do that. The conference experience, including light snow falling outside the Banff Springs Hotel, was awesome.

It was my experience of working with women like Elise, and others in our program, that confronted me with the reality of how pathetic my attitude towards women in Australia had been, and how powerful our culture had been to mould me this way. Respect for women was just another characteristic of Canadians I came to appropriate. As I studied and learned with this great group of professional men and women, there were many other aspects of our Australian culture that I began to see in stark contrast. I was also admonished to admit my ideas about women had been shaped by my working-class background. Education was extracting me slowly from degrees of ignorance to a more enlightened view of life.

As winter approached and it quickly became colder, I wondered how anyone could stay alive in this climate. I remember looking out of the window from my college accommodation and seeing trucks being loaded with snow by front end loaders, then driving down onto the frozen river, to dump their load. I had no concept of a river freezing enough to support a heavily loaded truck. Further, going outside was a major operation which included putting on warm boots, coat, scarf, beanie and gloves, all of which I had to search for and purchase. I was finding all this a challenge and I wondered how I was going to last like this for the winter.

Meanwhile, I was a Graduate Student with a full study program. I undertook the research route for my degree, which meant I had to complete a major research project. For this, I was fortunate to have Dr Eugene Ratsoy – a somewhat unusual name – as my formal mentor. He was part of a team contracted by the Alberta Department of Education to review the decentralisation of education in Alberta. Dr Ratsoy was leading the quantitative survey and analysis part of the team, and Dr Bob Bryce the qualitative component via extensive interviews. Both Dr Ratsoy and Dr Bryce were my assigned formal mentors for my Graduate Studies.

Mentoring 101

One of the things I loved about this process was our weekly meetings during which we discussed progress and shared information with all members of the research team. I was thriving in an atmosphere of mutual respect and trust. I also met regularly with the members of the Masters Course where we could encourage one another and share new knowledge. Overall, I was simply happy. I was thinking about education and discussing my ideas and vision for teaching with like-minded colleagues.

I was mentally and socially engaged in an atmosphere of formal and informal mentoring. Obviously, my research supervisors acted in the formal role as they taught and guided me through the preparation of my research proposal and the writing of my dissertation. Clearly, you would have to be insane to ignore the counsel and teaching of these people. On the other hand, I was thriving in a number of reciprocal informal mentoring relationships and friendship with my peers that were also invaluable in my learning journey.

When considering my ultimate success, the value of feedback and contributions my mentors provided in my studies, was incalculable. I also found my contributions were valued and respected by my peers, which also increased my overall self-efficacy. In short, my Graduate Studies Program was a time of significant learning, including gaining self-confidence in my academic abilities, and professional growth and development.

Graduate Studies 'Mach 11'

I was fortunate to have been awarded a Graduate Teaching Scholarship for my Masters that covered all my fees and weekly expenses, equivalent to what I was earning as a beginning teacher in Perth. Further, I was offered support to convert my Masters Degree to a Ph. D., with a Research Scholarship that was worth more than I was earning as a teacher in Perth. Although I understood this terminal degree would be far more intense than the Masters, and that I definitely lacked background experience, I also considered it as an opportunity for further study and research that would be of personal, and career benefit.

Since I was deeply engaged in my studies, and combined with becoming a competent skier, and being overawed with the chance to undertake more hiking in the Rockies in the summer, I accepted the offer. Who wouldn't accept an offer to stay in Alberta to ski, hike, and camp in the Rockies? I was ready and willing to embark upon a Ph. D. program.

During the Christmas break of 1974 I had grown a moustache and a beard, with unanticipated consequences. One evening in January as I walked to a local movie theatre, my beard froze, and as I entered the theatre, the ice on my beard thawed and I nearly drowned. Well, not quite. But it was a very strange experience to feel a frozen beard and then for it to quickly melt inside. I frequently wondered how people could live like this for six months every year. I mean, the mercury just went to the bottom and stayed there for weeks on end.

Work/Play Balance

In the February week-long 'study break' of 1975, I went on a ski trip with the P.E. Faculty to Sun Peaks, one of the best slopes in British Columbia. We stayed in chalets on the mountain, which meant you could step into your skis in the morning, ski down to the dining room for breakfast, and then straight to the lifts. Solid gold. I joined a ski school for a sixty-minute lesson every morning and then had the rest of the day to practice. My instructor was a brilliant teacher and with my P.E. background, I quickly picked up the basics. After that it was time to 'ski the outer limits.'

By the end of the week, I was tackling the difficult 'Blue Slopes' without any fear and I began to comprehend how people managed their winters. I was hooked on skiing. It is a magic feeling to be flying along and just hearing the skis dig into the snow as you turn. Learning the habit of leaning down the hill was against all instincts at first, but I quickly mastered the key principles. After a few undignified crashes, not unlike off road motor biking, you haven't tried hard enough if you haven't crashed.

Meanwhile, Fall Semester, 1975 heralded the beginning of Ph. D. Program. I found myself struggling a little. We had mountains of reading to prepare for classes and seminars, and without the background of teaching and leading schools my peers had to draw upon, it was sometimes tough to keep abreast of content in our weekly seminars. However, one advantage I had was just completing my Masters Degree and being confident preparing a Research Proposal for my Ph. D. dissertation. I had also developed an interest in the Community Education Movement across Canada and throughout the U.S., and I devised a plan to leverage that interest to my advantage.

Providence, or "The Right Place at the Right Time"

During the Winter Semester I happened to be in the right place at the right time. On this point I refer to helpful research and reflections by Malcolm Gladwell, [3] who identifies numerous people, including athletes, team players, IT gurus, ancient kings and the Beatles, as all being in the right place at the right time. Gladwell clearly demonstrates the:

> *"…beneficiaries of hidden advantages and extraordinary opportunities and cultural legacies that allow some to learn and work hard and make sense of the world in ways others cannot."*

175

There is no doubt hidden advantages and extraordinary opportunities came my way as I developed a proposal to report on the progress of the Community Education Movement which had schools in every Province and Territory in Canada. My proposal was accepted, along with a grant of $7,500 from the Government of Alberta, much to the amazement of my Canadian mates who asked:

> *"How does an Aussie manage to get an expense
> paid trip to visit the whole of our country?"*

I had no answer for that question. It was simply timing. I teamed up with a professor from the University of Calgary who was leading the total research project. By the time Fall Semester, 1975, came around, I was ready to journey across the country to conduct interviews for my research. I set off to interview select people in education about the development of community schools in their Province or Territory.

I began with Newfoundland where I witnessed huge icebergs floating offshore on their way to melt in the warmer Atlantic waters. I loved Newfoundland and the capital, St John. I had enough in my budget to rent cars in every city so that between interviews, I could do some exploring, including getting to know socially many of the leaders in education I was meeting.

Next was Prince Edward Island, the 'home' of Anne of Green Gables. The capital, Charlottetown, has such beautiful old homes and history. One of the people I interviewed took me on a flight in his light plane across and around the island. What a treat.

I flew on to Nova Scotia and Halifax. Nova Scotia is a stunning province of Canada, so breathtakingly beautiful in the fall colours. From Halifax, I flew to New Brunswick and the capital Fredericton. In order to complete all interviews, I stayed in each Province for approximately a week. Interviews had been previously arranged by mail, but circumstances occasionally changed. We had no email and mobile phones, so careful planning was a logistical necessity. I was fortunate because some of my colleagues had nightmares collecting data.

Following New Brunswick was Quebec and the capital, Quebec City, an amazing place. Quebec City is the only walled city in Canada and the U.S. I enjoyed walking around the city, especially since fall was approaching and leaves were turning. Since I didn't speak any French, Quebec was tough, but I managed to get the drift of what was happening in the province. Ontario and Toronto, where most of the Education Centres were located, were much easier and relaxing for data gathering.

From Ontario I flew to Manitoba's capital Winnipeg, allegedly one of the coldest places in Canada, and after my visit I wouldn't dispute that assertion. Next was Regina in Saskatchewan, then back to Alberta and Edmonton.

While I was back in Edmonton, I interviewed appropriate people in the city for my research. This included visiting the Alberta Department of Education to interview a young man I had previously arranged to meet. He knew I was coming, but when I announced myself at reception the woman had quite a concerned and worried look on her face; she almost ran to his office and exclaimed:

"Peter Proud is here."

During the time, there was a movie in town, *The Reincarnation of Peter Proud,* about a man, Peter Proud, who had died and come back to life to confront the person who had killed him. I understand the poor girl was quite discombobulated over the whole experience, and my contact got quite a kick out of the whole episode.

I transcribed all my interviews and had a unit to complete before heading off to British Columbia and Victoria on Vancouver Island for more appointments. It was getting cold as I headed to my last two destinations, Yellowknife in the Northwest Territories, and Whitehorse in Yukon. The Northwest Territories have been renamed Nunavit in recognition of the local people. I also visited Hay River on the shores of Great Slave Lake while in the Northwest Territories. It was outside Hay River that I experienced the Northern Lights up close and personal.

I was driving with a couple I knew from Edmonton, when we stopped in what appeared to be the epicentre of the Northern Lights dance. I could feel a hum in the vehicle as we stopped and just wondered at this awesome experience. There was a distinctly audible sound as the lights danced around us. I will never forget that moment.

Another memorable event of my research trip was in store. While we were sitting on the tarmac at Whitehorse waiting for the plane to be loaded, I saw a man coming to the plane in his winter gear and carrying a hunting rifle. He climbed on board, secured the rifle in a rack by the galley where the food is served, and nonchalantly took his seat. As you do. This was before September 11, 2001 and I just loved the idea that a man could walk across the tarmac with his hunting rifle under his arm and nobody cared.

Back in my office, with the goal of my Ph. D. almost completed, it was time to consider my next career move. I was walking the corridors of our Faculty Building one day when I had a chance meeting with another student, Dave Muttart, from Nova Scotia. Dave was just beginning his Masters study and he asked me what

I was planning to do when I finished in the Fall. I jokingly said I was going to take his job at Acadia University in Wolfville. Next thing, Dave came to my office and asked:

> *"Were you serious about going to Wolfville?"*
> *"No," I said, "but I am now!"*

Dave had twelve months leave from his teaching position but needed more time to finish his studies. He contacted his Dean at Acadia. I received an invitation to fly out to Nova Scotia for an interview, and I was offered a contract to teach Dave's Fall and Winter classes in education at Acadia University in Wolfville, Nova Scotia.

Back in Edmonton I was slowly writing up my research and completing courses. My Ph. D. supervisor was Dr Bob Bryce. I finally handed Bob a first draft of my thesis and when I went to see him for his feedback, he said there were two kinds of first drafts, those that were worth reading and those that were not yet ready to read. Mine was the latter. I was gutted since I had spent so much time on it already, but I appreciated his feedback.

Reflections

During my time of formal study, I was soaked in mentoring. It was an extraordinary time of learning and counsel, on behalf of a number of remarkable professors. Formal mentoring relationships had been instituted throughout the University of Alberta Graduate Studies Programs and included expectations for completing all research requirements to successfully complete a terminal degree. In this regard, lines of communication between myself and my university advisors were articulated in handbooks, and the finer points discussed as I progressed through the study program.

I was free at all times to seek clarification on policies and, as perceived appropriate by my study supervisors, to modify select roles and responsibilities for achieving my research goals. Working within this formal mentoring arrangement gave me confidence and security as I planned my study and research schedules. The lingering outcomes of my formal mentoring relationships included inculcating values of clearly articulated expectations of performance and responsibilities for all incumbents of teams within an organisation, and, effectively managing personnel within the organisation, or team.

Among my informal mentoring relationships were my peers in the Graduate Studies Program, and ski coaches in the mountains. In the context of my 'community of scholars' and the invaluable feedback from my formal and informal mentors, I have no recollection of any impacts of shame throughout my four years of study. I also benefitted from unique altruistic care by special people including Catherine, Terry and Leo, whom I will introduce in the final chapter of my story.

In addition, the volume of my 'voice of shame' was turned right down and 'drowned out' by all the affirmation and encouragement I received. My decision to leave home and travel to Canada to seek answers was justified 100%.

Upon reflection, I am grateful that in the short period of time that I left High School teaching, I was now highly alert to the benefits of mentors in my life. In their roles as formal mentors, Dr Ratsoy and Dr Bryce shepherded me through the maze of Graduate Studies, and informal mentors had honoured me, blessed me, taught me, encouraged me and enriched my life immeasurably.

I am also amazed at how much my academic and social skills grew. My emotional skills were still to be 'addressed,' and I share my spiritual growth in the final section of my story. For now, I was now launched into a world I had not anticipated or dreamed possible.

Chapter 18

A Year of Living Dangerously

During the first Semester at Acadia, I learned that the Annual National Community Education Conference would be held at the Hotel Fontainebleau in Miami Beach Florida. This is where scenes from the 1992 film *The Bodyguard* were shot. I thought it would be a great opportunity to go to the conference. The conference itself was stimulating and engaging, largely thanks to meeting a special man, Dr Don Weaver, from Western Michigan University in Kalamazoo.

Don was the Director of the National Community Education Centre at Western where candidates could complete an Ed. D. to qualify them to work in all kinds of development areas in Community Education, including the U.S., Canada, and Mexico. Don and I chatted about possibilities in Community Education, and he finally said to me:

> *"I think you should come and work for me for a year."*

I totally agreed with Don, so we wrote out a job description on a serviette in the foyer of the hotel. And that is how my successful Graduate Studies launched me into a twelve-month contract of immeasurable positive consequences! In August 1977, I wrapped up my responsibilities at Acadia and set off for Michigan.

Community Education (CE)

I had two key responsibilities in my new role as Associate Director of the National Community Education Centre at Western Michigan University. One was to arrange inner-city Internships for the fifteen students taking the Education Degree in Community Education and the other was to review the work of The Centre and provide a report for Dr Weaver at the end of June, 1978.

Community Education as a movement in the U.S. and Canada was sponsored by a philanthropist, Charles Stewart Mott, whose wealth came via the automobile industry in Detroit. Mr Mott, in consultation with a former teacher, established the C. S. Mott Foundation with Headquarters in Flint, Michigan with a mandate to support personnel and programs to extend community-based programs and activities designed to enhance community living for all citizens.

For my Community Education work, I had access to the university carpool and a budget to fly wherever I needed. By the end of the twelve months, I called my self 'The Freeway Child,' since I could navigate my way through cities like Chicago, Detroit, Minneapolis-St Paul, Cincinnati, Indianapolis, and all the freeways in between. I travelled to these places to arrange the Internships for our students, which they needed to complete during the winter semester of 1978.

Occasionally, I flew into O'Hare International Airport in Chicago to meet leaders from around the country working in Community Education. We would meet in a lounge in the terminal, plan future research and development actions, and return home at the end of the day. The Dean of the College of Education at Western Michigan, whom I admired and respected, pointed out this was extravagant behaviour, but he acknowledged it was the 1970s in the U.S., where everything had to be done by yesterday.

The Woodlawn Organization [1]

By far my most memorable and successful contact for internships was with a man named Leon Finney. Hailing from the south side of Chicago, Leon was the Director of The Woodlawn Organisation, so named after the suburb badly damaged in the 1960s riots. Woodlawn was made famous by a former powerful community organiser named Saul Alinsky who was called in by a predominately Irish community to halt the advancement of The University of Chicago along the northern borders of the community.

Leon was a charismatic man, and through him, I met many other community organisers who agreed to sponsor some of our students for their internships. Often, I would spend two or three days at a time in Woodlawn where I learned so much about the struggle of black people for equal rights, respect and dignity. I was always welcomed into their homes, and I just loved the little children who were fascinated by my soft hair and hairy arms.

Informal Mentoring Moments

One evening in Leon's office, I was privileged to sit on the floor eating fried chicken with Leon and Sam Saines who was another community organiser and disciple of Saul Alinsky. The reason for this 'meal on the floor' was I had been busy all day with the men conceptualising a grant proposal to the C.S. Mott Foundation to support ongoing work at The Woodlawn Organization. I was on warp speed, learning and thriving, and these were unforgettable informal mentoring moments. How could I not learn from these amazing men, and all the lived experiences they had to share?

After spending some time with Leon in Chicago, he indicated that he invested time and energy with me because, when I first approached him to take interns, I indicated that I believed he could teach them and that he had much to offer our program at Western Michigan University. I found out later that his previous experience with universities was they indicated they came to teach him what he needed to know. In my case, he appreciated someone acknowledging that there was much to learn from him.

In retrospect, I am grateful for my instinct to listen and seek knowledge and understanding. Further, during my time in the U.S., I would not have achieved what I did had it not been for the love, respect and care of so many who willingly engaged in mentoring relationships with me, including Don Weaver, Sam Saines and Leon.

Vulnerability and Mentoring

During my time at the Community Education Centre and Woodlawn, I occasionally felt the weight of 'imposter syndrome,' including the sense of vulnerability that is a typical symptom of believing you are an imposter. However, as I reflect upon the year in conjunction with Brene Brown's work on vulnerability, I appreciate the fact that I was, in a way, used to being vulnerable. I was always vulnerable in my dad's presence, and a common thread of my three years boarding at New Norcia was fear, loneliness and uncertainty, all common traits of vulnerability. However, I am now convinced that the flip side of vulnerability is courage.

For example, I cannot think of any instance of courage where the person or people involved in a courageous act did not first experience great danger and vulnerability. We only have to consider soldiers awarded merit for displaying courage in battle to appreciate how vulnerable they were in their acts of bravery. It took courage for me to leave home at age sixteen with limited education and an uncertain future.

At the time I didn't consider myself vulnerable or courageous, but I now see how embracing vulnerability such as asking for help and support from Leon at Woodlawn for example, was a doorway to a whole new world of experiences and learning. However, my occasional cavalier approach to vulnerability does not merit any award for courage or common sense.

More Work and Play

The National Community Education Conference was to be held in Las Vegas in early December, almost twelve months after I first met Don at the original conference in Florida. We presented our work at the Las Vegas Conference, and it was particularly gratifying to catch up with people I met in Miami, renew acquaintances and share the focus of my work in Kalamazoo. After the conference I had time to take a bus out to Hoover Dam and then on to the Grand Canyon. It was only an overnight stop at both sites, but I enjoyed the drive and of course the magnificence of the big hole in the ground.

The bus was scheduled to leave the hotel at Grand Canyon above Indian Springs around 11.30 am, so I set my alarm for 4.30 am, and literally jogged down to Indian Springs, which is almost at the bottom of the canyon, and looked over to the Colorado River. From Indian Springs I looked back up the canyon wall and I thought:

"Am I going to make it back in time?"

I didn't bring any water. I know. Really clever! At the time I was quite fit since I had been running indoors during the winter and enjoying lots of hiking during the summer. I had no time to rest, so I turned to face the wall. The path, by necessity was really narrow and zig zagged all the way. To my dismay, coming down towards me were people on donkeys and others walking.

By the time I was halfway back, I was wondering about the wisdom of my decision to do a 'down and back' in time to catch a bus. Since you actually 'walk through' climatic zones when climbing the canyon walls, I found myself begging for a drink. A couple of people, who also took the time to remind me how stupid I was to be walking without water, obliged. Nice of them really. Irresponsible of me though. By this time my tongue was stuck to the roof of my mouth, and the thought of dying of thirst crossed my mind. What a nuisance that would have been for all concerned.

Further, I had also borrowed a watch from a nice Singaporean man which I promised to return to him on the bus. Finally, I made it to the hotel, staggered into the bar and asked for litres of lemonade and a huge block of chocolate. How is that for your body knowing what it needs when under stress? Fluid and 'immediate energy.'

I made it to the bus and was glad to return the borrowed watch which I sensed both the man and his family were relieved to have returned. The bus took us back to Las Vegas, from where I flew to San Diego, then bus to Chula Vista which is right on the border with Mexico. I had been invited by one of our former Community Education graduates, Pat, whom I met previously, to visit a Community Education outreach for Mexican women in Chula Vista. These women were working in Southern California almost as slave labourers.

Pat is African American, so I was in a predominately black neighbourhood for about three days. It was awful to see the conditions under which these Mexican women lived, especially in such a wealthy country. However, it was encouraging to see how the women were caring for one another under Pat's mentoring, which was a vital touch point in this program.

Pat had two teenage children at school, and they allowed me to walk with them to school on Friday morning. Along the way, some white boys abused the children, which caused me great shame. Next day, being Saturday, Pat drove me with her children, across the border into Mexico. I was shocked as we drove through a couple of towns, to hear Pat's children in turn demeaning Mexicans. Only the day before, I heard them being abused by white boys, and now they were being disrespectful towards Mexicans. However, over cold drinks at a café before returning to Chula Vista, I was impressed by the children's responses as I shared my feelings about their comments. We agreed we all have racist tendencies, and it seems we sometimes enjoy putting down those who we think are beneath us.

Part Two

Back at work after Christmas/New Year break, I had the chance to attend a three-day training event in Montgomery in Alabama, which was the scene of great social upheaval in the 1960s, and the former home of the charismatic Dr Martin Luther King. Although I never felt uneasy or threatened, racial tensions still existed in the city. All the black people I met were among the most gentle and inspiring people whom I met in my whole time in the U.S. I met men and women who were strong in character and committed to seeking justice and peace in black neighbourhoods, and whenever these people sang of 'freedom' I knew it came from deep within their souls. At times when they sang, all I could do was just let the tears flow.

During my time in Montgomery, I was also invited by a white Superintendent of Schools to his home and when he invited me downstairs after dinner, I was shocked by the number of rifles and pistols he had hanging on the walls of the basement. Indeed, this was the only time I felt uneasy or scared during my whole visit to Montgomery.

The irony of being in a home packed with weapons and ammunition that belonged to a key leader of education in the state stayed with me for ages. My Montgomery experience was one of awe, wonder and richness in seeing the humility of so many amazing black leaders in Community Education.

Peoples' Express

My job establishing community placements meant I covered many kilometres driving, and even more flying. There was an interesting cheap airline operating in the 1970s called Peoples' Express. You just turned up to an airport from which they operated, got straight on board and off you went. Once in the air, cabin crew would come around with a credit card machine to accept payment for your ticket. Cool. They would ask where you were going, which always amused me, for as far as I knew, I was going where they were going.

Money, Sex and Power

During the January to April months, I flew into Washington, DC at least four times, twice to deliver community grant proposals for funding, once in April with our students, and another for some training. The April trip was organised by Dr Weaver for our Interns to meet a man named Paul who was a lobbyist on Capitol Hill for The Mott Foundation.

Paul's mandate, on behalf of Community Education, was to keep politicians apprised of the work The Mott Foundation was undertaking around the country, including the Community Education Training Centre. It was spring in Washington, so all the magnificent cherry blossoms were out and Paul provided me with a pass into the East Wing of the White House to meet with people about our Internship Program.

I was standing at one of the windows overlooking the lawn when the Air Force One helicopter landed and President Jimmy Carter walked across the lawn to the West Wing. As I witnessed this, I felt a shiver of 'imposter syndrome,' and thought to myself:

> *"How did I, a dairy farmer from Ferguson, get*
> *to be in the East Wing of the White House, watching*
> *the President walking across the lawn?"*

During my year of such frenetic pace and energy in the U.S., I appreciated how easy it would be to believe the 'meta-narrative' that I was special and important. During two visits to DC, I was to deliver plans and explain projects for Community Education work that included housing and other community services in poor neighbourhoods in Kalamazoo and Chicago. Paul found me accommodation close to offices for Housing and Urban Development, where we held meetings for those trips.

It was all exhilarating and at a crazy pace but at the time, was energised by it. I also knew, even as this was happening, that it would be impossible to expect another year of experiences and learning like the one. From a more sobering perspective, if I had stayed longer in the highly charged atmosphere of such power and seductive influence, I may have succumbed to the existential narrative that I was as good as the narrative was leading me to consider. I also understood why men and women from ancient times chose vows of poverty, chastity and obedience to help them focus upon serving God exclusively while on this earth.

Today we use the terms power, sex and money to acknowledge easy ways in which we can become entrapped in the seductive ways of the world. I concluded from my visits to DC, and my access to unlimited travel and decision-making that the culture of power, sex and money is palpable. You can almost cut it with a knife in Washington DC.

Reflections

My year working in the U.S. remains a 'revolving gift' in my life. I frequently reflect upon my experience of mentoring in terms of being a mentor to my students and being a protégé to remarkable people like Don Weaver and Leon Finney. In both instances my belief in the mentoring process helped me define and assess my own progress and success, and to appreciate the power of feedback accordingly. The benefit of counsel and learning in mentoring is also a major hallmark that I respect and honour.

In my five years living, studying and working in Canada and the U.S., I had not once been told I was useless and 'no good for anything.' Rather, I had been affirmed, encouraged, respected, honoured and loved. Finding a new social and cultural environment enabled me to firstly turn down the volume of shame in my mind, and to begin a process of unlearning the messages of Brene Brown's 'shame gremlins.' However, I was still 'captive' to the habit of impulsive actions that I had not considered had any agency in my life. This enlightenment was still to come. Another fork in the road.

PART FOUR

Coming Home

Chapter 19

"It's Not Easy Being Green"

Kermit from Sesame Street

Settling back in Perth was extremely difficult. I experienced the weird phenomenon of 'reverse culture shock,' feeling like an outsider and stranger in my own culture and 'hood.' I was also now married with an infant daughter.

I had accepted a teaching and research position in the School of Education at Murdoch University, but this wasn't effective until March, 1979. In retrospect, this time from our arrival back in Perth in mid-September 1978, until March the following year was a form of 'dark night of the soul' for me. I had left twelve months in the U.S. of frenetic activity where I went from traversing the country and meeting all kinds of engaging and stimulating people, to find myself back in Perth where I was lonely and suffering severe culture shock.

Socially and emotionally, I was wrung out and lost. I was often numb to all around me, and I felt like there was nobody who could possibly understand me, including friends I had before I left home. During my five years away, I had experienced mind-bending intellectual growth, and spiritual and emotional experiences that were simply 'off the scale.'

Coming down from a high of an over stimulating and seductive pace of my time at the Community Education Centre, was, in retrospect, a significant social and emotional crash landing. It was not until I sat down to write my story that I appreciated just how powerful and influential my experiences in Canada and, especially the U.S., had been. I was not ready for the shock that coming home to Perth presented.

In the process of this necessary withdrawal, I tried to recreate the stimulation I had fed upon in the U.S. Through a range of circumstances, I met a man in Perth who was a 'consultant', of which there were many in Perth in the late 1970s, and 1980s. I accompanied this man who offering 'power selling' training, which encompassed all kinds of topics. At one stage, I was 'consulting' with staff, regarding sales techniques and meeting customer expectations, in five specialist women's clothing stores in Perth city and suburbs.

This was over-stretching the 'can do' attitude I acquired in Canada and the U.S. I hated what I was doing which even included driving around town in a Mercedes coupe at one stage. I was making money but I was socially, emotionally and spiritually on empty. I am embarrassed to admit all this, especially after the quality times I spent over the previous five years with special men and women in Canada and the U.S.

Real Learning

As I settled back in Australia, I knew all was not well in my life generally, and in my spirit specifically. I contacted Dr Patrice Cook again and arranged to see her. During one of my first sessions Patrice asked me:

"How do you feel about that?"

I was now around thirty-four and I had no idea what she was asking.

"What was a feeling?" I asked myself.

I knew feeling tired and hungry, but that was about it. In the context of a counselling session, I had no idea how to identify or to express what I was feeling. I couldn't even articulate that I felt confused, ashamed or embarrassed. Nothing. I hasten to add that I do know how to do it now, albeit in a clumsy way, but as I reflect upon this time in my life, I appreciate Brene Brown's [1] counsel that:

> *"Shame derives its power from being unspeakable, but we beat it when we name it."*

When Patrice first asked what I was feeling, I recall my heart starting to race, my palms sweating, my tongue drying up and my testicles withdrawing inside for safety. One might say this was a significant 'fear response' to the challenge to be authentic and transparent. I was at pre-school level, and about to begin learning about and acquiring emotional intelligence.

I am grateful to Patrice for leading me through this next painful and exhausting stage of my journey. After seeing me a couple of times, Patrice suggested I join a group she was running. My group met each Wednesday evening and I entered into it with a passion to figure out what make me tick, or not. I remember it being emotionally exhausting, fronting up every Wednesday night for three hours with a group of around twenty people.

Participants could speak as they felt inclined and talk about things that were bothering them, and Patrice and her co-leader would work through issues with them. I recall we had a lovely couple in our group in their sixties, and I bonded with the husband. Sadly, during one of our term breaks, the man died and I remember being devastated when we came back.

That event opened a flood gate of sadness, fury and loss at being ignored and devalued by my dad. In the group process, I finally learned how to identify and name feelings, and there were lots of issues to work on that helped make sense of how I had been behaving. I recall one evening realising that I was like my dad in some ways, but that I did not have to repeat his lifestyle. That was a huge relief to know that I could change. Starting the counselling journey was the best thing I had ever done.

In the process of our group work, Patrice taught us how to listen with respect to one another, in effect, active listening. Naming my shame was a significant part of my emotional healing and I gradually developed a healthy self-love from this process. Learning to actively listening also promoted significant empathy for others in our group as they shared their stories of shame and pain. There was often joy in my heart as I was honoured to listen to others articulate their shame and find that awe of healing accordingly. I soon came to understand how, if we choose not to name our shame, we can easily get stuck in self-pity.

In my experience, we can only move on from self-pity and 'other blaming' to forgiveness and a determination to no longer allow the shame to rule our lives, when we name our own shame, and take steps to combat it. Even as I write, I found this to be a long and enduring struggle. Nevertheless, the chain of shame in my case was identified and I could begin dealing with it.

Mentoring: "Graduate Studies"

My Graduate Studies in Mentoring took place in a unique setting: St Matthew's Anglican Church in Shenton Park. Rev Dr

David Seccombe was the pastor. He was a fantastic person and brilliant teacher. Dave initiated a small group model for St Matt's that he called 'Outpost Groups.' People could volunteer to lead these groups and to choose, or not, to belong to a group. The groups met at different times over various weeknights and days, according to the needs of people involved. I was a member of a group that turned out to be an awesome, mutually supportive group for encouraging one another in our faith journey and our roles as parents and professional workers.

We followed all kinds of agendas for our Outpost meetings, including strategic studies, sharing one another's hassles and problems from work or home making and sharing our life stories. We encouraged honesty and vulnerability in meetings, including welcoming feedback on how each of us could work more effectively on our parenting, our marriages, and work issues. For example, we usually went away for a weekend together with our group members, in addition to an annual Family Camp for the whole church.

On one of our Outpost Weekends, my two daughters would get into scuffles and a bit of conflict. I always picked the wrong one for attention and blame. One couple finally said in exasperation:

> *"Can't you see what is going on between your*
> *girls? You are picking the wrong one for rebuking."*

As I write, I am still grateful to one of the men for pointing out this parenting 'fault'. I saw this action by the group as an act of great love and respect towards me, and most helpful in my subsequent parenting methods. The group had been invaluable in helping moderate my parenting for both daughters. The groups were 'formalised' at David's suggestion, but they only functioned as well as every member chose to participate.

In this case, from a mentoring perspective, our group was one I would describe as informal, but highly effective in teaching and counselling for each of us involved. I know my own mentoring skills were sharpened considerably during this period of almost fifteen years of belonging to our group.

Leading, Learning and Feedback

I continued teaching and supervising student teachers at Murdoch University. Meanwhile, I was feeling underutilised at Murdoch and was looking for something completely different. I became aware of a volunteer organisation in Perth that was part of a National and International Outreach to youth and children and families. After research and interviews, I was offered the position as WA State Director, and I commenced my duties in June, 1980.

Leading a volunteer organisation was a massive learning curve. Much of my prior work experience had been supervised generally in a 'formal mentoring' manner where I understood what was expected of me and I had job descriptions that outlined my duties and responsibilities. With my new work, members of the governing council outlined general expectations of me, which I appreciated. But these were of little value if I couldn't 'win over' paid staff, as well as a large number of volunteers who worked in a myriad of areas within the organisation.

Working with the paid staff was rewarding and, as we established protocols for achieving the goals of the mission, I soon established open dialogue, humour, and a shared passion with them. By contrast, leading our network of volunteers was another matter entirely. Within the first few weeks of assuming the State Director's role, I met as many groups of volunteers as possible in order to share my vision for the work with them, and to differentiate and articulate my formal and informal mentoring relationships.

During the process, I listened to their passion, their experiences, and their wisdom, and then set out to do all I could to honour their own expectations as volunteers, all within the overall mission objectives. I soon found this agenda of meetings and short-term training events to be an exhaustive proposition.

One of my early mistakes was to try and please as many people as possible, even if it meant 'tweaking' my own public vision for our work. In the instances where I endeavoured to accommodate a plethora of expectations, I became bogged in a maze of impossible expectations and confusion. People who volunteer for any organisational work can just as easily 'volunteer out,' especially if they perceive the leader is not going in the direction they desire.

Further, it is extremely difficult to thank a volunteer for their work, or 'fire' them. I learned quickly to consistently articulate the direction I believed we needed to take in order to successfully achieve our mission, particularly in the climate of the 1980s, and to respectfully defend that vision at all times. It was a steep and tiring learning curve.

My leadership style was raw and often 'found wanting.' I had learned from Patrice's teaching to become a good listener, and I succeeded in riding out several challenging individuals who rightfully viewed me as a newcomer who didn't know the history of the work of the mission. I was 'learning on steroids' and it was telling on my health as well as my family life. I was becoming increasingly worn out and eventually suffered from a serious bout of chronic fatigue, which slowed me down considerably.

Feedback

What I learned about leading a volunteer organisation in my own backyard was invaluable to me in a future role. Toward the end of my five-year role as State Director, the Council appointed a wonderful man from Canberra, Spencer Colliver, to conduct an exhaustive review of the work in WA, including my leadership. When Spencer finished his review, he called me and said he had finished and, before he reported to the council, he wanted to share findings with me. He indicated there were hard things he needed to say, and that some would be hard for me to hear. Both turned out to be true.

However, Spencer was loving and kind enough to point out the things I had done well and then areas where I had not done well, or actually failed. I appreciated some of the things were hard for Spencer to say, and they were tough to hear. But I will never forget Spencer for his generosity in sharing this feedback. How else was I to learn more effective leadership skills?

From this experience of feedback, my counsel is to consider all feedback as potentially invaluable for building our character and empowering us to improve our work. We don't have to do exactly as the person might say we should; what we do with feedback is entirely up to us but I suggest we listen carefully, no matter how hard the feedback may sound, then go away and think about it. We can always contact the person again and say:

> *"I appreciate what you said to me, can you clarify such and such for me?"*

Or, in the view of Sheila Heen, [2] you can say:

> *"Thank you for that feedback, could you suggest one or two things I could do in order that I can improve my leadership in some way?"*

In other words, don't make excuses, but always ask for clarification on the best way forward, especially if it is not immediately clear. Remember, feedback is about what you have done or failed to do, and we all fall into those categories. It is just that, not everyone is as fortunate as I was that day, to be given that gift of caring and precise feedback. I hope there will be people willing to do that for you throughout your life, and that in turn, you will be gracious in doing the same for others.

Finally, one of my behaviours Spencer noted was to work myself to exhaustion and not delegate responsibilities. If I found the going getting tough, I would just work harder rather than seeking help or delegating. My preoccupation with my work resulted in me not paying enough attention to my family, who also suffered during this time. I was still attending the counselling groups and learning a great deal about myself. However, depending upon my physical energy to achieve what I deemed sound outcomes for all concerned ultimately ended in disaster. During this time, I had not anticipated a major regret that was brewing.

How I Blew an Opportunity to Honour My Dad

I was continuing counselling when I made a fatal error which I have regretted throughout the following years. During one of our counselling sessions, it became clear that some of the things my dad had said and done were still stinging in my mind and heart. I was advised by my group to seek clarity with dad about these issues. Eventually, armed with what I believed were the right words to say, I drove to Bunbury to talk to dad.

As fortune would have it, dad was home alone when I arrived, and as I sat down to a cup of tea with him, he began telling me all kinds of experiences he had as a young man. These included working in the gold mines in Kalgoorlie, preparing horses for the 10th Light Horse Regiment during World War Two and other events I had never heard of or known about. He had never spoken of any of these occurrences in his life and I was fascinated. My big regret is that I should have just kept listening. The other could wait. But I didn't.

During a break in my dad's story, I asked why I had been treated so badly as a kid. Naturally when we are confronted by something we can't even understand ourselves, we immediately become defensive, which is what my dad did. The moment suddenly changed from dad sharing his past with me to having to confront things he clearly regretted. I don't know of any man who wakes up in the morning and decides:

*"I am going to be as mean as possible to my son
or daughter today".*

We just don't do that. I now appreciate my dad was swamped by his own feelings, and I am sure, regrets about the past. These are the kinds of things that play on our mind and emotions, and that can influence the way we respond to others, including hurting them when we don't set out to do that. I am not sure exactly when in the 1980s this happened, but it pushed back my relationship with dad to one of wariness and coldness. I only wish I had not been so keen to get some answers that day, especially when other richer answers were coming in a way I had not expected.

When I went to see dad, I was still learning about Emotional Intelligence (EQ), but obviously clumsy about accessing it. It is one thing to learn about a new concept, and another to actually incorporate it into our behaviour, particularly where emotions are concerned. It also confirms for me how deeply some of our hurts can lurk in our hearts, and how easily scars from those hurts can be torn away. Nevertheless, a reasonable EQ allows us to listen to the other and simultaneously hold our emotions in check as we endeavour to clearly hear their story.

Once this level of communication takes place, we can advance to understanding the other's experience, and eventually seek and offer forgiveness, and ultimately reconciliation. All this takes place in a perfect world where none of us reside. But we can persevere.

I only saw dad briefly after this event, and, if I had 'kept my powder dry' on the day, my girls may have experienced a rich relationship with their grandfather, just as they did with their gran. I will never have answers to these questions, but I have wisdom about deficits in my own behaviour at the time. At least I learned something from the experience.

Years after this event, my heart was completely softened towards my dad. I appreciated how hard it is to forgive and love one another. It is hard to avoid this tough idea of forgiving, but when I finally began the process of forgiving my dad and consequently beginning to understand his life, a great burden was lifted. This is because by not forgiving him I was carrying unnecessary pain and anger that was only hurting me, not him. I also know that this refusal to forgive and the hate I carried had contributed to my breakdown during my last year at university.

I eventually experienced forgiveness as a powerful 'cleansing agent' in my life. There is freedom of heart and soul as we release useless hurt, rejection, and pain in our lives, and embrace joy, freedom, celebration, gratitude and love. There are countless books, songs, movies, plays and scriptures about forgiveness. I have included reference to a lovely article by Australian Professor Everett Worthington [3] that also has other tips and leads for anyone seeking to forgive, or forgiveness.

Emotional Intelligence (EQ)

The term, Emotional Intelligence (EQ), was popularised by Daniel Goleman [4] who postulates that, while we cannot change our emotional responses to people, we can learn to respond more effectively to them. For Goleman, the key to developing our EQ is self-awareness. The more aware we are of our feelings, the easier it is to make effective personal decisions. EQ comprises knowing your emotions, managing emotions, motivating emotions, recognising emotions in others (empathy) and handling relationships, thus we become more intelligent in controlling our emotions.

It logically follows that, when are developing effective mentoring relationships, either as mentor, or protégé, we need a degree of EQ accordingly. There is an excellent review of EQ by Daniel Goleman in which he describes it as:

> "*...knowing one's emotions and the emotion of others, managing those emotions, self-motivation, recognising emotions in others, and effectively handling emotions.*"

Based upon all my life experiences to date, I have arrived at working understanding of EQ as:

Our ability to identify and understand what we are feeling at any given moment, including seeking to understand emotions in others, and to respectfully withhold expressing our feelings, until an appropriate and mutually beneficial moment for all parties involved in a discussion, or dialogue.

Whereas I believe in the efficacy of this definition, I caution that I don't always get it right in practice. I will elaborate upon this in a later chapter in my story.

Further, Goleman's expansive thinking and understanding in relation to the phenomenon of intelligence was influenced by Howard Gardner's [5] Multiple Intelligences (MI), originally a suite of seven relatively autonomous cognitive capabilities, or seven (multiple) intelligences. Unlike previously established theories which describe intelligence as a global mass, Gardner's basic tenant is that we are intelligent in different ways and that throughout our lives, we can draw upon and develop these individual intelligences. Accordingly, we can become more intelligent as we pursue interests and ideas that motivate us, and we have a natural affinity for. Therefore, with respect to intelligence, a valuable exercise can be to reframe the fundamental question:

How intelligent am I? to *How am I intelligent?*

We can also modify the mantra:

How smart am I? to *How am I smart?*

As we seek to hone our EQ it is helpful to consider in detail, the phenomenon Multiple Intelligence (MI), including the fact that intelligence is not a fixed order in our brain, rather our brain can change and grow in intelligence. For example, as we pursue and refine a particular skill or interest, we become increasingly intelligent in that area. This growth in intelligence can be influenced by many concepts, such as motivation to learn, passion or interest in something, and a desire to become more confident and skilled in our inter-personal and intra-personal relationships.

Multiple Intelligence criteria are listed in the following table.

Table 1. Gardner's Multiple Intelligence (MI).

Specific intelligence	Characteristics of intelligence for this person
1.Visual/Spatial	Read and write for enjoyment; solving puzzles; interpret pictures, graphs, and charts; drawing, painting, and the visual arts; recognize patterns easily
2.Linguistic/Verbal	Remember written and spoken information; enjoy reading and writing; debate or give persuasive speeches; explain things well; use humour when telling stories
3.Logical/Mathematical	Excellent maths skills; enjoy thinking about abstract ideas; like conducting scientific experiments; can solve complex computations
4.Kinaesthetic	Skilled at dancing and sports; enjoy creating things with your hands; excellent physical coordination; learn and remember by doing, rather than hearing or seeing
5.Musical	Enjoy singing and playing musical instruments; recognize musical patterns and tones easily; remember songs and melodies; rich understanding of musical structure, rhythm, and notes
6.Interpersonal	Communicate well verbally; skilled at nonverbal communication; see situations from a range of perspectives; tolerate ambiguity; create positive relationships with others; resolve conflicts in group settings; listen well
7.Intrapersonal	Understand your strengths and weaknesses well; enjoy analysing theories and ideas; excellent self-awareness; understand the basis for your own motivations and feelings
8. Natural	Understand living things; enjoy reading nature

As we have noted, in proposing his concept of Multiple Intelligence, Gardner never intended these cognitive capacities (brain skills) be taken as 'fixed concepts,' rather that we are intelligent in a range of ways. For example, I see myself as a 'mix' of 2, 4, 6, 7 and 8. On the other hand, while I love music, I couldn't carry a tune in a bucket, I can draw a stick person and colour between the lines, and I can almost understand my bank balance.

As I reflect upon my life journey to date, I started with low MI across most areas, but driven by the desire to examine life events that provoked anger within me, I appreciated that developing intelligence in different ways has proved valuable in viewing issues in from different perspectives. Consequently, my counselling and intentional reflective practice in examining my own behaviour and learning, has led me to considerably sharpen my overall Emotional Intelligence - EQ.

I am convinced that to become men of character and perseverance, we gain by seeking to engage as many areas of our brain as possible. Since everything we learn is accompanied by an emotional response, it would appear only logical that we should develop our interpersonal and intrapersonal intelligence accordingly. I have been part of a culture that claimed showing emotions was not 'manly', that only 'girls cry' and 'don't show your emotions.' That was a lie, and it still is a lie.

Men of my generation had been convinced of the need to appear tough and strong, and show no feelings. I rather embrace gentle strength and high Emotional Intelligence. Otherwise, I think we are condemned to become 'emotional cripples' who rely solely upon our physical strength and basic survival instincts. We no longer live in jungles or upon open plains where we have to fight to survive. But we are still called to be strong and gentle; strong and caring; strong and nurturing; and, strong and teachable.

In which areas do you see yourself as most intelligent?

Mate to Mentor

It was during this tumultuous time that I meet Bruce Robinson who ultimately became my life-long friend and informal mentor. Bruce is also a much-loved friend of my family. Over the years, Bruce and I have become great soul mates. Our families attended St Matt's Church and we often spent family holidays together, and sharing has included times of sickness and health. Bruce also visited and encouraged us during an extended sojourn back in Canada.

Initially, before we started our workdays, Bruce and I used to go running on the beach each morning. This was followed by a swim, coffee and a prayer for one another. Years later, the running morphed into a controlled stagger, so we dropped that in favour of swimming. Now we meet for an hour every Saturday morning for a 'splash and dive' in the ocean before our intentional check-ups that include our families, our spiritual well-being, our work and what we are currently wondering about.

We also check our 'half time' activities, which evolved from our desire to 'finish well,' considering all the gifts and opportunities we have received. This has been our routine since we met in 1984, barring the times I was away in Canada.

Contract Ending

I entered 1985 with six months to go on my contract at the volunteer organisation. During the early part of the year, I had my conversation with Spencer and our Council Chairman who asked me to continue for another five years. Meanwhile, through my work, I met John Allen-Williams who invited me to join his staff in 1986 at St Stephen's School in Duncraig, a new suburb to the north of Perth. St Stephen's had been established in Term One, 1984. Getting back to teaching was my primary goal and, during my last two years, I had been included in setting the initial culture of St Stephen's with John.

Reflections

By far my most significant memories of this action packed seven years were the births of our two daughters, both so different yet equally miraculous. Other key reflections include:

- Always plan to be reconciled with parents or anyone else. Equally, be prepared to listen first and forgo your plan for what may unfold. If I had been wise when I went to see my dad, the outcome would have been different, and far more constructive. Wisdom is hard to access when we are under heightened emotional pressure. We need to plan, but we do not control all events. However, our ultimate destiny is ours to shape.

- If I had gone to see my dad more focused on grace and love, I am sure I could have steered it towards his childhood and learned so much more about him. At a later date, I could then have told him I had a better understanding of who he was and that I could forgive him. I have since totally forgiven my dad and I feel a good deal of sadness and loss in relation to him.

- As I have come to reflect upon mistakes of my own life, I understand how difficult it was for my dad, working hard to provide for his family, especially in the midst of his own emotional turmoil. For a brilliant summary on empathic behaviour and loving lifestyle, I recommend Chapter 21 of Julia Baird's book *Phosphorescence.* [5] I hope my life is somewhat reflective of the grace and respect afforded to all people by men and women identified by Baird in this section of her book.

- Having people like Patrice, David and Spencer Colliver in my life was an awesome gift. They all spoke truth to me with love and respect and I became a stronger man for it.

- Being a father of three special daughters, all of whom brought me great joy and pride, was a significant part of my spiritual awareness and growth, and is something impossible to quantify.

Finally, with respect to learning shame 'busting' strategies, I proffer the following:

- Belonging to extended family, and to community is rich and immeasurable.

- Listening in order to understand emotions cannot be overestimated.

- Asking for help is a sign of strength.

- Listening to and seeking all feedback is life-giving.

- Vulnerability almost always ends in behaving with appropriating courage.

- Strength of character is manifest in courageous acts of 'other centredness'.

- Embrace your emotional safe, and become more intelligent in the process!

Chapter 20

Leading and Mentoring: St Stephen's School and Pioneer Ranch Camps

At the time that St Stephen's was established, Year Eight was the first year of High School and we began each year with an Orientation Camp for them. Accordingly, all Year Eight's began their school year in the same manner. Thereafter, I introduced an annual thematic camp for each year group. I appreciated John's support in establishing this 'camp culture' and former students will have their own 'war stories' about their camps.

I enjoyed the rhythm of each school year, including teaching my own classes and engagement in the School Leadership Team. My role on the team included recruiting and inducting new staff, and organising ongoing Professional Development (PD) for our whole school staff.

One of the first of these PD events was at The Institute of Human Development in Jarrahdale, a small town about forty-five minutes' drive southeast of the city, where I previously participated in group counselling weekends with Patrice Cooke. Accordingly, I engaged Patrice to lead our first school PD weekend. The staff loved Patrice and they gained a great deal from her wisdom.

Modelling Reflective Practice (our Examined Life)

My philosophy of leadership included intentional teaching at weekly House Assemblies, which were designed to lead students away from ignorance towards achieving academic success, and to developing their God given talents. In this way we encouraged our students to reflect upon their overall experiences and learning at school, and in their communities. In practice, we endeavoured to engage in reflective behaviour that reinforced their formal and informal learning.

In an effort to measure the impact on student values and learning, I conducted annual exit interviews with graduating students from Alethea House. In these interviews, I asked about memorable moments from their high school years. In one special interview, a boy responded that he didn't enjoy any of his high school and that he always missed his primary school days where, in his words, he could:

"...hang out with my friends and just be free."

I was quite shocked, but as he finished speaking, he sat back in his chair, breathed a heavy sigh, and was totally relaxed. It was as if a huge burden had been lifted from his shoulders. As we both sat in the quiet, this was a sacred moment for me. I felt a sense of sadness that we had failed a young man at High School, but a deeper sense of honour that he had trusted this information with me.

I also felt I understood, and that I had been in those places myself as a teenager. Upon reflection, I also appreciate the fact that we established a culture at St Stephen's and in Alethea House in particular, where all students felt free to express any sentiment they wanted. Another student said she would miss the:

"...faithful old school shoes" that she had worn all the way through High School.

I loved the comment and, as she looked down at her well-worn shoes, I was moved by the simplicity of her words in a life that I knew had been packed and successful for this special student. In all the pressure we face as teachers, a student was reminding me to never lose sight of the simple and mundane, and to take time to reflect and appreciate accordingly.

Both these experiences motivated me in later years to focus research upon the power of reflective practice, especially in relation to our ongoing intellectual, social and emotional growth and development. In later years, I jointly supervised a research project, along with two colleagues, where we asked a group of selected Australian teachers to keep a log of their reflections as teachers embedded in schools in an East African country. [1]

Reflections

This period of nine years was packed with many memories, but the most important thing I learned throughout this time was that a family surrounded by a church community and loving families and friends is rich indeed. I thank the range of people who extended love and friendship towards us during this stage of my life. I am also most grateful for the nine years I was leading and teaching at St Stephen's.

Pioneer Ranch Camps

At the end of nine years teaching and leading at St Stephen's School, I was invited back to Alberta by Tana Clark, the Director of Inter-Varsity, to act as a catalyst for change and renewal in the

Pioneer Camps. Tana was, and still is, one of the finest formal mentors, line managers and strategic thinkers I have encountered. I enjoyed Tana's trust, but I was not from the cowboy culture of Alberta, which I respected and honoured.

Pioneer Camp Director

My formal role in Alberta was Director of Pioneer Camps, [2] a ministry of Inter-Varsity in Canada. There were two permanent campsites, one approximately 150 kilometres south of Edmonton, close to the town of Rocky Mountain House, and another around 100 kilometres north of Calgary, near the town of Sundre. At both permanent sites we had major buildings for meals, meetings, and accommodation as well as log cabins for camper accommodation at Rocky. Activities for camping included ropes courses, climbing walls, a lake at Rocky and pool at Sundre, canoeing, mountain bikes, corrals and many horses for riding. The third camp program, Peace Pioneer, was exclusively for riding in the Rockies and around the Peace River area in the Grande Prairie Region of Northern Alberta.

There were Site Managers at Rocky and Sundre plus a number of paid staff, especially during spring and winter, for Outdoor Education Programs. During summer we had hundreds of volunteer staff engaged in running an incredibly diverse range of camps for children and youth, plus riding adventures for adults at the Peace Pioneer Camps in the Grande Prairie area. These programs had been successfully operating for fifty years when I arrived. I had previously experienced many of the benefits of Pioneer activities during my years of study in Alberta, and I knew much of the history of the mission.

I loved horses and from my days on the dairy farm, was a competent rider. However, as a result of my serious pelvic injuries from Borneo, I found long hours in the saddle extremely painful. Having an Aussie, who didn't have horse riding as his first love, appointed to lead the highly successful and cherished 'horse focussed' camping program in Alberta was always going to be problematic, and it didn't take long for me to appreciate just how far back on the grid I was as an acceptable leader for the Camps. I spent time listening to major stakeholders, and I began to see the significance of the issues I was confronting.

A glaring example of unintentional tinkering with the culture at Rocky occurred during my first winter. There were twenty different cabins in the woods on the edge of Crimson Lake, and in winter I observed huge gaps and holes in the timber walls where the winter wind charged into the cabins. In order to ameliorate the impact of the wind, the cabins had huge pot belly stoves for warmth (one cabin actually overheated and caught fire while I was in Alberta, much to the consternation of many who had strong emotional attachments to the said cabin).

I wondered aloud with a few people why we didn't just plug the gaps in the cabin walls with timber coloured silicone or a similar product, to keep out the wind and thus reduce the fuel load and potential danger of fire. 'Chinese whispers' took hold and I soon heard I was intending to line the cabins with plaster, thus hiding the rustic log effect. As I loved the log cabins, nothing could have been further from the truth. So, how did this blow up?

Simple. I had learned this from my time as a teacher and from leading activities in the volunteer organisation back in Australia. When we learn anything new or different, the knowledge is accompanied by degrees of emotional reaction from joy of success to dread from failure, and every emotion in between. In the case of the cabins at Rocky, many cowboys could tell of highly positive transformative changes in their lives, via teaching and counsel from mentors, in their cabins.

If I was to change anything in relation to those cabins, I could, in the minds of past campers, potentially ruin the chance for boys and girls to experience the same transformative experiences as men and women of the past. Consequently, the cracks in the cabins remained. It was a battle not worth fighting.

The costs associated with running the camps were escalating, and unnecessary insurance requirements were being demanded of the camps. The added bile to this factor was that these premium demands were coming from insurance brokers in Toronto, thousands of kilometres from Sundre and Rocky Mountain House. I was now seeing a clash of cultures within Canada. As an 'outsider' in Alberta I was on the side of the cowboys on this one.

There were other pressing and more sensitive issues of personnel to confront which caused me sleepless nights and angst. On the other hand, I was able to introduce some positive reforms. From this perspective I was grateful to draw on the feedback from Spencer Colliver during my time of leadership of a volunteer organisation in Australia, and from my rich nine years' experience of leadership in a highly successful High School in Perth.

The Emotional Phenomenon of Change

Throughout my time leading this volunteer organisation, I learned another invaluable lesson regarding change and the process of change. All organisations establish processes and protocols that ultimately form a culture of 'the way we do things' in our work. This way of doing things is normally developed over time and serves the vision of the organisation effectively and successfully.

As a newcomer, I asked questions to learn, and I questioned the efficacy of some behaviours and standards. It was my latter actions that, for some long-standing members, were tantamount to insurrection and caused consternation and grief. With the luxury of hindsight, I later understood and respected the feelings of those committed and dedicated volunteers. I was perceived to be challenging their culture.

For example, by questioning a number of prior decisions and routines, incumbents perceived my actions as criticism. Further, by suggesting alternative ways that could be more effectively measured and monitoring progress for future planning, I was charged, in effect, with claiming prior efforts had been fruitless and ineffective. After reflecting upon these reactions, often from elders I respected, I gradually understood that change is as much an emotional phenomenon as it is a routine 'tinkering' to produce more effective outcomes. I also learned that any change begins with an ending.

In the process of change, we need to modify, or completely abandon current practice, then travel a period of uncertainty as we learn a revised, or completely new and sometimes foreign way of doing things. This can be emotionally draining, indeed threatening for some. I confess, however, that at the time I became frustrated with certain members whom I believed resisted change for the sake of staying in their 'comfort zones' and being so set in their ways to embrace, what I believed, were realistic alternatives.

How easily a 'standoff' can occur under these circumstances. In some cases, I listened respectfully and did all I could to state my case, as an objective 'outsider,' for change. In other cases, I considered the battle wasn't going to advance the war, and in yet others, I 'let it be.' I learned a great deal from these experiences, and I claim I am wiser as a result. I now appreciate that, for all involved, change is emotional because it is transformative; we are changed in the process. Change requires us to cease routines and way of working with which we have been comfortable and knowledgeable, and we can spend time in the 'wilderness' as we learn a new way of operating. However, gradually we can embrace activities that have been planned to suit a rapidly changing culture and society.

Change for me is a powerful phenomenon that, if not fully appreciated, can cause havoc in relationships, or it can be a harbinger for collaborative efforts and constructive community building within organisations and communities. I will share more about this in my story, especially from a cross-cultural perspective.

As I began my work with Pioneer Camps, I sought out many people, including cowboys I respected as mentors, from whom I could learn and in whom I knew I could confide. Simultaneously, I initiated informal mentoring relationships with young people who had attended summer camps and others who had worked as volunteers as cabin leaders for camps. An advantage in being an 'outsider' was that I was able to recruit past and present volunteers in the camping program from all over the province to attend a weekend training camp at Rocky. Among this group of people were many who had been previously engaged in Pioneer Camping, and for a variety of reasons, had taken 'time out,' or felt excluded.

During this time, I was able to broker the healing of past relationships between a number of stakeholders, and to cast a vision for the camps into the future. This was a strategic weekend for me since I was able to establish credibility by listening respectfully and engaging all stakeholders in shaping future directions. After all, I came back to Pioneer Camps because I loved the people involved and I felt honoured to be asked to take a lead role for five years.

Reflections

As I write, I am grateful that I only recall rich memories of my time back in Alberta. I made mistakes in leadership and errors of judgement in the 'cowboy culture' and at the time, I tended to bash myself up over some of the things I did and regretted, or things I failed to do. There are often times when we hesitate to do something because we think it may not be safe, or we wonder what others might think. I believe there has to be a margin of doubt and the possibility for error in every decision we make. If we wait for 'the right time,' or until we have all the information we need, the opportune moment can likely pass.

On the other hand, I can see how my impetuosity sometimes ended in me having to backtrack, apologise and resolve to learn. Further, the battle against failure and shame is constant and I still find I need to be vigilant. There were many other moments throughout the five years where I battled the imposter demons of 'unworthiness' and 'who do you think you are'? Among the strategies employed to overcome these false accusations were spending time with mentors, and quiet times of reflection and being still. As a designated leader and change agent, I found it necessary to access these strategies and not to fall into the trap of exhausting myself as I had done previously in my home state and city.

I drew upon my prior experiences and in the process, gained increased self-confidence. As I reflect upon my formal responsibilities at Pioneer Camps, I am grateful for honest feedback and encouragement from my formal mentors, Tana Clark and Neil Graham, and informal mentors, Gordy Cunningham, Beth Schmidt, Ps Henry Schorr, and Carrie Herbert. Canadians are special people and living in Calgary with the Rockies filling our kitchen window every day, it wasn't hard to love the place and appreciate the privilege of leading the camping program. It was especially gratifying years later when one of my girls said:

> *"Dad, I appreciate all the time you spent taking us travelling, from which I learned so much."*

This feedback warmed my heart, especially since I wanted our girls to experience and learn from living in their mother's country and culture. It was rich and rewarding watching each of the girls grow in confidence in themselves, including enjoying horseback riding with their mother who also loved camping. All of these were special experiences, and a blessing to see our girls reaching for their own 'outer limits.'

Meanwhile, back in Perth, I was about to confront a hurdle and another new experience. I viewed my life and career at this stage as 'midway,' or 'half time,' whereby I would embark on a more permanent career path.

PART FIVE
"Half Time"

Chapter 21

Navigating Failure

I returned to Perth for an interview and was offered a position as Foundation Principal of a new school, which I believed was my next career move. I was immediately engaged in picking up roles and responsibilities at the school. But all was not well. I gradually felt I wasn't suited for this role and that it wasn't in my gifting. I was despondent and felt inadequate; I knew I was not in the right place. I was also struggling with the decision to leave Alberta. My decision to join the school in Perth was one that ultimately 'blew up' in my face.

After the first year of operation of the school, members of the School Board also felt I was not the person they wanted as principal, and at a specially convened meeting, it became clear I was no longer a part of the board's vision for the school. I took a redundancy offered by the board and, as I drove home, I felt total relief. I had failed the task, but I knew I wasn't a failure. Later in my time at university, a student of mine, who was a member of the National Hockey Team, indicated her coach once said:

"FAIL means 'first attempt in learning."

With respect to failing and confronting unexpected change in our lives, a cowboy in Alberta once said to me:

"Any good cowboy knows, when his horse dies it
is time to get out of the saddle!"

He was a funny man with a dry wit and a neat sense of humour. When I harkened back to his philosophy it helped me relax about my failure and to consider what I learned from it. Having the courage and intention to leave behind and take up anew implies we have the power to either act upon setbacks and disappointment and move on, or to stay in the saddle of what could potentially be, our recently deceased steed. Not so edifying.

Shame was a key reality hammering at the door of my soul during this time. I am convinced we need to plan and to have a vision for what we seek to achieve in our lives, especially in relation to talents we obviously possess. However, we always need to hold these plans lightly, and be ready to adapt to changing circumstances when they come. I also appreciate I can recover from my failures and become a better person for it. I am blessed that I have never been crushed in life, just banged up a bit, so I can recover, and by adopting the appropriate strategies, move on.

With respect to strategies for overcoming my shame of failing, Brene Brown teaches about "false stories" of "unworthiness" we have about ourselves that can keep us from fully recovering from setbacks. There were times when I found the reality that I was deemed unworthy as a High School principal scary. I had to re-examine my vision to one day lead a school and seek wisdom about my next step for if the horse has died, there is nothing to be gained by just sitting in the saddle and hoping.

I now believe that any commitments we have that don't turn out as intended are for a reason, which I will share in the final chapter of my story. Further, vital realities for me in recovering from this major setback, included family support, the reliable presence and counsel from my key mentors, reflections in quiet times upon what I had learned through the total unfolding of events, and recalling the satisfaction and joy of learning and success to date, especially in Canada and the U.S.

What happened next? One of the men on the task force to appoint the principal at the school was disappointed with the Board's decision, so he offered me tutoring work for pre-service primary school teachers at Edith Cowan University (ECU). Graham Johnston, the Senior Pastor at Subiaco Church also asked me to support him by helping his staff team. I had time to reflect and round up all my feelings of loss, failure, sadness and questions about my decision-making and wisdom.

Beyond Failure

I accepted part time work tutoring education students at ECU, where I eventually increased my time to almost full-time employment. I accepted the role of Co-ordinator of the Graduate Diploma of Education (Secondary). This connected me with graduate students with wide ranging backgrounds and prior work experience, including up to thirty per year from Canada. I delivered core lectures, followed by meeting many students in tutorial groups of up to thirty for workshops.

At last, I felt I found my niche. I have always been passionate about teaching and the value of work done by teachers. I revelled in the opportunity to encourage and model effective teaching to students. I was having an impact by encouraging and supporting students in their career choice, and, by inspiring them as beginning teachers. I also believed I was multiplying my effectiveness, especially if they took on their work with passion and vision. From 2001 to 2013, I contributed to developing our teacher training and education program, and although I wasn't engaged in any meaningful research, that would come.

My Mother Stumbles

On June 8, 2004, we had a party at Di's house for mum's ninetieth birthday and on that weekend, it seemed as though a switch had been flicked, and mum's mind began unravelling. Mum became increasingly forgetful and anxious so we encouraged her to sell her house in Bunbury and to move to Perth where we could all take care of her. Upon reflection, that may not have been the best idea since the move really seemed to unsettle mum. However, living two hour's drive away made it difficult for Di, Rossco and I to be there if anything suddenly went wrong with mum in Bunbury.

Mum lived with Di for a while and then moved in with us, where our kind and loving youngest daughter agreed to be her gran's main carer. At the time, our youngest daughter was nineteen and she left us all in her wake in terms of stepping up and taking care of her gran. Nurturing and loving her gran was instinctive for our daughter. It was so special watching her take care of mum, especially as it became more and more difficult for her to do so. As time passed, it became increasingly difficult to have mum in our house. She would often get up during the night and into all kinds of 'mischief.'

Finally, one weekend mum had a meltdown and we needed to call for experienced medical help. Consequently, she was admitted to hospital for specialist palliative care. I will never forget the trauma of making this decision on the weekend we 'lost' our mother. Later when mum died our youngest played her violin to accompany her equally talented sisters singing a beautiful reflection at the burial service for their gran.

Turning Towards the Final Quarter

There were all kinds of new things happening in my life at this stage, including things I didn't anticipate and that I wasn't necessarily ready for. I needed support from my key mentors, but I didn't share with them all that I was processing in mind and heart. I know this was partly because I was embarrassed to ask, and because I knew I was wrong in what I was doing. I also knew what they would say, and I don't believe I wanted to hear that. I was guilty and I knew it. It was also during this time that I heard from a Singaporean friend about:

"...making the rest of your life count."

My friend shared his thoughts on ways to make our lives count, especially in our sixties and beyond. He referred me to a challenging text by Bob Buford, [1] which stirred me to re-examine priorities, and how I might 'finish well.' Part of my reaction to my friend's conversation was to share ideas with Bruce, after which, we initiated a program called *21ˢᵗ Century Men,* where we defined topics that we believed would be 'attractive to men.' We formalised topics, a venue, and a range of speakers we both knew, and we ran monthly seminars.

The format for each meeting was to ask well known men to share their life stories, specifically about how they dealt with difficult times in their lives. After the brief presentation by speakers, men attending the evening would be placed in tables of six, and would share their own ways of dealing with similar issues. Those we consulted about our plan believed we would not get men to share at tables, but we found it was always difficult to get them to stop talking at the designated time. Among topics we presented during these sessions were:

"Tips for being a dad to our sons"	"Facing our perceived inadequacies"
"Making our marriage work"	"Being dads for our daughters"
"Dealing with conflict – home & work"	"Finding mentors"
"Being mentors"	"Health issues & dealing with them"
"Asking for what we need"	"Active listening"

The age range of men was usually thirties and above. Some dads came to select sessions with their sons. It was a time of raw emotions at times, joy at others and overall, a gratifying experience for Bruce and I. Sadly, after three years, we had to stop the meetings because we simply could not keep up the pace and energy required to keep going. We tried to inspire others to take over the project, to no avail. Maybe the idea had also run its course.

Reflections

I harken back to my failure as a principal. I was gutted at the time, and I was extremely grateful for my good friend Rod Lewis and his wife, Marg for their support and care during the months following my demise. Through a lengthy process of developing friendship, and sharing similar values, Rod became one of my valued informal mentors. For years Rod managed my personal and family financial affairs and, like Bruce, he endeared himself to my family.

Rod and I forged a deep friendship whereby we developed a seamless interface between friendship and a mentor/protégé relationship. The trust and respect I have for Rod is immeasurable and invaluable. As I write, I trust other men will find ways of mining a rich friendship into a life-long mentoring relationship.

Chapter 22

Mentoring in East Africa

My only East African visit to Tanzania took place with colleagues from ECU, Geoff Lowe and Karen Murcia, as part of a research project in Dar es Salaam. Karen secured a Rotary Grant for us to travel to a unique cultural setting to test the efficacy of reflective practice by Australian teachers. We pre-selected five teachers from Perth, and arranged for them to work in various schools in Dar es Salaam, keeping a journal of their experiences.

We tutored the teachers on the way we wanted them to report their experiences, and we later published the findings for our research. With a focus on reflective practice based upon intentionally thinking about incidences in the classroom, how they initially responded to those incidences, and listening to one another as they deconstructed events of the day, we added the mentoring skills of effectively listening to one another to offer counsel on each other's experiences.

Beer O'clock

A key facet of the project was meeting every day for an hour after school with the five teachers to guide them as they conducted the deconstruction process of that day's teaching. A hidden agenda for these meetings was to teach active listening skills, one of the first steps in effective mentoring. This proved to be a successful project and a significant learning curve for all of us involved. As I listened to the teachers' discussions, it was also further evidence for me as to the agency of mentoring among school staff. A link to the research can be found in the notes section. [1]

The Tanzanian research project was an important experience for me, especially as Geoff, Karen and I later prosecuted the role of our embedded teachers as mentors for their Tanzanian peers. Mentoring and reflective practice were obvious concepts we noted as we carefully read the extensive journals our teachers had compiled. At the time of reading our research notes, I was not conscious of any intention to embark further upon extending research into the efficacy of mentoring among teachers. However, with the benefit of hindsight, I appreciate just how personally formative the experience was.

Humbling Learning Experiences in East Africa

During the years 2001-2004, my church had established an outreach in East Africa, and our Senior Pastor, Graham, invited many of us to accompany him in teaching and training outreach in Western Kenya, Uganda and Rwanda. The goal of these ventures was to respond to requests for teaching and training from hosts in East African countries, and to acknowledge we were providing this service from a Western perspective. Our hosts would then consider our ideas and decide which ones, if any, would fit their context.

These were inspiring and humbling experiences and I quickly developed a love for remarkable people in these countries. I always emphasised to team members that we should plan a fifty-fifty outcome from these events, with fifty percent of our effort in presenting and fifty percent in listening and learning from our hosts. An outreach I led to Rwanda in 2004, including all the experiences getting to the retreat centre, was packed with the fifty percent learning. All team members were struck by the beauty of the country of Rwanda. It is known as a land of a thousand hills, and the bus ride from Kigali to the Retreat Centre at Ruhengeri in the northwest of the country was spectacular.

The Rwandans we met and worked with were such hospitable and gracious people, and I could never work out how their terrible ethnic cleansing took place in 1994. I felt it was justification alone for the members of our teams to learn as much about the culture of the people who invited us, as it was for us to share our knowledge and experience with them.

One of the most inspiring men I met from almost a decade of travel to East Africa was Stephen Bamuleke (Bamo) and his wife Siriake. Bamo and Siriake have packed more into their lifetime than I could in three. During the Rwandan genocide of 1994, Bamo and Siriake lived just inside the Congo side of the border with Rwanda, and would constantly have large numbers of people sheltering and seeking refuge on their property.

Siriake had her own mission to women in Rwanda and the border region of the Congo. All the women we met in regional areas of East Africa worked incredibly hard and if anyone believes people are poor because they are lazy, let them visit any African country and see how hard women work. In one day, I saw women dig a field of potatoes, using their fingers and hands to 'dig,' and then load the bags on trucks. Some of them also carried a baby all day on their back. Their payment for the day's hard work was to carry home a sack of potatoes for their families. Without the hard work of women in East Africa, I am sure countries in that region would shut down. [2]

Along with our numerous trips to East Africa for training and teaching, we developed the vision and a project to establish a school with a training wing attached in Western Kenya. The project, named *Kenya Youth Futures (KYF)*, encompassed teachers being released from duties to come to the school to watch and learn about effective teaching, and sharpen their own teaching skills accordingly. However, we were first faced with a challenge to find land for building a school and other facilities, raise money for scholarships for poor students and find local staff who were sufficiently skilled to become the lead teachers at such a school.

Exploring a Vision for Kenya

In February 2014, I travelled to Kenya to assess the prospect of actually bringing such a vision to reality. From my exploratory time in Kenya, I have numerous rich and humbling memories of learning, particularly in towns and schools. For example, I was returning once from my early morning walk when I was greeted by two children, a boy around five years old and a beautiful little girl around three. They both did the usual:

"How are you?"

But the little girl held out her hand, and as I stooped to take it, she looked at me with magnificent brown eyes that reflect the depth and wonder of this Nation and she said:

"Thank you, teacher!"

I looked down at her tiny brown hand in mine and I was mesmerised. I had done nothing to deserve such honour and respect; she didn't know me and I may never see her again. As she and her brother walked on, I just could not move. I was filled with awe and wonder at the solemn respect and innocence of the children. The joy and gratitude they extended to me was precious beyond description.

On the other hand, a disturbing factor of life for Kenyans in some areas outside major cities, is pockets of intense witchcraft. One school in particular that I visited, was confronted by this to the extent that some children were afraid to come to school; a number of teachers were also afraid. The syncretic nature of belief in these areas is that if God doesn't answer your prayers (normally related to illness or death), the witch doctor will fix it. I was assured by a village chief and a school principal that the witch doctor's influence normally prevailed, accompanied by great fear and reluctance to attend school.

I confess I was exhausted and disillusioned from my three month's exploration, especially in relation to negotiating in a complex matrix of relationships and expectations among tribal groups and families. I was encouraged in this respect by my Kenyan friend and mentor, David Waweru. Dave assured me that, after spending a weekend with his family and relatives in regional villages, he also returns home to Nairobi exhausted from negotiating all the machinations of nuclear and extended family. I felt better after Dave's honesty and encouragement.

I also grew to understand that our vision for a school and training centre would not be achievable. We could see the need, but we had to respect the importance of ancestral land ownership to Kenyans. To part with some of their land for muzungus to build a school was anathema to tribal Kenyans who love the land and who honour their ancestors who passed ownership down through families. Further, we did not have the resources or backing to bring our vision to fruition. However, in partnership with my ECU colleague, Geoff Lowe, I published some of the work I completed while in Kenya. [3]

Reflections

A key revelation emanating from my experiences over ten years travelling through East African countries was the power of shame in those cultures. This was especially true in Kenya, although wider reading and discussions with Kenyans I love and respect, confirmed for me that shame is a phenomenon well known to most African people. Indeed, all the definitions and outcomes of shame I shared in chapter two of my story are evident in peoples' lives in Kenya.

Publicly shaming someone is common practice in Kenya, particularly in local villages. It is used as a 'weapon' of control over people. It can also be dangerous for some. For example, if a woman is shamed in a village, she can be excluded from joining the group walking each day to a well or river, to fill water containers. In turn, she becomes vulnerable to attack, including serious harm from animals such as lions, and tragically, assault and rape.

Further, men in the cultures where we taught, will go to any lengths to avoid being shamed, either personally, or publicly. As social research asserts, shame is a factor of human experience, and not restricted to people living in Western countries. It is a matter for us to find constructive and effective ways of combatting the effects of shame, spanning all cultures and people groups.

Returning to Academia

As I was planning to leave Kenya, I heard from Henry and Rosco that, in August, they were planning a four-week trip into Australia's hinterland.

"Pick me," was my immediate thought, followed by my written request accordingly.

And they did. Consequently, I was about to embark upon another transformative experience, this time with my brothers. This included growing closer to them, learning more about them and with them and gaining a deeper connection after feeling separated from them all those years ago on the farm.

Throughout our journey, as I intentionally reflected each evening and morning upon my relationship with Henry and Rosco, I appreciated how we all 'suffered' from our dad's relationship with each one of us, how the power was now in our hands to address issues, and how we could benefit immeasurably by sharing our insights and learning with one another.

Chapter 23

A Brotherhood of Mentoring

On August 1, 2014, my brothers and I upon a journey of awe, almost unspeakable beauty, laughter, rest, wonder, and an experience of mutual love and delight. We travelled four thousand kilometres from Perth to Alice Springs, then Halls Creek, Kununurra, Gibb River Road, Derby and Broome, Karijini and finally home to Perth. All this in four weeks. We had my 4x4 Nissan Navara for this venture, equipped with long range fuel tank, two extra spare wheels, spare fuel cans, spare water cans, and all the necessary camping gear for the three of us. At first, I had no specific plans for learning more strategies for dealing with facets of shame on this trip, but as we travelled and sat around campfires at night and talked, I realised I was in a petri dish of fermenting ideas for personal growth and confidence. Let me share what I mean.

We arrived in Kalgoorlie on our first night, and after dinner, it was off to see the Super Pit, [1] the largest open cut gold mine in the world. Next morning was Leonora, Gwalia, [2] and Laverton, all original gold rush towns but with little mining activity now. We then drove the Great Central Highway which leads eventually to Uluru. On our first night camp we endured a freezing breeze all night. Dingoes howled all night and tried to tear us to pieces during the night, but we fought them off, and then I woke up.

Next, we drove by the awe-inspiring Kathleen and Schwerin Mural Crescent Ranges.

As we did, the sun was setting behind us and shining on the ranges. It was so beautiful with stunning white barked gums, and the ranges in the background. I felt the presence of awe during this period, and such a peace in my soul, especially after my exhausting time trying to make sense of the complicated cultures of Kenya. I always find the stunning beauty of my homeland so refreshing for both soul and spirit, more so on this occasion as I was still processing the disappointment of 'failing' to launch the Kenyan project.

We crossed into the Northern Territory, and on to the Docker River Aboriginal Community where the campground had been wrecked by camels looking for water. We had seen a mob of twenty camels on the road during the drive, and we trusted they would stay away from us during the night. We understood camels can be aggressive if they are thirsty and we were camped in an area where there was water. We slept under the stars with a freezing cold wind for company, and it was not much warmer during the day. With plus 0° humidity, our lips cracked and our hands became so dry that our finger nails were cracking. At this stage my reflections were more about survival than pondering upon the beauty of the land.

Our first view of the Olgas (Kata Tjuta), [3] was amazing. Again, the sun was behind us and thus highlighted the hot red colour of this special outcrop of rock. We pulled into the car park and took a walk through the rocks up to a lookout. Hundreds of Zebra Finches, grey in colour with blood red beaks, were flitting about. Beautiful little birds. The white trees, including coolabahs with their green leaves, were spectacular against the background of the massive rocks and bluest sky I have ever seen.

Wildflowers were hanging on and still fresh in areas away from the direct sun. The Kata Tjuta seem to be made of rocks squeezed into mud – amazing. Walking in the quiet with my brothers was incredibly special, and more than I can express, as was leaving the sense of unworthiness of the past in the beauty of this place with my brothers.

A Special Place

Next was Uluru. [4] What a breadth-taking experience to see it for the first time from fifty kilometres away. We booked into camp at Ayres Rock Camp Site, then back to the rock for sunset; people everywhere waiting for the sun to set and the colours of the rock to change. An international community of people taking photos of one another. Awesome. A deep-down headache and overall body ache had taken the edge off the day for me. However, a shower and good night's sleep, plus drugs and I was good to go next morning. A lady in the tent next to us warned us she snored. She did, all night. When she wasn't snoring at night, she was talking nonstop when awake.

Our first stop before going back to Uluru itself, was at the Cultural Interpretive Centre in the National Park. We spent ages there, including watching two aboriginal women painting. I sat close to Elsie and thanked her as I left. She proffered me a huge smile that made my day, at least for that moment. Back at Uluru, we walked to specific areas around the base of the rock, beginning with Mala Puta and Kanju Gorges. The latter is not to be described, just experienced. There is a little pool at the foot of the rock, and we just sat there in silence listening to the birds, the breeze, and the past.

I could have stayed there all day. As I sat at this spot, I realised I was getting older, that I knew so much less about things and I embraced that fact. I am most at peace now when I am in a place where I sense the magnitude of our Creator God, and how good it is to know I don't need to be perfect, or to have all the answers.

Mala Puta is a place of significance to the Anangu people; we saw caves where people gathered for ceremony and special law. One of the stunning features of Uluru is this massive rock suddenly arising out of flat land three hundred and fifty metres high. The walk around the rock is level and beautifully set out to experience the magnificence of this place.

From there we drove around the rock to Mutijulu Waterhole which was also breathtaking in its beauty. The waterhole is permanent, so all kinds of animals and birds drink there; again, it was a place where you didn't want to talk, just be. There were magnificent white gums against the red rock and blue sky, all kinds of native plants and amazing birds.

So sad Rosco couldn't hear the birds as he is partially deaf and can only hear certain sounds, which doesn't include birds. I admire my brother, since the impediment to his hearing does not diminish his love of birds in the wild. Reluctantly, we left Uluru in mid-afternoon to head for Kings Canyon, about three hundred kilometres away, and set up camp for the night.

Moving On

The morning was amazing; I woke at 5.00 am as the sun was rising. My stretcher was level with the spinifex, and as I lay there the spinifex was turning gold in colour. As the sun rose the spinifex turned lighter shades of gold, then into a beautiful rice colour. The river gums were pure white and the river sand the same; all for no cost. The birds were going crazy with song, and the cicadas and frogs joined in. The walk around Kings Canyon itself was stunning and multitudes of birds kept us company. Driving away from Kings Canyon we saw a dingo, many horses, donkeys and fabulous vistas. Iconic Australia with the ranges and open plains.

We next camped by the Fink River, supposedly one of the oldest rivers in the world. I don't know how 'they' work that out, although it flows into Lake Eyre in the middle of the continent which seems to be an undignified end for it. I slept under a magnificent gum tree that night and I could see the moon shining through the canopy of leaves as I went to sleep. Sun rose at 5.30 am and my tree was full of birds, all singing away. Why wouldn't you love this country? At this stage of our journey, the disappointment of Kenya was becoming a distant memory. The therapy of travel in our beautiful land, plus the company of my Bros, was taking full effect.

Next stop was Alice Springs, [5] known with affection in Australia as 'The Alice'. It is a quaint town with a mix of old and new but seemed to be quite depressed with new malls but numerous vacant shops. We rested for a couple of days before leaving The Alice at 7.30 am to drive on the Tanami Track through five hundred kilometres of spinifex plains, some tress, and land sometimes so flat we couldn't see the horizon. At some point we saw a crazy German tourist cycling along the unsealed road, and waving an empty water bottle at us. We stopped and gave him some water, reminding him respectfully that this was not Germany with water everywhere. I am not convinced he believed us.

On one of our overnight stops along the Tanami, the moon was so full I had to pull covers over my head to sleep. I woke at midnight and the moon was directly above and so bright; I could have read my kindle, if I felt so moved. In the morning was a phenomenon I have rarely seen before; the moon setting and simultaneously, the sun rising. The moon was a massive ball of red reflected light as it set, and the Eastern sky was blood red as the sun rose. Rosco shared this beautiful moment with me. I wished it would not stop or at least slow down. So special sharing these unique moments with my brothers.

A "Spiritual" Place like Uluru

We stopped at Wolf Creek Crater [6] on our way to Halls Creek. The crater is an impressive site and we agreed we were glad not to have been around when the meteor landed. Next was Halls Creek which has special significance for us, being the town where our mother nursed for a short period of time in 1946 – 1947. From Halls Creek, we drove north to Purnululu National Park. [7]

The drive from the main highway to the camp site took us over an hour. It is beautiful country and I could see why the squatters loved this land, and of course the First Nations people here revere the land. We camped by a dry creek bed, had lunch and squad rest. Next day, we visited Echidna Chasm on the northwest corner of Purnululu.

How to describe the beauty of the place? To walk up to the chasm, we traversed a rocky creek bed; either side of the chasm were palm trees. Seeing these out in the Kimberley is fascinating. Some were clinging to the rock face high above us and others towered above us on the creek floor. After about four hundred metres, we entered the chasm. The walls were as many shades of red that you can imagine.

After another two hundred metres we entered the chasm proper, and my claustrophobic metre began to climb. Once we entered the walls where I could touch both sides with my arms, I hit five out of ten on the claustrophobic scale, then eight out of ten as it became shoulder width with the wall seemingly reaching to the sky.

Still, we proceeded until we entered a grotto with nowhere else to go. Fortunately, we were alone so we could be quiet and hear the wind in the palms on the rim of the chasm high above us. The area where we stood was about as big as a normal living room. I found the experience almost intimidating. I mean, we were standing in this small space in the centre of this incredible edifice of rock which had been there way before our land was inhabited by people. On the drive back to our camp, the sun was setting behind us affording us a spectacular 'fireworks' of colour; one rock face in particular appeared to be in flames. In the foreground were a host of blue leaved trees with white trunks accompanied by white gums and wildflowers. A simply magnificent garden.

I was up at 5.30 am next morning as it was getting light and the birds were going nuts. After breakfast we hiked to Picanniny Creek and Cathedral Grove which is now my equal first favourite spot in central Australia, although nothing can surpass Uluru. It is where a Qantas commercial 'I Still Call Australia Home' was filmed. We were informed by Park Rangers that concerts are occasionally performed in this place; it would be awesome to be there for that.

The Kimberley: Such a Timeless Part of Australia

Next stop was Kununurra and Lake Argyle, [8] the latter is spectacular but is man-made and can't possibly match the natural beauty and quiet of the hinterland that embraced us. After Kununurra, we camped out on the banks of the Pentecost River, far enough up the bank to avoid the crocodiles who also like the river. To cross the river, we forded in water up to tire level of the vehicle. The uneven river floor made this a bumpy ride and a tad concerning for 'first timers.'

On a previous visit to the Kimberley, I had swum in this part of the river, swimming on the road so to speak. I discovered later that crocs consider the river their territory so I didn't feel inclined to take another swim, especially following that vital piece of information. I passed this information on to my Bros and they felt the same, tempting as the water looked.

We drove south, down the mighty Gibb River Road, to Mt Barnett campground. From the camp, we walked out to Manning Gorge, [9] a stunning place. After climbing around, I found a hot spring coming out of the rocks so we had a lovely warm bath on the rock wall. Climbing around together on the rock walls of the falls and finding gushing hot springs reminded me of some of the best times we had swimming together in a dam on the family farm. I felt like a teenager again, rather than sixty-nine. After our swim at Manning Gorge, we drove on down the Gibb River Road to Bells Gorge [10] where we enjoyed another swim in the pool; yet another magic place. We had a couple of hours at the pool and then on into Derby to set up camp.

From Derby, we drove south to Broome and Port Hedland, and eventually into Millstream National Park, [11] which was the prettiest drive to date. The plains were flat and covered in wild oats coloured spinifex, which is my attempt to describe the colour of the spinifex. In addition, red to burgundy coloured dirt and hills, green trees with white trunks and blue sky. if you don't like any of those colours you are screwed.

The drive into Millstream Homestead was spectacular and as we came into the park, we stopped at one of the gorges for a swim, nobody around so we went in as we were born. This was the Fortescue River, an oasis in the Pilbara. The river spot is part of the park and the stretch of river for swimming must be over a kilometre in length. After our swim, we went on to the old Homestead that is now operated by National Parks Australia, and snooped around. Visitors can walk into the beautiful wet area around the Homestead where the pools are clear enough to see right to the bottom. Water lilies grow under the water since the sun gets all the way down to them through the crystal-clear water. I could have stayed there reading a book all day and spent a week in the park, being among the water lilies, swimming in the pool, hiking along the river. It is beautiful. So quiet. So peaceful. Restorative rating? Eleven out of ten!

As I relived moments of the trip, I realized just how personally restorative it had been. We were now on our homeward journey, visiting the mining town of Tom Price and then back to Karijini National Park for a couple of days before we made our way down through the wildflowers and home.

Reflections

Many people we met on our trip commented upon how good it was that the three of us chose to undertake this journey together. I understood what they meant. We had discussed numerous times along the way what we had learned from our childhood. In a way, I lost contact with my brothers from age twelve when I went to boarding school. Later, when I was on the farm they were at school and by the time they were ready to leave school, I had left the farm and was on another trajectory.

Henry and Rosco have good memories of childhood on the farm, which I respect. However, it had been difficult for them as younger brothers navigating my dad's relationship with me. Henry once said he determined as a kid to stay clear of me to avoid getting hit by the same lightening. A good analogy, but sad for my younger brother. Similarly, Rosco had the pressure of being seen as the 'favoured one' by dad, and I recall an incident clearly on the farm where that was so unfair on him.

I also recall a dinner we had together in Northbridge in 1979 when I returned from my time in Canada and the U.S., where we agreed that we were just getting to know one another as adults. I had fish for dinner that night just to reinforce how important the night was for me.

Since that evening, I have shared many rich memories of travel and family gatherings with my brothers and our families, especially with Henry selflessly embracing the role of 'unc' for our children.

However, it hasn't been until after I turned seventy that I have come to appreciate just how fortunate I am to have the brothers and sister I have. Growing older for me has been an experience of peace and reflection beyond my expectation, or imagination. Our 2014 road trip added to that knowledge and understanding in my memory bank. It was a special time and I thank Henry, Rosco, and God for every moment of it.

Chapter 24

Guilt to Shame

"If you do not transform your pain, you will always transmit it" Richard Rohr

Upon arrival home from my trip with my brothers, storm clouds were gathering in my marriage. As I reflect upon my marriage, quite possibly the most important phenomenon I learned is that attempting to live in the shadows of guilt is never going to end well. Hiding my guilt and duplicitous behaviour of infidelity was a breach of trust, commitment and responsibility, and it caused hurt and pain for my wife, and my daughters.

In addition, my guilt drained me of joy, creativity and physical and emotional health. I knew I wasn't teaching as well as I could, I felt lonely in my family and among my academic colleagues, and I was deeply ashamed to share my position with my mentors. I had fallen into what Brene Brown[1] refers to as:

"...the swampland of the soul."

Such a bleak picture of a nowhere place to be. In this environment, I gave credence to all kinds of self-destructive stories about myself. I felt unworthy, unsafe, deceitful, to name a few. It took quite some time to crawl out of the swamp towards wholeness and healing.

The first critical step was to acknowledge my guilt. In a session with a counsellor, I declared I could not believe I could have behaved in such a way. His reply floored me:

> *"You must be a proud person to believe you are above the potential and ability to sin!"*

His comment helped me 'own' my behaviour, rather than trying to rationalise it and hope the guilt would go away. Here I am helped by Brene Brown [2] who views shame as 'believing I am bad' due to a flawed belief in myself, and guilt as understanding 'I did something bad.'

I spent ten years living with the logical consequences and loneliness of my undisclosed wrongdoing. In order to reshape my destiny, it was time to seek forgiveness and grace. I was guilty and I knew it, and I had chosen to hide my guilt for ten years, therefore giving shame free range in my mind. This was also the event I vividly recalled of my dad walking alone to the dairy to milk the cows. In relation to my own family, I was excruciatingly aware of how my behaviour had impacted upon them, and how ashamed and sad I felt about that.

My behaviour resulted in living with shame and painful consequences. And it was mercy, forgiveness and grace that ultimately helped me deal with my guilt and confront my shame. To be perfectly clear; I understand that guilt is essential for us because it prompts our heart and conscience that we have breached the 'Golden Rule,' [3] and that we need to be reconciled accordingly. On the other hand, shame can follow unresolved guilt, and continue to 'accuse us,' even after we seek forgiveness for our guilty action. Interestingly, in the view of singer/songwriter Nick Cave: [4]

"...it is difficult to deal with shame in our current Australian cancel culture where mercy and forgiveness are hard to find."

However, Pete Walker [5] offers some hope in this regard by noting:

"We live in an emotionally impoverished culture, and those who stick with a long-term recovery process, are often rewarded with EQ far beyond the norm."

In light of Nick Cave's insights, I consider myself most fortunate, in this lowest point in my life, to have mentors and close friends who offered me mercy and forgiveness. Further, my experience confirms Pete Walker's assertion that, as I finally confronted my guilt, I noted a deeper well of EQ in my heart that enabled me to extract myself from the swampland of shame in my soul.

My earlier counselling experience with Patrice, along with my willingness to be vulnerable and to learn about and understand the source of shame in my life, eventually enabled me to acknowledge my guilty behaviour and to seek forgiveness accordingly. Upon deeper examination of my actions, however, I acknowledge that my tendency to impulsive behaviour was an additional factor in my actions.

Shame was a consequence of my actions but failing to deal with other mitigating factors in my life, contributed to my experience of temporarily, 'living in the swampland shame.' Further, if we don't admit our guilt, and identify and work on our shame, I am sure shame is instrumental in us 'lashing out' at others, thus avoiding dealing with the hurt within our heart. This is where my mentors were invaluable in loving me and granting mercy, and where grace was a balm of healing for my soul.

I hasten to point out that Bruce and Rod were instrumental in walking with me back to seeing myself as a champion again, albeit that Bruce and I had some tough conversations on why I hid my previous behaviour from him for so long. I appreciated that he told me he was hurt by that.

I moved out of the family home in November 2014, and began living in a one-bedroom unit. I was processing all I learned from my counselling, including regularly seeing a psychiatrist recommended by the Department of Veterans Affairs. The latter contact was invaluable as I negotiated my way through the early years after my marriage breakdown.

Meanwhile, after my time in Kenya, I had been invited back by ECU in 2014 as an Honorary Lecturer/Researcher.

PART SIX

Exiting the Swampland Of Shame

Chapter 25

A Pilgrimage of Hope

In January 2015 I was influenced positively by two significant events. In the first I watched a TED talk by Robert Waldinger [1] outlining a longitudinal study based out of the Harvard Graduate School of Medicine which piqued my interest for a potential research project. The second was a movie, *The Way*, about a man's pilgrimage on the Camino de Santiago.

With respect to the former, I discussed my ideas for a research project with two of my wonderful colleagues at ECU, Geoff and Christina, who agreed it had agency. As I shared the vision further, I was also encouraged by key educational leaders in government and the Department of Education to progress my ideas. I then set about, with Geoff and Christina, planning the early stages of our vision, including writing Research Proposals for our wide- ranging project.

Meanwhile, the movie, *The Way* inspired me to do my own Camino, which I decided to undertake the following year, 2016. However, during coffee discussing my Camino plans with a dear friend, she asked:

"Why not now?"

That was all the extra encouragement I needed, and I immediately began planning for my Camino Pilgrimage. After Semester One, 2015, I was able to book a flight to Barcelona and then train and bus to southern France to begin my Camino via the Way of St Francis, beginning in mid-May to the end of June. I walked eight hundred and ten kilometres from St Jean Pied de Port in southern France, across the Pyrenees to Roncesvalles in northern Spain, and west to Santiago de Compostela.

Camino Pilgrimage

The first day of thirty kilometres across the Pyrenees was probably the toughest of all days. It was stunningly beautiful at the 1400 metre summit where dense fog made it difficult staying on the path. It brought back images of the beginning of the movie *The Way* but can't say any more and spoil it for you. On my first morning I met young men from Brazil who adopted me as their 'Aussie mascot.' By day three, they left me in their wake. Along the way I met so many other fantastic people, generally when I stopped for a coffee during the day, or in the evening wherever I landed for the night.

This process was repeated day after day. Sometimes I would see the same people for a few days, then never again. Other times, I would meet people over a coffee and at the end of the time we felt we had known one another all our lives. I loved these interactions as much as I treasured the quiet to walk on my own. Further, I found the rhythm of walking precious, as each step revealed a slightly new vista. It was like having a metronome to measure my thoughts and reflections.

Sometimes, I was acutely aware and conscious of my reflections and at others I was just 'in the moment,' and enjoying the beauty of the pathway we all followed. ANZAC Day had not long passed so when I first saw poppies along the track, I felt so overwhelmed. I was seeing them as our Diggers did in country just north of me. I choked up for a bit as I reflected upon the fact that I was so close to where all the horror of World War One happened. Funny how something like that can 'take you there.'

Walking into Spanish Culture

I passed through the town of Los Arcos at 10.00 am one morning following the 'running of the bulls,' the night before. As I entered the town, I couldn't figure out why all the doors to houses in the main street were solidly boarded up. Then I saw bull droppings on the cobbled road, and I understood. You don't want bulls charging in your front door during the running in your neighbourhood.

Entering the town square there was a group of young people still 'celebrating' from the night before. I found a chair and table among the upturned and scattered furniture, and sat down for a coffee to take in the atmosphere. I watched one young man in awe and amazement. His body was erect in a chair. He had a stubby in one hand and a cigarette in the other. He seemed conscious, but his body appeared to be shut down, as if his cognitive capacity had almost totally shut down. He appeared to be trying to decide between a sip from his stubby or a drag on his smoke, but his brain was not helping. This was fascinating for a teacher to watch.

I asked the rest of the group if I could take a photo. They indicated in the affirmative, as best they could. As I was taking a photo, another young man approached me carrying a wooden table on his head. Should I be concerned? Too late. I was now under the table with him and he had his right hand in his mouth, while I believe, he was trying to communicate with me. After unsuccessfully trying to reciprocate on my part, he walked away and I left the square in peace to continue my Camino.

One of Many Breathtaking Camino Experiences

My next memorable experience of awe and wonder followed an overnight stay in the village of San Juan de Ortega, population of around twenty people. I sought accommodation and evening meal in an ancient monastery in the village. In the evening, we celebrated Mass in the monastery chapel for anyone who chose to go, and Mass included a gift of a Patriarchal Cross which I now wear. I decided that evening that I would begin walking next morning at 4.00 am, before dawn, so I would have the rising sun at my back. The awe and wonder of the next morning was continuous until the sun was quite high in the sky. As I left the monastery to head west, the mood and scene was mesmerising, and I was reminded of the Alfred Noyes [2] poem, *The Highwayman,* the only significant memory of learning I have from my three years at New Norcia!

As I walked in the pre-dawn light the road was indeed:

"…a ribbon of moonlight across the purple moor."

Although no highwayman came riding, later in the day a man and a woman on horseback overtook me on the track. On the previous day, I had the words of the song: *The Lord of the Dance,* [3] acting as a metronome as I paced myself and soaked in the beauty of the land.

As I left the monastery, along the path there were thousands of spectacular poppies, interspersed with all kinds of stunningly beautiful indigenous flowers. This array of flowers was about a metre wide on each side of the track and stretched from one rise to the next, then the next, and so on. In addition, cascading from the border of flowers, north and south of the track, were fields of ripening wheat, green stalks with heads just turning light gold in colour, all gently caressed by a breeze that caused rhythmic waves of grain as far as the eye could see.

I walked slowly and felt like I was on one a mobile 'walkways' commonly found at large airports. I was conscious of my heart beating and my soul being embraced by the whole experience. This kept on until the sun's warmth caused me to attend to drinking and focussing on walking.

Where Hemingway Trod

On a more sobering note, I am a Hemingway fan, and one of his books; *For whom The Bell Tolls,* 'came to life' on one of my days. I was walking through Basque Country where many battles from the Civil War took place. I could feel the reality of the place from Hemingway's description of the area, and as I walked up a hill, I saw rows of rusted barb wire, still in place from the war. Just prior to this, I walked past a recently erected memorial for many peasants who had been killed in the Civil War. During the conflict, their bodies had been deposited in a shallow grave that had recently been revealed after wind and water erosion. So many past conflicts and wars on the Iberian Peninsula.

I was also taken by cathedrals housing exquisite examples of skills of people from the past including, blacksmiths, glass makers, fine metal workers and more Many consider the Catholic Church should sell all these treasures, but I believe they miss the point. These tradespeople used their unique skills to honour God and to acknowledge their gifts and talents in a way that was meaningful to them.

Today we reach into our wallets and give what we have left over. These people of former times gave all they had which was their time and skill and we get to enjoy and appreciate their gifts of beauty, long after they passed them on to the church for posterity. At least, that is how I see it.

As I drew closer to Santiago de Compostela and realised I had one hundred and fifty kilometres remaining, I felt another sense of awe and wonder. How could I possibly fully grasp being in places where legions of Roman soldiers had marched, knights of the Crusades rode, El Cid fought the Moors and the brutal Civil War of the 1930s had taken place. This was a place of the earliest known human habitation on earth; and where inspired art and architecture was present for viewing. There was so much to process as I walked. I need to do this again.

Further along the way, I stayed for two nights at the Benedictine Monastery at Samos; the very place from which Bishop Salvado set out to establish Australia's only Benedictine Community town at New Norcia in my own state of West Australia and the site of my three years of High School.

I confess that finally walking through the old city of Santiago de Compostela was underwhelming. It was full of grey buildings with cobbled streets and little sunshine. Leaving the beauty and history of the *Camino Way* was bittersweet. It was wonderful to finish and get my certificate, but there were places along the way where I would have loved to have lingered and explored. Next time. Every day of my pilgrimage, my spirit soared, even when it rained. It was a time to think of only positive things, and to wonder about 'what next' in my life. I felt refreshed and energised. I was also looking forward to what lay ahead, including navigating 'single life' again.

No Longer Shackled by Shame

At this stage in my life, I am grateful for so much and, after seventy-seven years of experiential learning, I wonder what lies ahead? How many more years do I have? How will I spend those years? How do I wisely and compassionately 'spend' the intellectual, emotional, and spiritual capital I have acquired? How would I now live after 39 years of married life?

These were questions that I formulated and attempted to prosecute in my mind and heart as I engaged in, and completed, my Camino. Further, I was looking forward to developing research ideas I had shared before my Camino with colleagues, especially since I believed that the topic and strategies we identified for a sound research project, had gravitas and agency. I prosecute this case further in following chapters.

Chapter 26

Shaking the Research Tree for Mentors

I mentioned watching the TED Talk by Robert Waldinger who was then currently leading one of the world's longest ongoing longitudinal studies into what made life worthwhile and meaningful for people. Since I was in the process of reflecting upon what events and people had shaped my life so far, including how invaluable I was now seeing the role of mentors, Waldinger's research piqued my interest. Of specific interest were Waldinger's key findings regarding men over sixty years of age which included:

- *"Specific ways in which men alter themselves and the world around them in order to adapt to life."*

- *"Close relationships, not our culture, shape our adaptive processes."*

- *"The quality of sustained relationships," is the most important consideration in these relationships, and,*

- *"Human development continues throughout adult life."*

Waldinger's summary spoke powerfully to me. As I examined my life to date, I realised that, in many ways, I shared the traits identified among men outlined in the above four 'dot points. I had just turned seventy and I was more passionate than ever about the role of realistically sustainable work that involved sharing the wisdom I had gained from my life experiences. I had been 'battered' somewhat by prior experiences, but I have also been fortunate to have mentors in my life who cared enough to 'call out' my blind spots and to counsel me through reparation and healing.

These were the key factors in attracting me to the results of Waldinger's research, and to the potential for further insights into the formal role of mentors in teaching and learning. I was fortunate that colleagues more experienced in research than myself also saw the potential research opportunity, and they prosecuted a vision with the required order and structure. Our research project had 'wheels,' a purpose, and a plan.

Throughout 2016 – 2017, we identified veteran teachers as those over forty years old with twenty years of teaching experience, who were still passionate about their work, who valued close relationships in formal and informal mentors, and who saw themselves as mentors for beginning and struggling colleagues. I interviewed teachers in Western Australia, and in late 2018, I travelled with Geoff and Christina to Pennsylvania and New York City to interview veteran teachers in both locations in the U.S.

Findings

Our research affirmed that: [1]

> *"...veteran teachers we interviewed remain passionate and enthusiastic in their work when they were actively engaged in collegial social networks."*

I am therefore confident that formal and informal mentoring relationships was a significant practice among these passionate veteran teachers. In addition, our veteran teachers:

> "...employed strategic adaptive processes within their social networks which resulted in them reporting high job satisfaction and mental and physical wellbeing. This ability to adapt anchored positive veteran teachers in a view of reality that contributed to their passion and altruism towards their teaching."

These findings confirmed my own experiences of feedback I received from mentors in my life, enabling me to 'reality check' when I was unsure of myself, and to heed advice on sound practices to maintain healthy and balanced work/life practices. I was also reminded of learning in my 30s, concerning altruistic habits from my early group counselling with Patrice Cook.

Sharing the Research

In March 2019, I was invited to report our findings in Melbourne to leaders of the Australian Institute for Teaching and School Leadership (AITSL), and in July, travelled to Majorca in Spain for an International Conference in Education to present our research with a colleague from Pennsylvania, Dr Denise Meister.[2] In the process of our visit to Pennsylvania, I had met Denise who had also published work from her own research with veteran teachers.

Another wonderful researcher, Dr Jenni Wolgemuth, [3] was also gracious in helping me get our work published in the U.S. I was now really encouraged to see how our research was supporting my passion for mentoring and the role of mentors in my life.

Further support for our research came in October 2019 from the governor of our state, Hon. Kim Beazley AC, who invited all the teachers we had interviewed in WA to a reception at Government House. This was a lovely gesture and such an encouragement for these wonderful exemplary teachers. It also gave us as researchers a chance to thank our research participants who, in turn, reported feeling honoured at the Governor's encouraging words of appreciation for their work.

Finally, in January 2020, I attended the Annual Conference of *The Qualitative Report* at The University of South Florida to present further on our research with veteran teachers. As always, I was able to expound my views that mentoring was a common thread throughout all our research findings.

Sharing our Research More Widely

I re-married in 2019, and as my wife, Sonja read drafts of the manuscript for my story, she noted my working career was generally characterised by mentors setting expectations for me, and then allowing me to 'get on with the job.' Further, as he read drafts of my story, my brother Rosco pointed out that a great deal of my childhood and teenage learning had been experiential in nature and content.

Upon further reflection I realised this was generally true and thus a further motivation for promoting mentors, as I appreciate it was the commitment of these men and women in my life that was so important to my success.

This acknowledgment goes back to my childhood, where I experienced community in Ferguson as a group of people demonstrated by their actions that they were committed to maintaining the welfare of one another. Thus, community as I experienced it, was based upon close relationships that included:

- Teaching one another.
- Sharing ideas and equipment.
- Working with and for one another.
- Celebrating common community goals and events.
- Celebrating births and mourning death and loss, and,
- Attending a small local church where they honoured God.

This was a rich incubation for me, especially since I believe that I was blessed as a child with a sensitive and enquiring spirit. At this point, I harken back to behaviours outlined by Pete Walker, [4] especially as we respond to shame. Walker notes these are positive behaviours we adopt in dealing with shame, and he labels them as: Fight, Flight, Freeze or Fawn (the Four F's). I have represented these criteria in Table 2 below:

Table 2. Positive Characteristics of the Four F's

Fight	*Flight*	*Freeze*	*Fawn*
Assertiveness	Disengagement	Acute awareness	Love & service
Boundaries	Heathy retreat	Mindfulness	Compromise
Courage	Industriousness	Poised readiness	Listening
Moxie	Know-how	Peace	Fairness
Leadership	Perseverance	Presence	Peacemaking

As you scan this table you should be able to identify characteristics that most fit your adult profile. For example, most of my traits are in the Flight and Fawn column. In other words, during my adult life as I have worked through shame issues, I have often *disengaged, retreated, persevered and worked hard* (The Flight Behaviour). I also identify with *love and service, compromise, listening, being fair and peacemaking* (The Fawn Behaviour). I do not claim, however, to be totally successful in these endeavours. In summary, I consider Flight and Fawn, as those traits that most typically represent my ongoing coping behaviour.

With respect to the traits of Flight and Fawn, I believe this is what Bill Hybells [5] identifies as 'Holy discontent,' whereby adult learners identified by Waldinger, seek to "develop (and serve) throughout their whole adult life. It grieves me to hear of people on their death bed asking if their life 'meant anything.' I also believe 'retirement' is highly overrated, as is working until we are exhausted and 'worn out.' Much better to stay engaged in meaningful work, as long as we are able, especially if it is work that entails sharing our wisdom and experience in mentoring relationships. Clearly volunteer work is a key to healthy growth and healthy relationships for 'seniors,' whatever the term, 'senior' means.

The research project led me into a world of engagement and satisfaction that I could not have imagined. It was fulfilling mentally and socially, and inspired me to share what I have learned on a wider scale. Let me explain further.

Mentoring is no Place for Lone Wolves

On a personal level, I believe I have made the case for the agency and efficacy of mentoring as a way of establishing and maintaining:

- Supportive relationships for personal, emotional, cognitive and psychological growth

- Imparting knowledge, providing support, and offering guidance to protégés

- Personal and professional growth of protégés

- Spiritual growth and understanding by mentors and protégés

The question I still wrestle with is:

Are these criteria relevant at the macro or societal level?

Australian social researcher, Hugh Mackay [6] reflects on the social changes of the 1990s, and the breakdown of social cohesion in the country. He suggests seven main causes of this breakdown and calls us; "back to the tribe," to renew communities of harmony and cooperation in our country. When we consider the benefits of mentoring relationships, Mackay's thinking is sobering. I have paraphrased his seven causes as follows:

1. The struggle over gender roles and potential *adversarial relationships* between the sexes.

2. A rising divorcee rate that has *scattered the herd.*

3. The 1970s and 1980s focus upon personal development that has led to an *obsession with personal gratification to the exclusion of social cohesion.*

4. Multiculturalism and a focus on *diversity rather than unity.*

5. Politics of economics to the *exclusion of social justice and human values.*

6. IT and data transfer confused with communication; thus, *personal relationships have suffered accordingly.*

7. Technology has *fragmented the herd.* (Italics all mine)

Mackay adds:

> *"History suggests that it is virtually an axiom
> on human nature that, when the tribal sense is in
> decline, the moral sense is similarly threatened."*

Bearing in mind I have paraphrased Mackay, I stand by my assertion that the focus of my definition of mentoring stands in stark contrast to Mackay's "mind and mood" of Australians in the 1990s. I am in no way suggesting that mentoring is the panacea for our nation, but I stridently suggest that mentoring relationships offer some way "back to the tribe." If we consider the outcomes of mentoring from research, it is evident that they are about harmony and generosity towards one another, rather than disconnection and alienation. From my own research I prosecute this case further.

An International Perspective of Informal Mentoring

After working closely since 2015 in research into the role of veteran teachers as mentors, I invited Geoff and Christina and colleagues Jenni and Rachel in the U.S. and another colleague, Vicki Thorpe in New Zealand, to share their own experiences of collegiality in their work. [7] In conversations with all five colleagues, I elaborated upon collegiality as our way in academia, of referring to informal mentoring or collaborative relationships.

In the course of these discussions, we agreed it was becoming tougher to work collaboratively in the face of isolation, and an increasing demand for conformity and adherence to rules in our workplaces. I asked each person to share their experiences of connectedness and community in their research, including strategies they adopted for confronting isolation and neo-liberal challenges that we encounter in our research endeavours. In her submission Jenni noted:

> *"We suggest a sharing about community and care that tentacles across our individual reflections, but does not insist on consensus or stable definitions. This is the kind of (qualitative) research community I crave, an entangled community that stays with*

269

troubles (Haraway, 2016) of ideology and identity in neoliberal contexts, even as it pulses with care, creativity, and risk" (p. 4).

Jenni's point was that we don't need consensus of ideas to be part of a collaborative and caring community, yet we can still tackle contentious ideas and issues, thus learning from, and teaching one another in the process. Christina submitted that:

> *"I have felt lonely and overwhelmed in my research endeavours and often fearful of asking for help. Developing a research community with like-minded colleagues, Geoffrey and Peter, has profoundly affected me both personally and professionally. I have gained a much-needed safe place to belong. My community provides me with friendship, mentoring, and meaningful discussions to learn and think about possibilities"* (p. 5).

Christina's summary aligns perfectly with my passion for scholars working in mentoring relationships. In reference to his early teaching Geoff notes:

> *"Our collaborative endeavours were underpinned by trust in our disparate abilities and we in turn were trusted by our school management that what we did was in our students' best interests"* (p. 5). *I draw inspiration from our common purpose, unique skill-sets and shared communion based upon openness, trust and mutual respect. Each of us brings unique insights to our research where the whole is greater than the sum of its parts"* (p.6).

Geoff was recalling fond memories of past collaborative work that was fostered by school management. Sharing from her experiences in New Zealand Vicki notes:

> *"Previously my colleagues and I met several times a day working and teaching in specialised curriculum education classrooms. We rarely see each other now… Routinely I see no one, only to discover a colleague with whom I exchanged emails was in the building too. I am pedagogically isolated and professional wounded"* (p. 7).

Clearly, in terms of collegiality and anything close to mentoring relationships, Vicki's experiences with like-minded peers, are far from ideal. Finally, in reference to her current workload as an academic Rachel declares:

> *"This myriad of neoliberal-related expectations translates to emotional and psychological pressures to meet outcomes that are meaningless in relation to the work we are doing. This pressure is compounded when some administrators use dominant and aggressive behaviours to generate performance outcomes from their staff. The aggregate impact of neoliberal expectations causes suffering. I have cherished compassionate colleagues and communities for processing, managing, and emotionally regulating so that I could remain engaged in my work"* (p. 8).

Rachel's experience is sad, to say the least, especially when we consider community expectations of university teaching and research are still encompassed in the belief that universities are places where initiative, collaboration and creativity are fostered and valued.

My own experience over the last twenty years in university teaching and research, and those of my colleagues in Australia, the U.S. and New Zealand, paint a bleak picture. As lead author of this part of our research I conclude by noting:

> *"Each contributor to this article identified neo-liberal tendencies that are characterised internationally by managerialism, lack of support and isolation as major challenges they face in their work"* (p. 9).

Indeed, as I reflect upon my fifty years of formal working life, I have seen a significant shift from a more relaxed and generous lifestyle and working conditions in Australia, to the frenetic and impersonal environment of the Twenty-first Century.

Reflections

When we consider MacKay's analysis of Australia in the 1990s, it is not surprising that, as the five researchers I contacted assert, from a macro perspective, there has been a noticeable shift away from the cooperative relationships in organisations, to suspicion and, in some cases bullying staff, by administrators. But let us not despair. At a micro level our research indicates that informal mentoring relationships sustain us and help us feel connected and belonging in our local communities. As individuals we can all contribute to this community sense of belonging, connectedness and meaning.

I maintain that, if the empowering traits of mentoring were to be practiced generously in our schools and universities in Australia, this would go a long way to combatting many of the wicked problems we are facing in our country. After all, if students graduating from our High Schools and tertiary institutions are taught and inspired by staff who are protégés to committed mentors, this example would inspire our Youth to embrace a more relaxed and gracious attitude towards themselves and one another.

On a personal note, I celebrate the fact that I am bold enough to proffer the afore-mentioned reflections from my engagement with generous colleagues in teaching and research. I am still the boy from a farming background who (eventually) became a man, and who was blessed with a spirit of seeking to know and understand. I credit all the people I list at the beginning of my story for caring enough about me to counsel and teach me. I am also grateful for all the chances I had to travel and to learn in other cultures.

I was compelled to write my story in the hope I could encourage boys and men to boldly examine their own lives, for I am convinced they will be blessed as they do. I am grateful for all of life's lessons, including the opportunity for formal study and the consequences thereof. Moving on towards considering; "Where to from here?"

Chapter 27

The Practice of an Examined Life

One of the findings reported by Waldinger from the Harvard University longitudinal lifestyle study was that passionate and enthusiastic adults maintained a love of learning in their senior years. [1] As one in his 'seventies,' I was profoundly encouraged when I read that. I learned and I understood. I was also inspired to direct my understanding towards becoming a person of influence and mentor, and to constantly examine my behaviour in a disciplined reflective process.

Reflective Practice

In an honest endeavour to support any person seeking to understand their own behaviour, especially as it may be impinging upon their lives, I developed **LUBE**, the four-step process described in chapter two:

- **Learning** about shame

- **Understanding** the impacts of shame

- **Being** intentional and confident in adopting new ways of 'being'

- **Examining**, or 'reflecting upon' people and events that have influenced us, including ways in which we have inspired and mentored others.

It took me years of learning through failure to arrive at this reflective process although I am encouraged that Sheila Heen reminds us that "there is no pain free learning environment". Hugh Mackay [2] purports an interesting process for experiencing what he refers to as *"freedom from entrapment in our lives,"* and suggests three great therapies of everyday life:

- *to listen attentively,*
- *to apologise sincerely, and,*
- *to forgive generously.*

He then adds:

- *...to develop a keen sense of humour."*

I concur with all four habits, including the fourth. We can't take ourselves too seriously. I learned that as an eighteen-year-old on a shearing team when I was locked in a wool press and naively submitted to having my balls painted blue. Additional reflective strategies I know that work for me in combatting the invasion of shame include:

- regular exercise,

- checking with my mentors,

- rest,

- music,

- mentoring (where I am being 100% present to another, or at least as close to 100% as I can!),

- caring for the other,

- gazing at the stars on a clear night in the outback, especially around a campfire,

- being in nature,

- skiing,

- being close to Uluru (so special), and,

- being anywhere, or in the moment, when I let awe and wonder embrace me.

A wonderful book, packed with ideas that will help you find other strategies is *Phosphorescence,* by an author and journalist I respect and admire, Julia Baird. [3] Baird's work is inspiring and awesome soul food. It is a book I highly recommend. Speaking of soul food, I also recommend as further strategies for combatting shame, drawn from some of the practices of mystics and contemplatives. Robert Ellsberg [4] cites three such contemplatives, including Thomas Merton's defines of contemplation as:

> *"The highest expression of intellectual and spiritual life. It is spiritual wonder. It is spontaneous awe. It is gratitude for life, for awareness and for being"* (p. 10).

Catherine De Hueck Doherty believes what she calls 'desert silence' is an essential practice for us to be fully present to others. She notes:

> *"If we are to be always available, not only physically, but by empathy, sympathy, friendship,*

understanding and boundless caritas, we need silence" (p. 78).

Howard Thurman claims 'being human' implies:

> *"...the individual must have a sense of kinship to life that transcends and goes beyond the immediate kinship of family. To be a human being, then, is to be essentially alive in a living world"* (pp. 95-96).

I know all these strategies well and I attempt to use them often. However, I still regularly, fall for the old shame attacks.

Identifying Mentors

With respect to seeking mentors in our lives, John Maxwell [5] refers to what I understand is a ten-point check list we can adopt, in the process of:

> *"...finding the right people for your journey."*

I paraphrase the list and advocate seeking people who:

1. Are known for their integrity. Their "yes" means, yes, and "no" is a legitimate answer.

2. Nurture other people.

3. Have faith in people.

4. Listen carefully.

5. Understand people.

6. Encourage others to become more than they are.

7. Walk with others to help them find their own way.

8. Connect easily with people.

9. Empower others.

10. Develop others' gifts.

Mackay speaks of leading a "good life." I don't concur with the idea of being measured against the criterion 'good.' What is the measure of being 'good enough in life?' To whom, or what, do we compare ourselves for measuring goodness? I prefer to look at actions that take us out of our own navel gazing towards altruism. This relates to exercising Mackay's "therapies," including his suggestions of:

1. *behaving respectfully towards everyone,*

2. *tuning into the needs of people in our community and beyond,*

3. *becoming alert to disadvantages and unfairness in families, the workplace, the neighbourhood and the wider society, and,*

4. *showing concern for others' wellbeing.*

My Three Themes

In my prelude, I identified three themes for my story. Let's review them here.

Firstly, I set out to share impacts of shame throughout my life including, failure, loss, fury, and remorse. I noted that, in varying degrees, we are all impacted by shame in our lives. We all stray into the swampland of shame, and we need support in identifying and exiting our swamp. I also stress that 'failure' is not an end in itself. Rather it is an opportunity to review and to learn. Some of my best learning has emanated from failure.

I also acknowledge that some of my best learning is by observation and experiencing, in effect, 'giving it a go.' As I reflect upon my life, I realise I learned so much from watching, often in fear of my dad, and at other times, in safety and encouragement from others. I also stridently believe that real men seeking to be leaders in their families, workplace and community, constantly go through a process of self-examination, all in the endeavour to become 'better men,' and to sharpen every level of their intelligence.

Second, there are numerous people and events in my life that contributed to my intellectual, social, emotional and spiritual growth. I believe it is edifying, wherever possible, to identify those people and to take time to thank them for their impact upon your life. Similarly, special events always come to mind as I examine my life and consider numerous ways for exiting the swamp of shame. These disciplines of reflective practice through self-examination ultimately led me to healing, and to the authentic life I now embrace.

Finally, I acknowledge that significant achievements in my life have been due to mentors who gave me honest feedback and guidance. Mentors have been key in guiding me out of my swampland of shame towards a life of fulfillment and service in my community.

I began my story with the analogy of feeling like I was consigned to lane eight as a 'has been,' stuck in the swampland of shame. I could easily have stayed there, but by the grace of God, and all those along the way who reached out to me with straight feedback, teaching and counsel, I now identify with Kieran, the

'Champion from Lane Eight.' I sincerely hope this has helped you also believe in yourself as a champion.

As I write I hope you will be motivated, encouraged and emboldened to reach out to elders who have blessed and encouraged you. It will mean the world to them, but don't expect them to respond immediately with enthusiasm. You will need to establish a degree of agency with them first. Some will reject you outright. Don't be discouraged by that. Just move on, but don't give up. The time and effort are worthwhile and rich beyond your wildest expectations.

Summary

Overall, I submit there is ample evidence to defend the proposition that having mentors in our lives to teach and counsel us, is an invaluable tool for combatting shame, albeit that this combat is an ongoing battle in our lives. The main objective is to learn how to identify shame and to apply the most appropriate strategies for defeating the intrusive thoughts accordingly. The incident below is an example of my ongoing battle, at age seventy-seven, with chasing shame from my thoughts:

- As I was writing my story in September 2021, my wife began experiencing extreme pain from a protruding disc at L4 vertebrae. The disc was pinching her sciatic nerve to her left foot, resulting in no feeling in her foot, accompanied by intense and continuous pain. On a particular Sunday morning, when the pain was extreme, I sent a text to Bruce, my key mentor and friend, asking for advice re pain killers for my wife. Bruce didn't reply. I didn't try again.

- Eventually, we called an ambulance, and my wife was taken to hospital overnight where she received pain killers and short-term relief. She was discharged next day for an MRI and referral to a surgeon. All week I felt sick about Bruce not responding, believing he had ignored me.

- On the following Saturday at our weekly coffee, I workshopped with Bruce about the text. It transpired he didn't receive it. It was still in my phone! Possibly, in my distress, I neglected to press 'send.' Bruce assured me he would have responded in a heartbeat. And I know that is true. We share mutual love and care for one another, and deep down I always know that.

- What happened that caused me to momentarily lose faith in our relationship? We both agreed I was so stressed that I allowed the *"You are not worthy"* message to convict me. We have been close mates since 1984, and we have been through so much together. Yet, after all those years of mutual support and care for one another, my shame beat me in a moment of need.

- Bruce suggested: *"You need to include this event in your story."*

Shame is very hard to combat so don't let it get you down when it has an occasional win.

There is a beautiful song written for Clint Eastwood's character in the movie, *The Mule*, in which Clint plays an old man duped into carrying drugs. As a result of his actions and past lived experiences, Clint's character, Earl Stone, is wracked with guilt and shame, plus his ongoing reality of growing older. Thus, the words of the soundtrack:

"Don't let the old man in."

Earl adopted habits to keep himself *thinking young and useful* (italics mine*)*, including keeping the thinking of an old man out. We can do that with shame. Keep the shame thinking out. You are not all the things shame says you are. I can guarantee that.

Finally, in my story to date, I have shared my intellectual, social and emotional 'growth points,' including how I understand these concepts have arisen from my knowledge, understanding, being intentional in subsequent learning, and maintaining a discipline of examining my behaviour and beliefs as they impinge upon my future behaviour. In the final section of my story, I share my spiritual growth and development which is of paramount importance to me.

PART SEVEN

How God Intervened

Chapter 28

By the Grace of God

From my earliest memories of stories by mum, my awe of Father Cunningham and the love of the nuns at Bushy School, I formed an impression of a strong yet gentle God. A God surrounded by mystery, but benign. A God 'up there,' and impersonal. A God to be feared and revered. A God who would forgive, although with conditions (penance) that as I grew older made little sense. I had limited knowledge about a supreme God, and I had no understanding of a personal God.

Further, my years at St Ildephonsis College in New Norcia reinforced the impossibility of being able to please God, so why try? Like many Catholics, I 'retired' from my faith stance at my earliest opportunity, in fact immediately I escaped my parents' authority. My beliefs were of a child's understanding, which did not stand the prosecution of an angry teenage mind. This factor was compounded by cruel and bullying treatment by some of my Marist teachers, all wearing habits and large crosses, and by the alcoholic priest who replaced Father Cunningham.

I was hearing words from these 'people of God,' but I was not seeing the walk of faith, character, humility, service, love and gentle strength I experienced from Father Cunningham's life, or the nuns at Dardanup Convent and my mother. I had a childish notion of God but a unique experience of love, acceptance and warmth in his name through Father Cunningham, Keith and Sheila Butcher and my mum. I *knew* these people whereas I only knew *about* God. This was my faith reality as I ran away from home at age sixteen.

My Spiritual Awakening

The major reason for my increased self-confidence occurred when working with Ross and Jeff in the early weeks of arriving at my cousin's farm in Dalwallinu. It stemmed from a transformative time of amazing grace and happened thus. It was a cold June winter's night, around 9.30 pm. I was driving a Fordson Major tractor pulling an 18-disc plough to prepare land for seeding wheat.

I was sitting on an open tractor with no real protection from the elements. The tractor's headlights gave just enough light to see the furrow to follow and another shining back on the plough only covered the plough itself. It was dark and I admit I was a tad scared and jumpy. All I could hear was the tractor and an occasional loud bang as the plough uprooted a stump from the ground. I wasn't thinking about anything specifically at the time but I became aware of a quiet presence and voice saying to me:

> *"You are OK. This is not all there is for you. There will be better for you. I love you and you are OK."*

As you might imagine, at age sixteen, this was a profound experience I have never forgotten. It filled me with awe and peace. Yet I asked myself the following question:

"How can this be? I have little education. I am far from home and family. I have nothing and I am nothing."

Fortunately, I had enough rudimentary knowledge at that time to believe I was receiving a message from God. My confidence in this belief includes the 'rescue moment' of Father Cunningham in church where I felt the phenomenal security of protection and affirmation from him. Both these experiences were early landmarks in my journey of advocacy concerning the power of mentoring relationships in my life.

In addition to all I learned on the farm with Ross and Jeff that year, God called me on that cold night in June, 1961 to assure me that I was OK, and that I would be OK in the future. I later understood that, in God's perspective, I was not useless, no good, or unworthy. This was a massive emotional and spiritual growth year for me. My physical growth became obvious to those who knew me but I never told anyone about the incident on the tractor, but neither have I ever forgotten it. As a result of this intellectual, spiritual and emotionally charged transformation on the tractor, I understood without doubt that God was calling me, just as the apostle Paul wrote to people of the church in Corinth, nearly two thousand years before I was born:

"...think of what you were when you were called" (1 Cor. 1: 26a).

Before I heard this gentle but firm call from God, I believed I was 'no good' and that all the previous phrases I heard contributing to my shame, were true. Rather, I was now beginning a whole new journey of hope that would ultimately lead me to healing, piece by piece.

It was true that I had little education and seemingly bleak prospects, but I wasn't consciously thinking too much about my future at this point. I since learned that God never forgets us and he understands exactly who we are, including the gifts we have to share in our lives. I also appreciated God has given me gifts and, as I am prepared to offer them throughout my life, he will multiply them for the good of so many other people. It is not unlike the stories of Jesus feeding crowds of people with little food available. As the disciples trusted Jesus and began handing out fish and bread, Jesus made sure there was enough to go around, including plenty of leftovers.

"Experience" Alone Will Not Last

In retrospect, I am amazed that my 'tractor experience,' may have only lasted until next morning. I honestly do not recall any further growth in my spiritual understanding, or any time I actively sought counsel on what I experienced. What is even more profound is that by the time I returned to the farm for my parents to travel, I was already in the process of discarding all I had learned about God in my Catholic faith. Clearly, I needed facts and knowledge to accompany my emotional experience.

Lake St Clare

Fast forward through my spiritual desert in my university years to age twenty-six, and the incident by Lake St Clare in Tasmania. The time of quiet and reflection, early one morning sitting on a log at lakeside, left me in no doubt that this was another call of love from God. It was not exactly like my tractor experience at age sixteen, but it filled me with a 'supernatural' sense of quiet, comfort, peace and love. A belief I was OK, and that I was where I was meant to be, for now.

My main reflection here is based upon a story from First Century Palestine about a man who had two sons. The youngest son, in effect said to his father:

"I can't wait for you to die, so I would appreciate my share of your inheritance now."

The father acceded to his son's wish and the son travelled off to cities where he eventually squandered all his fortune, including losing all the 'friends' he made with his money. He was reduced to hiring himself out to pig farmers where he ate the corn fed to pigs. Finally, he knew he needed to return to his father, believing his father would expect him to work as a hired hand. Instead, when his father saw his son approaching the village, he ran out to meet him and organized a huge celebration to acknowledge his son's return.

This story has agency for me because I realized I had basically ignored God since Father Cunningham's influence and my transformative experience, age sixteen on a tractor. God had been looking out for me during my tumultuous university years, and he spoke softly to me when I was quiet and listening by a lake in the early morning. As a result, I claim my most consistent and reliable way of dealing with whispers of shame is simply to place my faith back in God and to listen always to his quiet, still voice. I wish this for every person who reads my story.

Lake Tukarnah

It was while I was walking alone along the shores of Lake Tukarnah in the South Island of New Zealand that I experienced my third beautiful blessing from God. The first age sixteen, the second age twenty-six and now the third age twenty-eight. The lake shore was made up of small pebbles with small waves about three centimetres high and ten centimetres apart, gently lapping the shore.

As I walked and listened to the sound of 'waves' breaking on the lake shore, I had the same experience of deep peace and joy I experienced on the log at Lake St Claire the previous summer. This continued for quite a while as I walked, to the point where I can still 'feel' that sensation as I write about it. It was a beautiful day and so peaceful walking alone along the shore. By the end of 1974, these three experiences would explode into transformative significance.

Despite these three incredible experiences, at the time I departed Australia for Canada in 1973, I was still lost in terms of my faith. I am humbled now by the fact that God never abandoned me, especially as I had ignored the unique calls, he made to draw me into his permanent love and relationship.

Edmonton Retreat

Once I arrived in Edmonton and settled into accommodation at St Joseph's Catholic College on the University of Alberta campus, clear memories of Father Cunningham's love and going to Mass in Dardanup drew me to explore once more the reality of God in my life. I figured that men like Father Cunningham were not easily fooled and that if he believed in God and dedicated his life to serving him, there must be something there to understand. As I began studying the life of Jesus, during my formal studies at university, I loved the apostle, Peter, but not just because of the name. For example, consider the following with me:

- Peter and his crew are out on the lake and they saw Jesus, walking on the water towards them. Peter was an experienced fisherman, and he knew very well fish are built to swim and he was built to stay in the boat and catch them. So, upon an invitation from Jesus, Peter stepped out of the boat and began to walk towards him. On the water where fish swim. How crazy was that. Then he figured:

"Holy smoke, I am not built for this!"

And he began to sink. Surprise, surprise. You may know the rest. Jesus said:

"Mate, your faith would have kept you going."

Imagine the talk around the campfire with his mates later that evening. Peter 'just did it,' and he always had that experience to reflect upon in later years. We sometimes need to step out of the boat to really experience the fullness of life.

A Mentor's Life-Changing Advice

One afternoon, as I walked into the dining room of the college, I was greeted by a man with wild long hair, a beard, and the softest blue eyes I had ever seen. He stood up as I entered and said:

"Hello, my name is Terry."

We exchanged introductions and the basics such as:

"What are you doing here? Where do you live, etc.?"

It transpired that for thirteen years, Terry had been a missionary priest in the Philippines where he had been commissioning men and women in remote villages to lead Mass and give communion to their people. Terry saw this as multiplying his effectiveness, but some in the church hierarchy didn't agree, therefore he was 'called home' to Canada. I thought Terry's idea was great strategic thinking. I mentioned to Terry that I had seen a poster in the college chapel indicating a Retreat was planned for a weekend towards the end of November, to which he replied:

> *"I know, I just put it there. I am running the*
> *Retreat."*

I signed up. Subsequently, I saw quite a bit of Terry over the next few weeks. Finally, on the Friday night of the Retreat, I travelled with Terry to the location. Part of the process of a Catholic Group Retreat is to gather in a large group for direction by the Retreat Leader, Terry in this case, to hear a reflection on Scripture and suggested direction for each person to go away and ponder the meaning and implication for their life.

After Terry's introduction, I met a nun, Sister Catherine, and asked if I could speak with her. She graciously agreed and I spent ages sharing with her my frustrations with the Catholic Church with the exception of the amazing Father Cunningham and some of the nuns in Dardanup. I mentioned to her that, apart from these examples, I could see no point in the church.

However, I was convicted that, if men like Father Cunningham and Terry, believed in God, there had to be some evidence for that. I concluded that not all these quality men and women could be deluded or wrong. I also recognised that I still had a child's understanding of God, and that once I left school, this knowledge and understanding of God didn't mean anything to me.

As a skilled mentor, Sister Catherine listened patiently to me, and then she offered counsel that was as wise as any I have received. She looked at me and said:

"Peter, if you want to know if God is real, ask him to show you in a way you will understand. But don't ask the question, if you are not serious about the answer."

I was serious. And I wanted to know. For the rest of the weekend, I listened to all Terry had to say and I went away simply wondering and asking God how it could all be true and what sense it made to my life. The final Mass for the Retreat came and just before communion, the major focus in a Catholic Mass, I asked God to show me if he was real. Just as communion began, I became aware of a genuine sense of being washed clean with waves of warm water, almost exactly the size and distance apart as the gentle waves at Lake Tukarnah in New Zealand. Here I was in Edmonton, halfway around the world from Lake Tukarnah, and I was feeling those warm waves washing me clean along with a gentle voice saying something like:

"I love you. You are not useless; you are my child."

I can't remember the exact words now, but I will never forget the undeniable experience. Almost the same words as the night on the tractor in Dalwallinu and the same unbelievable peace and joy I felt at Lake St Claire and Lake Tukarnah. At the most sacred time that I would understand in a Catholic's life, when we receive communion, God chose to visit this experience on me. Again. At that moment I no longer doubted that God is real, that he is alive, and that he is personal to me.

I didn't make it to communion because I was just overwhelmed with joy and peace, probably silently weeping tears of joy too. I know for days later I would go to the chapel to pray, and only tears of joy would flow from me. God had been calling me. He had forgiven my transgressions and faults. He loved me. He had washed me clean on the inside and he was ready for a long-term relationship with me.

I shared my experience with Sister Catherine, Terry and others I met over the next few weeks. I still remember reading for the very first time Paul's epistle to the Roman church. In this letter we are assured of our place in the kingdom God has prepared for us. It is only by faith we are assured of this truth. There is nothing we can do to earn God's love, or to be 'good enough' to find our place with God.

Rather, we are justified before God because Jesus paid the price of our behaviour that would never be tolerated in heaven. And so much more. All my prior emptiness was making sense and I felt healed and ready for a new life as a follower of Jesus. Going back to my near-death time in Borneo, I now know the difference between knowing *about God* and *knowing* God.

Responding to Grace

Why was I searching for answers at the Retreat? Firstly, my two faith heroes as a child were my mum and Father Cunningham, both of whom I loved and trusted, and saw in their lives what knowing God meant to them. I figured if God was real to them, there was the possibility he could also be real for me. As I study the Scriptures now, I note the Apostle Paul once encouraged his young disciple Timothy to:

> *"...continue in what you have learned because you know those from whom you have learned it"* (2 Tim. 3: 4).

Here Paul is assuring Timothy that he can continue, in confidence, in his search to know God in a deeper way because of his trust in, and love for, his grandmother and his own mother, both of whom first taught him about God. I knew I benefitted similarly from my relationship with my own mother and Father Cunningham, including their teaching and their unconditional love for me.

Secondly, I appreciate the importance of heroes, especially since I have learned numerous things from some of my own faith heroes. Heroes influenced my desire to know God, but it was up to me to embrace the unconditional love and acceptance that God offers. We cannot live a risk-free life, nor can we be sure of all the facts, but we acquire enough evidence to have confidence in what we know, to trust in what we don't yet know.

This is the enticing mystery of faith, for me at least. It is impossible to align all the facts before we make a decision. At some point we simply make decisions based upon the facts at hand, and upon our faith from past experience. We then step out of the boat. Further, my life changing experience at a Retreat outside Edmonton, was based in part upon best advice ever by a mentor, Sister Catherine:

> *"If you want to know if God is real, ask him to show you in a way you will understand. But don't ask the question if you are not serious about the answer."*

Following the Edmonton retreat experience, I was convicted with every fibre of my body, that God is real and that we are spirit beings in a physical body. I would go to pray and I would just weep soft tears of joy and healing. I was now convinced of God in my life, his love for me and acceptance of me as his child. I was blessed to have Terry to consult and Sister Catherine and her community at *Stillpoint,* which was a house of prayer that I visited weekly, to pray with the community to strengthen my faith journey.

I devoured books on Christian living and I began an exhaustive study of the Bible. I experienced other amazing one to three-day Retreat's under Sister Catherine's leadership, and I discovered a deep knowledge and understanding of God, and my relationship with him. Terry and Catherine were highly influential mentors for me during this time by teaching and counselling me along the infant stages of my faith journey.

One further insight, apropos my extraordinary spiritual experiences. There is a story of Jesus being followed by a large crowd, when a woman who had suffered bleeding for twelve years, reached out and touched the hem of Jesus' coat, believing as she did, that she would be healed. We are informed by the eyewitness to this event that, as the woman touched Jesus' coat:

> *"Immediately, her bleeding stopped and **she felt in her body** that she was freed from her suffering (Mk. 5: 29).* (bold mine)

Every time I reflect upon this story, I am filled with awe that God would bless me in a similar way. On all four occasions when I know it was God calling me, *I felt it in my body.* For me, this is amazing grace.

Alberta: Cowboys as Mentors

Before semester one of my second year of Graduate Studies commenced, I had time free and decided to drive out to Pioneer Camp in Sundre for a weekend camp of riding with a group of cowboys. We rode around the foothills of the Rockies, through creeks and amazing mountain meadows where flowers and shrubs were just beginning to turn yellow and red at the end of summer. There was always the need to be aware of grumpy bears and hungry cougars.

Being in the company of these highly competent and tough men was as good as it gets. In my studies at university, I was growing in confidence academically and here on camp I was blown away by the informal mentoring, watching and listening to these awesome and humble Canadians. Sleeping out and watching the dancing Northern Lights at night, and singing around a camp fire at night was where I wanted to be.

These men, who seemed without fear and capable of surviving everything they encountered, sat around the campfire on the two nights we were out and sang songs of praise to God, as if they meant it. I was in my infancy in my faith journey, so seeing these men sitting around joyfully singing hymns and choruses of praise to God, was another confirmation I had not been confused and deluded by my heart and soul experiences of God. God was real to these men too.

Walking into Deeper Faith

By now, I had a firm understanding of the calling I felt to get out of Perth and away to a totally different place to learn more about the world and a purpose God had for me. I was gradually slowing down. I saw the folly of my belief I had to be the 'life of the party,' in order to be accepted in a group. I also appreciated my significant motivation to continue studying to prove to my dad that I was not incompetent. I needed to confront and let these false beliefs go. Then I could celebrate my desire to serve God and our community.

I continued to devour books on Christian lifestyle and to study the Scriptures. Terry still helped me a great deal in this, as did another priest Leo Floyd, whose church we were attending. In addition, I had rich contacts with fellow students and professors at university that inspired and encouraged me.

Nova Scotia: "Cursillo"

I joined a Catholic Church in Wolfville and, through the church, I learned of a new movement in the Catholic Church called Cursillo, pronounced 'Cur see o', a Spanish word meaning 'short course in Christianity.' I jumped at the opportunity to do the coiurse and loved the weekend. It was packed with men telling their own faith stories, lots of jokes being told, lots of singing and great conversations. There were two priests and two lay men running the Cursillo. However, on the last afternoon, all the windows to the Retreat Centre were blocked with paper; we had no idea why.

Towards the end of our time on that Sunday afternoon, we were sitting at tables in small groups when we heard people singing a theme song we had learned for the weekend. Then the door burst open and people came in singing our song and surrounding us at our tables. We were all weeping with joy by then. It was such a magnificent experience, and the hymn *How Great Thou Art* still brings me to tears. I have asked that it be sung at my funeral.

Since ours was the first Cursillo in Nova Scotia, people from as far away as Ontario came to be this 'invasion' of others who had completed their own Cusillo. This was such a moving time for those of us who had just completed our own Cursillo. It was another boost to my faith journey, and every weeknight, as a follow up, I met with a group of men to pray and support one another. Faith for me then was, and still is, about community, mentors and deep friendships.

Miracles in the US

I have referred to how God has blessed me, including my moment at sixteen, on a tractor in Dalwallinu. At that time, I believed I was a nobody. I was wrong. We are all born in the image of God; therefore, we are never a nobody. I refer to my twelve months contract working with Dr Weaver as an example of blessing undeserved, or, as previously noted by Malcolm Gladwell, being in the right place at the right time. I prefer the blessing option.

A further blessing was seeing President Jimmy Carter land on the lawn of the White House. It was a moment of wonder and awe, and another time when I remembered clearly back to that cold June night when I was 16. How could I have planned to be standing in the East Wing of White House? You recall this that God whispered to me on the tractor:

"This is not all there is for you."

I believe that with every fibre in my body that He was delivering on his promise.

During my time in the U.S., I also experienced spiritual tension. On the one hand, knowing my place in God's Kingdom, and on the other, believing I was as good as the 'worldly existential narrative' said I was. It was only two years since my transformative experience of grace in Edmonton, and I needed to lean heavily upon that fact to remind myself that the existential narrative was not real. True, I was working with and meeting amazing people, but the pace and energy was frenetic. I knew I was caught up in a whirlwind that was not real to me; no time to pause, to reflect, to be still and to listen to what God might be saying to me.

The Reality of Spiritual Warfare

At the conclusion of my contract with the Community Education Centre, it was time to 'go home.' It was during a layover in Auckland where I experienced a frightening and nasty experience.

I need to digress a little here and say when I left Perth five years previously, I was known as the 'life of the party' and a bit of a rebel. In my mind, when I left in July 1973, there was no need for or evidence of God in my life. Now it was the end of 1978, and I was a much more settled and a changed man with a deep understanding of the power of grace in my life. I knew I had been changed by grace, but I also knew I was the same person, if that makes sense.

Obviously, the devil believed I was changed because he attacked me big time that night in the motel. I awoke, at some time, feeling like a huge weight was on my chest and I was being choked. I also saw a definite shape at the end of the bed, and my body went freezing cold. I woke with this feeling of total dread, cold and being smothered. It was as powerful as my experience of being washed clean in warm water at the Retreat in Edmonton, five years previously. For me, this was just another confirmation of how powerful it is to be called by God and to be protected accordingly. As the apostle John says:

> "...the one who is in us is greater than the one
> who is in the world" (1 Jn. 4: 4).

In other words, as followers of Jesus we can expect attacks from the evil one at any opportunity, but greater is the grace we are given by God to combat this evil. I began to grasp the power of grace and the meta-narrative of my new-found faith in my story. I appreciate that God sometimes opens doors wide enough to drive a Mack truck through, yet I sometimes still want more evidence.

Marriage Breakdown

Following a major life-changing event such as a marriage breakdown, my journey from the swamp to purpose and vision was sometimes lonely and often sad. I never imagined, or planned, that my marriage would end. After all I have shared about how much I know God loves me, I found myself terrified to approach God as my Father for forgiveness, mercy and grace, all of which I knew was there for me. I just had to ask.

I found my way back to God by adopting an intentional practice of daily prayer that I still follow today. I was recommended a book, *Prayer: Experiencing awe and intimacy with God,* by Tim Keller, who shared his own way of renewing his prayer life. Each day he read one psalm and then kept a journal of how the content of the psalm spoke to him. I adopted this practice and I love it.

I now re-visit daily my own reflections of the psalms and I am blessed mightily as a result. I have gone through other books of the bible with the same practice of taking a chapter and recording my reflections and recommend this as a way of staying out of the swamp and, in my case, getting back into Lane Eight.

Camino

Part of my learned practice is habitual reflective thought, or from my Catholic background, 'examining my conscience,' Undertaking the Way of St Francis appealed to me as a brilliant opportunity to 'walk with God' as I contemplated my life so far. During my early teaching career at St Stephen's School, including times working in church-based ministry and pastoral care, I had numerous opportunities to sit with students and adults as they shared intimate thoughts and reflections about their lives. It was now time for me practice what I had recommended. I could never have imagined the benefits and blessings I was about to experience from an eight-hundred-and-ten-kilometre pilgrimage across northern Spain.

Grace and Guilt

Freedom from guilt comes from a profound Scripture that assures me/us:

> "...*your guilt is taken away and your sin is atoned for*" (Is. 6: 7b).

In other words, in all my human relationships, as guilt does its work and helps me take responsibility for my actions or behaviour that is wrong and hurtful, I can 'own up' and seek mercy and forgiveness. Exactly the same process takes place between me and God. The exception is I can count on God's promise to release me from the guilt I know I deserve, and to leave it alone. He has taken it away.

Corrie Ten Boom [1] says God flings our guilt into the deepest ocean and then puts up a 'No Fishing' sign. I love this analogy. Once I 'own up,' and seek forgiveness and mercy, guilt no longer has a purpose in my life. But, if I continue to hold on to guilt, it is an entrapment of shame and my own making.

If you made it this far in my story, I do pray you have been blessed accordingly. I would also love to hear from you, and your story. If you have faith questions, or you have felt abandoned, or 'burned' by the institutional church, I will spend all the time you need, to hear them and care for you.

Shalom

APPENDIX

This section contains tips and strategies for (1) developing and maintaining effective relationships between mentors and mentors and protégés, (2) recognising shame, and (3) combatting the impact of shame in our lives. It includes tips and strategies I find useful, and many more I have gleaned from the literature. The essential criterion that I consider bedrock to all the following suggestions is that we are absolutely clear about the difference between **guilt** and **shame**.

Guilt is an understanding we have breached standards of behaviour for which we accept accountability, and we know are unconscionable. Further, we acknowledge and accept our accountability as we are remorseful and, as we seek mercy and forgiveness accordingly, we rest assured our guilt is taken away (no longer held against us) and our behaviour is forgiven.

Shame is a false view of ourselves that regularly leaves us plagued by emotions such as unworthiness, sadness, incompetence, rejection, loneliness, despair, failure, inferiority, and being attacked, often unmercifully, by these and many similar emotions.

Part 1: Mentor/Mentor and Mentor/Protégé Relationships

The most practiced framework I use (unconsciously now) when I meet with my mate Bruce for our Saturday morning catchups is based upon the *See, Think, Wonder Visible Learning Strategy* developed by the Harvard Graduate School of Education. This involves:

- What **key things** have happened for you personally, in your family, at work, and spiritually, this week?

- What did you **think about** these things (i.e. believe, or judge)?

- In relation to the above, what are you **wondering**? Unsure of? Needing to talk about?

In this process, we aim to share the time, but if something really important is nominated, we allocate time accordingly. In order for this process to work we:

- Listen carefully to one another without judgment or jumping in with suggested solutions.

- Respond with ideas, suggestions, questions of clarification/ checking for understanding, and, encouragement and support.

- Offer counsel, only when asked.

- Commit to pray for one another, including, with respect to any important and ongoing issue, and, checking on one another during the week(s) following.

- Agree on confidentiality and being honest with one another.

This framework is the best we have identified and it works for us. However, any intentional process, similar to the one above, would work. In my view, valuing and being committed to the relationship, is the most important criterion to protect. A useful text I have accessed in adopting this approach is:

Kerry Patterson, Joseph Grenny, Ron McMillan & Al Swizzler. (2012). *Crucial conversations: Tools for talking when stakes are high.* (2nd ed.). NY: McGraw Hill.

Part 2: Recognizing Shame

Numerous, but not definitive signs of shame in our lives <u>may include</u>:

- Unaccountable weariness or exhaustion.

- Loss of appetite and healthy eating habits.

- Loss of fitness.

- Disinterest in hobbies, and activities that we normally enjoy.

- Distancing ourselves from friends/family.

- Sleep deprivation, or inability to fall asleep.

- Anxiety and lack of confidence in social situations.

- Risk aversion.

- Sensitivity to feedback – in relation to some areas of our behaviour.

- Negative view/belief in ourselves.

- Feeling we are being "attacked" when friends/family ask, or remind us of something.

- Knowing we are guilty, and refusing to admit and confront our action(s).

- Lethargy, and gradually withdrawing from people, events and activities that bring us joy, hope, and, good physical and mental health.

- Avoiding our spiritual "maintenance."

Feel free to add your own to this list. Then talk to your mentor about it.

Part 3: Combatting Shame

- My most important action is to sit with a psalm or passage(s) of Scripture I know, and to meditate accordingly i.e., listen to what God will say for you. Ask God. Open your heart to God.

- Raise the issue with your mentor.

- Act upon what you learn from the previous dot points.

- Release yourself from any grudge or blame of another(s). Let it go. Ban shame by forgiving. Don't let shame in or it will occupy all your head space, thus leaving no space for joy and wonder.

- In order to learn strategies for combatting shame, set SMART goals (Specific, Measurable, Achievable, Realistic, Timely), for learning these skills.

- Smile at your shame including its pathetic attempt to gain (temporary) control of your mind.

- Spend time in quiet, in nature, or just reading a book and relaxing.

- Give yourself "you time."

- Exercise in moderation, with the goal to relax and get your body moving.

- Manage your diet for balance and nutrition.

- If possible, take a nap during the day.

- Make a covenant with yourself to deny the lies of shame.

I like what Stephanie Davies offers about mindfulness as a strategy for combatting **pain**, which I embrace for combatting **shame**, namely:

> *"Mindfulness means paying attention to what is happening in the present moment. Awareness of the present involves many different sensations. If thoughts and feelings about the past or future arise, they are calmly acknowledged and accepted. Gently, you focus on the sensations of the present moment."*

Stephanie Davies, Nicholas Cooke, & Julia Sutton. (2015). *Rewire your pain: An evidence-based approach to reducing chronic pain.* Cottesloe: Western Australia. WA Specialist Pain Service. (p. 60).

Mindfulness is also highlighted by:

Kirk A. Bingaman (2014). *The power of neuroplasticity for pastoral and spiritual care*: MD: Lexington Books. (pps. 101-118).

There is also a generous range of resources offering tips and strategies for combatting shame, including:

Brene Brown. (2012). *Daring greatly: How the courage to be vulnerable transforms the way we live, love, parent and lead.* UK: Penguin Random House.

Julia Baird. (2020). *Phosphorescence: On awe, wonder and things that sustain you when the world goes dark.* Sydney: Australia. Fourth Estate.

Barry K. Weinhold & Janae B. Weinhold. (1989). *Breaking free of the co-dependency trap.* (Revised ed.). Novato, CA: New World Library. (Chapters. 5, 11, 14, 15, 18)

Scriptures (NIV Version), I have paraphrased that I find helpful in being quiet and reflective when I am challenged by shame:

- Is. 43: 18-19. "Forget the former things; do not dwell on the past. See, I am doing a new thing!"

- Is. 43: 2-5. "When you pass through waters …they will not sweep over you; When you are surrounded by fire; you will not be burned…For I am the Lord your God, the Holy One of Israel, your Saviour. Since you are precious and honoured in my sight, and because I love you… Do not be afraid, for I am with you."

- Is.49. 16. "See I have carved your name on the palms of my hand."

- Is. 55: 12. "You will go out in joy, and be led forth in peace; the mountains and hills will burst into song before you, and all the trees of the field will clap their hands."

- Ps. 119: 105. "Your word is a lamp to my feet and a light for my path."

- Ps. 119: 33-39. "Teach me, O Lord...Give me understanding...Direct me in your path...Turn my heart towards you...Turn my eyes away from worthless things... Fulfil your promise to me...Take away my disgrace (shame)."

- Ps. 51: 10-12. "Create in me a pure heart, O God, and renew a steadfast spirit within me. do not cast me from your presence or take your Holy spirit from me. Restore to me the joy of your salvation and grant me a willing spirit, to sustain me."

- Ps. 46: 10. "Be still and know that I am God..."

- Ps. 139: 23-24. "Search me, O God, and know my heart; test me and know my anxious thoughts. See if there is any offensive way in me, and lead me in the way of everlasting."

- Prov. 3: 5-6. "Trust in the Lord with all your heart and lean not on your own understanding; in all your ways acknowledge him, and he will make your paths straight."

- Mic. 6: 8. "...And what does the Lord require of you? To act justly and to love mercy and to walk humbly with your God."

NOTES

Prelude

1 See this link for the story of Kieran's inspirational race at Atlanta 1996 Olympic Games:

https://www.inspire-fitness.com.au/blog/2012/07/kieran-perkins-inspirational-olympic-moment/

2 Hugh Mackay (1993). *Reinventing Australia: The mind and mood of Australia in the 90s.* Sydney: Angus and Robertson. (p.297).

Part One: People, Events and Destiny

Chapter 1

1 For a comprehensive history of the town of Katanning I recommend:

https://lostkatanning.com/early-history/

2 For a comprehensive review of Carrolup Settlement I recommend

https://www.findandconnect.gov.au/guide/wa/WE01142

3   For more detail on the role of Marribank I suggest:

https://www.findandconnect.gov.au/ref/wa/biogs/WE00136b.htm

4   To view examples of this beautiful art I suggest: https://www.carrolup.info/gallery/art/

5   For a modern and comprehensive review of the history of Halls Creek the Halls Creek Tourism Brochure is a good place to start!

https://www.hallscreektourism.com.au/information/halls-creek-history

Chapter 2

1   For more detail on this phenomenon see:

Daniel Goleman. (1995). *Emotional Intelligence: Why it can matter more than IQ.* London: Bloomsbury Publishing. (Chapt. 2).

2   Pete Walker. (2014). *Complex PTSD: From surviving to surviving.* USA: An Azure Coyote Book/2013. (p. 28).

3   Brene Brown. (2012). *Daring greatly: How the courage to be vulnerable transforms the way we live, love, parent and lead.* UK: Penguin Random House. (pp. 68-69).

*Brene Brown TED Talk (2010)

https://www.ted.com/talks/brene_brown_the_power_of_vulnerability/transcript?language=en

*Brene Brown see TED Talk (2012) https://brenebrown. com/videos/ted-talk-listening-to-shame/

4   Edward T. Welch. (2001). *Shame interrupted.* Greensboro, NC: New Growth Press. (p.23). I also recommend Chapter 4 of this same text where the author discusses the phenomenon of shame leading to self-disgust.

5   Jon Ronson (2015). *So you've been publicly shamed.* NY: Riverhead Books. (p. 249).

6   Among the best references on how our brain works in learning are:

•   P. Eggen & D. Kauchak (2007). *Educational psychology: Windows on classrooms.* (7th ed.). NJ: Pearson Education, Inc. Chapt. 7. (pp. 200-222).

•   Anita Woolfolk (2013). *Educational psychology.* (12th ed.). NY: Pearson. Chapters 2, 8, 9, 11.

•   Michael Nagel & Laura Scholes. (2016). *Understanding development and learning.* Victoria, Australia: Oxford University Press.

•   Patricia Wolfe. (2010). *Brain matters: Transferring research into classroom practice.* (2nd ed.). Alexandria, VA. USA: Association for Supervision and Curriculum Development. Part 11, pp. 71-104 of this publication, is particularly helpful in explaining brain development from birth through adolescence.

https://www.readpbn.com/pdf/Brain-Matters-Translating-Research-Into-Classroom-Practice-Sample-Pages.pdf

7 Neuroplasticity in learning is well described in the following publications:

- John Media. (2014). *Brain Rules: 12 principles for surviving and thinking at work, home and school.* Australia: Scribe Publication Pty. Ltd. (pps. 158-159).

- This section on Medina's 12 Brain Rules is fascinating, and worth considering.

  https://catalogue.nla.gov.au/Record/6486708 Or file:///E:/brainrules_summaries.pdf

- Kirk A. Bingaman (2014). *The power of neuroplasticity for pastoral and spiritual care*: MD: Lexington Books. (Chapt 1, pp 9-26).

8 Rick Churchill. et al., (2016). *Teaching: Making a difference.* (4th ed.) Milton Queensland: John Wiley & Sons Australia, Ltd.

9 Norman Doidge. (2007). *The brain that changes itself: Stories of personal triumph from the frontiers of brain science.* NY: Penguin books.

10 A comprehensive review of Arrowsmith School can be found in Wikipedia:

https://en.wikipedia.org/wiki/Arrowsmith_School

Chapter 3

1 Bruce Robinson. (2001). *Fathering from the fast lane: Practical ideas for busy dads.* Sydney: Finch Publishing.

* Bruce Robinson. (2008). *Daughters and their dads: Tips for fathers, adult daughters and father-figures.* Perth: Macsis Publishing.

2   Steve Biddulph. (1994). *Manhood: An action plan for changing men's lives.* Sydney: Finch Publishing.

3   For further resources on parenting, and being father-figures in children's' lives go to; The fathering Project: https:// thefatheringproject.org/about-us/our-mission/

Chapter 4

1   For my Ph D dissertation in later years I studied community schools and community education in Canada. I have no doubt that my interest in this topic was sparked to some extent by my positive and nurturing experience of community in my childhood.

- Prout, P. F. (1997). *Community Schools in Canada.* Toronto: Canadian Education Association.

- Prout, P. F. (1977). *General and specific environmental conditions in relation to community education developments in Canada's provinces and territories.* Unpublished PhD dissertation. The University of Alberta, Canada.

2   For a vivid description of this fire see: The West Australian, 15 Apr 1950:

https://trove.nla.gov.au/newspaper/article/47841614

Chapter 5

1   For more detail on this exceptional man's life go to: https:// www.wikitree.com/wiki/Cunningham-8428

2   For comprehensive detail on the Shire of Dardanup
     see: https://www.dardanup.wa.gov.au/wp-content/
     uploads/sites/105/2014/05/LHS_2016_final-
     issue_November_2016.pdf

3   See: https://www.wikitree.com/wiki/Cunningham-8428

4   "Bushy School" was a week-long program offered every
     school holiday in August. It was run by the nuns at the
     Dardanup Catholic church for kids like myself who went
     to local public schools. Father Cunningham would see us
     every day for various fun activities, including taking us for
     rides in an open trailer behind his car. He would follow
     bush tracks and swerve along the road so the trailer would
     sway sideways, much to the delight of all of us! No focus
     on safety protocols in those days! Thank goodness! He also
     showed Charlie Chapman movies for us almost every night.
     My fondest memories of the movies (I don't think I was
     old enough to appreciate them!) was hearing and watching
     Father Cunningham's belly laughing throughout the movies!

Chapter 6

1   Catherine McLaughlan asking: Mentoring: What is it.....

     https://www.ncbi.nlm.nih.gov/pmc/articles/PMC2875765/
     pdf/hesr0045-0871.pdf

2   Lillian T. Eby and others asking the question: Does
     mentoring matter......

     https://www.ncbi.nlm.nih.gov/pmc/articles/PMC2352144/

3   Mary Abbajay writing for Forbes Magazine suggests three
     essential elements for success in mentoring:

https://www.forbes.com/sites/
maryabbajay/2019/01/20/mentoring-matters-thre
e-essential-element-of-success/?sh=d7a9d45a9fcc

4   Stephen Covey. (2013). *The 7 Habits of highly effective people.*
London, UK: Simon & Schuster Ltd.

5   Sheila Heen TED Talk:

https://alumni.opcd.wfu.edu/2019/05/tedx-talk-how-to-us
e-others-feedback-to-learn-and-grow/

6   James Clawson. (2003). *Level three leadership: Getting below
the surface.* (2nd ed.). New Jersey: Pearson Education Inc.
(p. 58).

Chapter 7

1   The best option I suggest for more information on this
unique town is Wikipedia:

https://en.wikipedia.org/wiki/
New_Norcia,_Western_Australia

2   A "shirt front" is a term from Australian Rules Football,
where you crash an opponent with your hip and shoulder as
he is contesting possession of the ball. The end result you
seek is that you win the ball and he is left 'wishing he had
the ball', and conceding minor victory to you. All in the
game!

3   For a great description of blind spots see Sheila Heen's TED
Talk:

https://alumni.opcd.wfu.edu/2019/05/tedx-talk-how-to-us
e-others-feedback-to-learn-and-grow/

4   See the following site for more information on Sputnk: https://history.nasa.gov/sputnik.html

Chapter 8

1   Brene Brown. (2012). *Daring greatly: How the courage to be vulnerable transforms the way we live, love, parent and lead.* UK: Penguin Random House. (Chapt. 3).

2   Brene Brown. (2012) shares interesting observations with respect to potential responses to shame by social-cultural researcher Dr Linda Hartling. (p.77).

3   Pete Walker. (2014). *Complex PTSD: From surviving to surviving.* USA: An Azure Coyote Book/2013. (p. 13).

Chapter 9

1   I recommend the following text and books for further understanding of how emotion is engaged as we learn:

- Rick Churchill, et al. (2011), *Teaching: Making a difference.* Qld: Australia. Wiley. (Part 2).

- Norman Doidge. (2007). *The brain that changes itself: Stories of personal triumph from the frontiers of brain science.* NY: Penguin books.

- Philippe Douyon. (2019. *Neuroplasticity: Your Brain's Superpower: Change Your Brain and Change your life.* Izzard Book.

- John Media. (2008). *Brain Rules: 12 principles for surviving and thinking at work, home and school.* Australia: Griffin Press.

[2] Matthew McConaughey. (2020*). Green lights*. UK: London. Headline Publishing Group.

I thoroughly recommend pp 61-84 of this book where Matthew shares his experiences as an exchanged student in Australia, a remote town in the state of New South Wales to be exact. How an 18-year-old from home was dropped into an "alien culture" (when you read the story you will understand what I mean here!), and triumphed through his emotional strength, is amazing.

Chapter 10

[1] One of the most reliable references concerning the death of JFK:

https://www.jfklibrary.org/learn/about-jfk/jfk-in-history/november-22-1963-death-of-the-president

[2] Ray Sorrell Sandover Medal https://australianfootball.com/players/player/ray+sorrell/15840

[3] Vietnam War. I suggest *Wikipedia* is a good place to start for researching this conflict:

https://en.wikipedia.org/wiki/United_States_in_the_Vietnam_War

[4] Details of the Indonesian Confrontation in Borneo can be found at:

https://www.awm.gov.au/articles/atwar/indonesian-confrontation

[5] The Two-Year National Service Ballot https://www.awm.gov.au/articles/encyclopedia/viet_app

Part Two: A Second Chance

Chapter 12

1   Lance Armstrong doping himself with his own blood:

https://www.theverge.com/2013/1/17/3886424/programmin
g-your-body-lance-armstrong-and-doping-technology

Chapter 14

1   The Tet Offensive from US Army
perspective https://www.army.mil/
article/216671/a_harrowing_tale_of_the_tet_offensive

2   I have chosen an article from the Smithsonian Institute to
share this story

https://www.smithsonianmag.com/history/
ghosts-my-lai-180967497/

3   I consider this video of Senator Robert F. Kennedy
announcing the death of Dr Martin Luther King a moving
testimony to the vision and character of both men who were
assassinated in 1968:

https://www.youtube.com/watch?v=_bDlET_gK68

4   I recommend Wikipedia as the best place to start for
information on this tumultuous event.

https://en.wikipedia.org/wiki/Prague_Spring

5   I recommend this article by James Montague for a summary
of this historic event. The DVD *Salute* is also a "must see!"

https://edition.cnn.com/2012/04/24/sport/
olympics-norman-black-power/index.html

6   See details of the Meckering Earthquake in the following:

https://www.slwa.wa.gov.au/SLWA-on-ABC-Radio/
meckering-earthquake

7   I chose a NASA page for details of this historic event in
    1968:

https://www.nasa.gov/topics/history/features/apollo_8.html

Chapter 15

1   See an official NASA description of this extraordinary
    achievement:

https://www.nasa.gov/mission_pages/apollo/apollo11.html

2   Powell, John. (1969). *Why am I afraid to tell you who I am?
    Insights on self-awareness, personal growth and interpersonal
    communication.* Chicago: Angus Communications.

Part Three: Canada: And Grad Studies

Chapter 17

1   Pennebaker, J. & Smith J. ((2016). *Opening up by writing:
    How expressive writing improves health and eases emotional
    pain.* (3rd ed.). US: Guilford Publications.

2   Pete Walker. (2014). *Complex PTSD: From surviving to
    surviving.* USA: An Azure Coyote Book/2013. (p. 102).

3   Malcolm Gladwell. (2008). *Outliers: The story of success.* NY: Back Bay Books. (p. 19).

Chapter 18

1   Three useful resources for more information on *The Woodlawn Organization*, including a profile of (Dr) Leon Finney

https://interactive.wttw.com/dusable-to-obama/woodlawn-organization

https://en.wikipedia.org/wiki/Woodlawn,_Chicago

https://en.wikipedia.org/wiki/Leon_Finney_Jr.

Part Four: Coming Home

Chapter 19

1   Brene Brown. (2012). *Daring greatly: How the courage to be vulnerable transforms the way we live, love, parent and lead.* UK: Penguin Random House. (p. 67).

2   Sheila Heen has excellent insights regarding feedback in her TED Talk:

https://alumni.opcd.wfu.edu/2019/05/tedx-talk-how-to-use-others-feedback-to-learn-and-grow/

3   Prof Everett Worthington (14 Feb 2021) Radio National Sunday Extra interview. Sophie Kesteven and Skye Docherty https://www.abc.net.au/news/2021-02-14/forgiveness-benefits-health-justice/13141296

[4] Daniel Goleman. (1995). *Emotional Intelligence: Why it can matter more than IQ.* London: Bloomsbury Publishing. (pps. 36-45).

[5] Howard Gardener. (1983). *Frames of mind: The theory of multiple intelligence.* NY: Basic Books

[6] Julia Baird. (2020). *Phosphorescence: On awe, wonder and things that sustain you when the world goes dark.* Sydney: Australia. Fourth Estate. (Ch. 21).

Chapter 20

[1] For further detail on research into reflective practice see:

- Lowe, G., Prout, P., & Murcia, K. (2013). I See, I Think I Wonder: An Evaluation of Journaling as a Critical Reflective Practice Tool for Aiding Teachers in Challenging or Confronting Contexts. *Australian Journal of Teacher Education,* 38(6). Article 1

[2] The following site gives a comprehensive, current overview of Pioneer Camps, Alberta:

https://www.albertacamping.com/qry/page.taf?id=22&cid=76

Part Five: Half Time

Chapter 21

[1] Buford, Bob. (1994*). Half Time: Changing your game plan from success to significance.* Grand Rapids, Michigan: Zondervan: www.Halftime.org

Chapter 22

1   Lowe, G., Prout, P., & Murcia, K. (2013). I See, I
    Think I Wonder: An Evaluation of Journaling as a
    Critical Reflective Practice Tool for Aiding Teachers in
    Challenging or Confronting Contexts. *Australian Journal
    of Teacher Education, 38*(6). http://dx.doi.org/10.14221/
    ajte.2013v38n6.6

2   I have three books to recommend here, from among many I
    have read:

- Martin Meredith. (2021). The state of Africa: A history of
  the continent since independence. UK: Simon & Schuster,
  Limited.

- William Easterley. (2007). *White man's burden: Why the
  West's efforts to aid the rest have done so much ill and so little
  good.* US: Penguin Putman Inc.

- Steve Corbett & Brian Fikkert. (2009). *When helping
  hurts: How to alleviate poverty without hurting the poor and
  yourself.* Chicago: Moody Publishers.

3   Geoffrey M. Lowe & Peter F. Prout (2018): Reframing
    Teacher In-service

    Training in Kenya: Recommendations from the Literature,
    Africa Education Review, DOI:

    10.1080/18146627.2017.1340803 https://doi.org/10.1080/181
    46627.2017.1340803

Chapter 23

1   The Kalgoorlie "Super Pit" is awe inspiring in terms of magnitude.

https://www.superpit.com.au/

2   The town of Gwalia claims fame because former US President Herbert Hoover was a former manager of the mine. https://www.mindat.org/loc-23188.html

3   I don't think any photo can capture the beauty of this mountain range in the desert.

https://parksaustralia.gov.au/uluru/discover/highlights/kata-tjuta/

4   Even this range of photos cannot match being there in person.

https://www.gettyimages.com.au/photos/uluru

5   This is a nice collage of "The Alice." https://www.istockphoto.com/photos/alice-springs

I also recommend a wonderful book by Neville Shute called *A Town Like Alice*, which is available online.

6   Walking into the crater is an eerie experience.

https://www.sciencephoto.com/media/177057/view/wolf-creek-crater-australia

7   Purnululu is one of my favourite places in WA. Part of the spectacular QANTAS commercial was filmed in Cathedral Grove. https://whc.unesco.org/en/list/1094/

8 Lake Argyle and Kununurra, including Lake Kununurra (the latter being one of my favourite camping spots at Lake Kununurra Campsite: https://www.dreamstime.com/photos-images/lake-kununurra.html

9 Spectacular manning Gorge https://www.alamy.com/stock-photo/manning-gorge.html

10 Almost as spectacular Bells Gorge – both worth the visit.

https://www.alamy.com/stock-photo/bell-gorge-western-australia.html

11 The drive in to Millstream from the Great Northern Highway is spectacular, and the drive is worth it.

https://www.shutterstock.com/search/millstream+chichester+national+park

Chapter 24

1 Brene Brown see TED Talk (2012) https://brenebrown.com/videos/ted-talk-listening-to-shame/

2 Brown, Brene (2012). *Daring greatly: How the courage to be vulnerable transforms the way we live, love, parent and lead.* UK: Penguin Random House. (p. 71).

3 "The Golden Rule" has a number of interpretations, namely; "Walk in another's shoes;" or Immanuel Kant's. "Don't create rules for yourself that you wouldn't apply to others;" or, "Do not do unto others as you would not want done to you."

However, the most understood definition of "The Golden Rule," stems from Jesus' teaching: *So in everything, do to others what you would have them do to you, for this sums up the Law and the Prophets."* Matthew 7:12; and, *"Do to others as you would have them do to you."* Luke 6:31.

Thus, the Golden Rule encompasses the empathic essence of morality. It is a simple yet powerful way of saying that we should recognize the respective dignity of all people, and not forget we all are capable of inflicting immoral actions.

[4]   Nick Cave. (2020). What is mercy for you? *The Red Hand Files.* Issue # 9, August.

[5]   Pete Walker. (2014). *Complex PTSD: From surviving to surviving.* USA: An Azure Coyote Book/2013. (p. 80).

Part Six: Exiting the Swampland of Shame

Chapter 25

[1]   For more on this Waldinger's TED Talk see:

https://www.ted.com/talks/robert_waldinger_what_makes_a_good_life_lessons_from_the_longest_study_on_happiness

[2]   Inspired by the poem, *The Highwayman,* by Alfred Noyes.

Alfred Noyes. (1906). *The Highwayman.* Blackwood's Magazine.

[3]   A lovely melody, *The Lord of the Dance,* based upon the American Shaker song, *Simple Gifts.*

Sydney Cater. (1963). Acknowledged author. Source. *Wikipedia*

Chapter 26

[1] For more detail on our research see:

- Prout, P. F., Lowe, G. M., Gray, C. C., & Jefferson, S. (2019). An Elixir for Veteran Teachers: The Power of Social Connections in Keeping These Teachers Passionate and Enthusiastic in Their Work. *The Qualitative Report, 24*(9), 2244-2258. https://nsuworks.nova.edu/tqr/vol24/iss9/10

- Prout, P. F., Lowe, G. M., Gray, C. C., & Jefferson, S. (2020). Examined Lives: The Transformative Power of Active Interviewing in Narrative Approach. *The Qualitative Report, 25*(1), 14-27. https://nsuworks.nova.edu/tqr/vol25/iss1/2

- Lowe, G., Prout, P., Gray, C., & Jefferson, S. (2020). Reappraising the AITSL Professional Engagement Domain: Clarifying Social Capacity Building for School Leaders to Enhance Overall Teacher Job Satisfaction and Career Longevity. *Australian Journal of Teacher Education, 45*(9), 63 – 79. http://doi.org/10.14221/ajte.2020v45n9.4

- Gray, C., Lowe, G., Prout, P., & Jefferson, S. (2020). Growing through life's bumpy moments: Key experiences transforming the careers of positive veteran performing arts Teachers. NJ: *Drama Australia Journal*, (44), 2, 106–119 https://doi.org/10.1080/14452294.2021.1886287

- Gray, C., Lowe, G., Prout, P. & Jefferson, S. (2021). 'Just like breathing': A portrait of an 85 year old veteran teacher. *Teachers and Teaching, Theory and Practice.* https://doi.org/10.1080/13540602.2021.1977275

2   Articles from Denise and Jenni related to my passion for mentoring that inspired me are:

- Meister, D. G. (2010). Experienced secondary teachers' perceptions of engagement and

  effectiveness: A guide for professional development. *The Qualitative Report, 15*(4), 880-898. Retrieved from http://www.nova.edu/ssss/QR/QR15-4/meaister.pdf

- Meister, D. G., & Ahrens, P. (2011). Resisting plateauing: Four veteran teachers' stories.

  Teaching and Teacher Education, 27(4), 770-778. Retrieved from http://dx.doi.org/10.1016/j.tate.2011.01.002

3   Wolgemuth, J. R. (2013). Analysing for critical resistance in narrative research. *Qualitative Research, 14*(5), 586-602.

4   Pete Walker. (2014). *Complex PTSD: From surviving to surviving.* USA: An Azure Coyote Book/2013. (p. 106).

5   Hybels, Bill. (2004). *Holy discontent: Fuelling the fire that ignites personal vision.* Grand Rapids, MI: Zondervan.

6   Hugh Mackay (1993). *Reinventing Australia: The mind and mood of Australia in the 90s.* Sydney: Australia. Angus and Robertson. (pps. 271 – 273).

7   for further details regarding this research see:

- Prout, P., Wolgemuth, J., Gray, C., Lowe, G., Thorpe. V., & Killam, R. (2021). I was wondering: reflections on collaborative practice by five researchers in Australia, New

Zealand and the United States, *Reflective Practice,* DOI: 10.1080/14623943.2021.1938998

https://doi.org/10.1080/14623943.2021.1938998

Chapter 27

[1] I recommend two resources from my research for further detail here; Waldinger and Vailant:

Waldinger's TED Talk:

https://www.ted.com/talks/robert_waldinger_what_makes_a_good_life_lessons_from_the_longest_study_on_happiness

Vaillant, G. E. (1977). *Adaption to life.* Boston, MA: Little, Brown & Coy.

[2] Hugh Mackay (2013). *The Good life: What makes a life worth living?* Sydney, Australia: Macmillan. (pp. 207-233, p. 190).

[3] I highly recommend this awesome book for inspiration and teaching about what sustains us physically, emotionally and spiritually:

- Julia Baird. (2020). *Phosphorescence: On awe, wonder and things that sustain you when the world goes dark.* Sydney: Australia. Fourth Estate.

[4] There are summaries of 12 special people contained in this useful book on teaching and suggesting life skills we can consider for more effectively overcoming shame through service to others.

- Robert Ellsberg. (Ed), (2008). *Modern spiritual masters: Writing on contemplation and compassion.* Maryknoll, NY: Orbis Books

5   John Maxwell. (1997). *The success journey.* Nashville, USA: Thomas Nelson Publishers.

Part Seven: How God Intervened

Chapter 28

1   The moving story of Corrie ten Boom who helped Jews escape persecution during Nazi occupation of Holland in WW11 has a powerful message of forgiveness. Corrie spent years in the notorious Ravensbruck Prison for women. Her sister Betsie died in prison, but Corrie survived. Her story can be found in: "The Hiding Place" (2004). London: UK. Hodder and Stoughton.

Tables

Table 1: "Gardner's Multiple Intelligence", in Anita Wolfolk. (2013). *Educational Psychology.* (12th ed.) NJ: Pearson. (pps. 120-122)

Table 2: "Positive Characteristics of the Four F's", in Pete Walker. (2014). *Complex PTSD: From surviving to surviving.* USA: An Azure Coyote Book/2013. (p. 106).

ACKNOWLEDGEMENTS

My Mentors and Significant Peers

My mother, Eva Prout, Fr. Cunningham, Keith & Sheila Butcher, Jeff Eldridge & Ross Harvey, Bob Haymes, Sergeant Sartorius, Len Pavey, Jim Davies, Brian Brand, Robbie Young, Rod and Marg Lewis, Ernie (Jacko) Jackson, David Andrich, Mike and Katie Irvine, Prof. John Bloomfield, Bob Horseman, Sr. Patrice Cooke, Fr. Terry Gallagher, Sr. Catherine, Don Posterski, Prof. Ed Segar, Gordy and Nancy Cunningham, Marj Long, Neil Graham, Don Weaver, Leon Finney, Prof. Barry McGaw, Prof. Brian Hill, Michael Beech, Rev. David Secombe, Graham Mabry, John (Chappo) Chapman, Spencer Colliver, Jennifer Turner, Bruce Robinson, Vincent Leung, Tana Clark, Carrie Herbert, Beth Schmidt, Bob Balisky, Ps. Henry Schorr, Jen Argue, Ps. Graham Johnston, Rod Cousins, Dr. Francis Ndgu, Steven Bamoleke, David Waweru, Damian Doyle, Christina Gray, Geoff Lowe, Karen Lloyd, Bill Allen, Denise Meister, Jenni Wolgemuth, Hunter and Alice Beattie, Ray Sorrell.

Family

Thanks to my brothers Henry and Rossco, and sister Di.

I also wish to acknowledge those who encouraged me to write and those who gave me insightful feedback and explicit direction that enhanced the clarity of my story.

- For ongoing encouragement to complete the task I thank Sonja Botma, Christina Gray, Geoffrey Lowe, Bruce Robinson, Bruce Davis, Marg Pownall, Tony Quinlan, Ivor Davies, Tana Clark, Jen Argue, Luke Pownall, Dan Hribernik, Sue Vanderhaeghen.

- For in-depth, explicit ideas and direction I am indebted to my wife Sonja, my brother Ross, my mate and mentor Prof. Bruce Robinson, my colleague and friend Dr Geoffrey Lowe, and David Waweru, Zanthe Hand, and Dr Bill Allen.

I acknowledge the professional direction and in-depth counsel by personnel from *Tellwell Publishing Australia.*

- In particular I am indebted to Despina MacLaren, Publishing Consultant at *Tellwell*, for her initial guidance and direction in preparing my story as a manuscript for publishing.

- In addition, I thank the Project Manager at *Tellwell*, Jun Mark Vertudazo for keeping me on track, including his insights and counsel in preparing my draft for publication.

Finally, I acknowledge Brene Brown whose research and writing inspires me, including her phrase in relation to shame, ...*the swampland of the soul,* which I adapted for the title of my story.

Contact

I welcome any feedback or questions in relation to my story.

You will find further insights on my website:
www.peter-prout.com

You can also contact me by email:
peter.prout3929@gmail.com

or phone:
+61 (0) 433 567 235

Manufactured by Amazon.ca
Bolton, ON

27977650R00192